Fourteen Writers Explore What Illness Means in the Context of Their Lives

- **Andrew Sullivan's** HIV diagnosis forever changed the way in which he viewed the world, his relationships, and his own life.
- **Mary Swander,** proud of her independent and solitary life in rural Iowa, learned to accept the kindness and help of friends and neighbors when viral myelitis left her immobilized.
- Seven months after she had her first baby, **Kris Vervaecke** became violently ill and unable to move. Diagnosed with rheumatoid arthritis, she was incapable of even holding her own son. Through her recovery process, she began a journey of return: to her mother, to Nebraska, to the body's story of reconciliation.
- When **Patricia Foster** developed a debilitating environmental illness, she and her husband together gathered the strength needed to battle her almost constant fatigue and pain while overcoming the stress her illness placed on their marriage.
- **Linda Hogan,** suffering from an unusual form of multiple sclerosis, movingly meditates on the meaning of physical pain, recognizing that it "isn't just an event; it is a country—one whose citizens recognize each other on daily streets just by the expression of their faces."

THE HEALING CIRCLE

PATRICIA FOSTER has an M.F.A. from the Iowa Writers' Workshop and a Ph.D. in women's literature from Florida State University. She has edited *Minding the Body* and *Sister to Sister* (Anchor). She now teaches nonfiction writing at the University of Iowa.

MARY SWANDER is a widely published poet and essayist best known for her books *Driving the Body Back* and *Out of This World* (Viking). She is the winner of the 1994 Whiting Writers Award and a professor of English at Iowa State University.

THE HEALING CIRCLE

Authors Writing of Recovery

EDITED BY PATRICIA FOSTER
AND MARY SWANDER

A PLUME BOOK

PLUME
Published by the Penguin Group
Penguin Putnam Inc., 375 Hudson Street, New York, New York 10014, U.S.A.
Penguin Books Ltd, 27 Wrights Lane, London W8 5TZ, England
Penguin Books Australia Ltd, Ringwood, Victoria, Australia
Penguin Books Canada Ltd, 10 Alcorn Avenue, Toronto, Ontario, Canada M4V 3B2
Penguin Books (N.Z.) Ltd, 182–190 Wairau Road, Auckland 10, New Zealand

Penguin Books Ltd, Registered Offices: Harmondsworth, Middlesex, England

First published by Plume, an imprint of Dutton NAL, a member of Penguin Putnam Inc.

First Printing, April, 1998
10 9 8 7 6 5 4 3 2 1

"Blue Baby" by Lauren Slater reprinted by permission of the author.
   "When Plagues End" by Andrew Sullivan reprinted by permission of the author.
   "The Gift of a Normal Life" by Tracy Thompson reprinted by permission of the Putnam Publishing Group from *The Beast* by Tracy Thompson. Copyright © 1995 by Tracy Thompson.
   "Musée des Beaux Arts" from W. H. Auden: *Collected Poems by W. H. Auden*, edited by Edward Mendelson. Copyright 1940 and renewed 1968 by W. H. Auden. Reprinted by permission of Random House, Inc.
   "I Find You, Lord, in All Things and in All" from *Selected Poetry of Rainer Maria Rilke* by Rainer Maria Rilke, edited & translated by Stephen Mitchell. Copyright © 1982 by Stephen Mitchell. Reprinted by permission of Random House, Inc.

Ⓟ   REGISTERED TRADEMARK—MARCA REGISTRADA

LIBRARY OF CONGRESS CATALOGING-IN-PUBLICATION DATA:

The healing circle : authors writing of recovery / edited by Patricia
   Foster and Mary Swander.
      p.   cm.
   ISBN 0-452-27756-6 (alk. paper)
   1. Self-efficacy.   2. Mental healing.   3. Mind and body.
   I. Foster, Patricia.   II. Swander, Mary.
   BF637.S38H43   1998
   155.9'16—dc21   97-40276
                                                   CIP

Printed in the United States of America
Set in Goudy
Designed by Eve L. Kirch

BOOKS ARE AVAILABLE AT QUANTITY DISCOUNTS WHEN USED TO PROMOTE PRODUCTS OR SERVICES. FOR INFORMATION PLEASE WRITE TO PREMIUM MARKETING DIVISION, PENGUIN PUTNAM INC., 375 HUDSON STREET, NEW YORK, NEW YORK 10014.

CONTENTS

ACKNOWLEDGMENTS

We wish to acknowledge the generous assistance of the University of Iowa and Iowa State University for departmental leaves that allowed us time to complete this book, and the Whiting Foundation for its support to Mary Swander.

In addition, we wish to thank Jennifer Moore, our editor, for the clarity of her vision and her thoughtful comments. Crucial help was provided by agents, Kimberly Witherspoon and Lizzie Grossman. A special thanks to David Wilder who provided computer assistance.

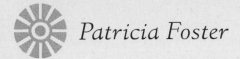 *Patricia Foster*

INTRODUCTION: THE MIDDLE PASSAGE

When I was six, I loved to go with my father, a doctor, to the hospital to look at the newborns. I'd put my face close to the nursery window and watch their tiny fists curled over a blanket, their fragile heads covered with crocheted bonnets or the soft fold of flannel. I liked to look at the babies because my own survival after birth had seemed such a miracle, first a human miracle, and then a medical miracle. Even at six, I knew that I'd been born with erythroblastosis, a word I loved to pronounce to adults who oohed and ahhed over "such a big word for such a little girl." Mother said only that I'd had a prolonged stay in the hospital with blood transfusions given in my neck and head, something I tried to imagine—that needle piercing my cool, delicate skin. I never knew the more intimate details of this event, for my mother kept it all hush-hush until I was in my thirties. Maybe it shamed her to remember how vulnerable we both were, innocents caught in the medical gulag of male practitioners of the late 1940s; maybe she worried that I would be upset over the condition of my birth, memories that would taint each successive birthday, leaving me saddened and angry as I blew out the candles on my cake. Or maybe she didn't know how to resolve the story of medical miracle with medical mishap, and so told only one-half of the story, the more familiar one of diagnosis, treatment, and recovery.

I was born in a private, one-doctor clinic in a small Alabama town, a child so pale I was almost no color at all. On the day of my birth, my father had just finished his army duty in Augusta, Georgia, and though he'd always wanted five boys and one girl, he and my mother weren't disappointed at a second daughter's birth, for I was a silent, sleeping child who looked so fragile— with fine blue veins spiraling across my forehead, a soft stem of a neck, and bright orange spots beginning to freckle my cheeks— I elicited everyone's sympathy. And yet as the day lengthened, Mother began to worry; I seemed so listless, so quiet there was something odd in this absence of frustration. Why didn't I cry when I was hungry, when my diaper was changed? Where were those sly, subtle smiles, those gurgles of flirtation with the world? And what about the strange little freckles, the spots sprinkling my cheeks like diluted Mercurochrome? Mother read medical journals in her spare time and followed the new theory about the Rh factor—a condition in which a fetus creates antibodies to the mother's blood source, resulting in brain damage, lethargy, and, ultimately, death. She knew that many doctors discounted such a theory, considering it only a hypothesis, provocative but unproven, still involved in research trials. And yet my apathy alarmed her: When she tried to imagine me at age three picking up my teacup or playing with my favorite dolls, she saw me vanishing into the walls of the house, becoming ghostly, invisible, leaving only the faint rhythm of my breath.

Frightened, she told the doctor the next morning that she was worried about my listlessness, my luminescent paleness. "She doesn't cry," Mother said, "and that's not normal." The doctor, gray-haired and gentle, a man well thought of in the community, leaned over to examine me. He was so close Mother could see the part in his hair, could smell his aftershave, could hear the starchy crackle of his white coat. He felt my pulse, checked my lungs, then studied my chart. "She's fine," he said confidently, straightening, his stethoscope gleaming in the light. "She's just pale, but she's eating well. Now don't you worry." I imagine that Mother sighed, retreating into the world of hopeful endings, wondering if she might just be anxious, overzealous, *that kind of mother*. She'd been well-trained to respect doctors. In every hospital where she'd worked as a nutritionist, the doctors were treated like gods, autocratic, omnipotent, their authority never questioned. At City Hospital in Mobile, the entire staff had stood when a doctor entered the room.

But in the hushed early light of morning, she noticed once again that I was ghostly white as if the blood flowed weakly below the surface of my skin. Outside her hospital window the sharp cries of robins and bluejays in the mimosa trees made a distinct contrast to my infinite silence. Only occasionally did I whimper as if too exhausted to protest, and for the second time Mother saw me leaving, a child who simply couldn't hold on, who turned her cheek to the wall and stopped breathing.

The next morning she asked the doctor specifically about the Rh factor, explaining that she was A negative, my father B positive (knowledge she'd acquired only because of metabolic tests during this difficult pregnancy), mentioning that she'd read recent articles in medical journals which described some of my symptoms. "Like those little orange spots," she said, staring at the spray of iridescent freckles splattered across my cheeks. Again the doctor bent over my bassinet, studying me, checking my chart, until finally he straightened and looked thoughtfully at my mother. "You just read too much, Mrs. Foster," he said in his soft-spoken Southern voice. "There's nothing wrong with your baby." Then the nurse bustled in with water and fresh towels for Mother's sponge bath. The doctor patted her hand.

Surely for a few hours my mother relaxed, perhaps falling into that trance of deep sleep where nothing is retrieved, a black hole, a hidden well. After all, the doctor had said I was fine, no need to worry. And yet something happened to my mother that night, a change in the current of her thoughts as she watched the shadows of the trees brushing against a moonlit sky. It was as if she were waking up, seeing the world for the first time, knowing that her impression of me was indispensable; without her help, I might die. Medicine, after all, was a frail structure, knowledge a tiny pinprick in the fabric of danger. On impulse, she dressed quickly and told the nurse she was leaving, taking me to another hospital to have my hemoglobin checked.

"Lord, you can't be getting up yet," the nurse said, ready to tuck her back in (women usually stayed in the hospital seven days after delivery), but my mother was already putting on her shoes, clasping her belt. Her insistence was like an alarm clock shattering the clinic's quiet, methodical air. As a result of her defiance, an immediate hemoglobin test was done; when my red blood cells were discovered to be dangerously low (so low I was expected to die), I was rushed in an ambulance to City Hospital in Mobile. It's here in Mobile that the medical miracle begins, for it's here that I'm diagnosed with erythroblastosis and kept alive with donor blood for two months until the correct match can be found. I am transfused again and again in the tiny veins of my neck, my forehead, the soft strata of my scalp, my body mummied down on a board to keep me absolutely still.

"You were sick for several months," Mother told me succinctly when I begged her for the story, "and then you were cured."

Sick, and then well. It was this story of metamorphosis I grew up with, the body repaired, restored, "fixed up as good as new," healed by medical expertise. I witnessed this daily when I stood at the nurses' station in my father's clinic and watched the kids come in for their polio shots or when I saw a cast removed from a child's arm. This was the predominant story of modern medicine, the story we all long for—the silver bullet, the magical drug or surgery that restores us to our former lives. It wasn't that people didn't die or have chronic illness in the fifties (there were children in town who'd gotten polio before the vaccine was discovered), but rather that, as a culture, we divided people into two categories—the sick and the well. You were in one or the other, rarely in both.

Today this story is completely revised: We've entered a new citizenship, a landscape where many of us traverse the territory between the sick and the well. We live our lives as commuters, one month overwhelmed by the sheer gravity of a diagnosis, by the dismay of a new symptom, the next bouyed up by a new diet, a new drug, a new resolve. Some of us have chronic, long-term illnesses that make us dependent on regimens of treatment to keep us active in careers and family life despite our disease; others have periods of remission, considered well but not completely cured. With our dual citizenships, we go back and forth, hitchhikers on this strange highway, taking whatever risks prove necessary for the trip.

When we began this anthology, my co-editor Mary Swander and I wanted essays that would investigate this landscape, personal stories that would help us map a journey new to our cultural mythology, stories about possibility *within* illness, about the dailiness of recovery and the strategies that have allowed us to turn paralysis and self-doubt into insight. These are stories of the body—not the medical facts (though many such facts are included in these essays), but the hidden story of the body wounded, the mind fractured, the spirit grasping to understand the nature of suffering. Our desire was to find essays that illuminated what was not known about the path to recovery, for illness remains a private exile, a disruption from the life of stability and achievement, something we've been taught to be ashamed of as if it's a personal failure. And yet all of us, at some point, will pass through these narrow gates, will have to contend with the meaning of descent and reconciliation.

Since my own life began as a battle over an unproven theory, the Rh factor, it seemed ironic that my health after age thirty depended on another unproven diagnosis: environmental illness. Like my mother, who read about Rh factor complications as theory before applying them to her child, I read about the breakdown of the immune system, how chemical sensitivity to environmental toxins and candida overgrowth inside the intestines could make the body ill, resulting in a host of symptoms, from exhaustion, migraine, fibromyalgia, and loss of memory to more profound cognitive dysfunction.

At first I was merely bewildered by my illness, a condition whose onset seemed as sudden as the Rh factor at my birth. And yet, upon reflection, I saw that Environmental Illness had had an incubation period, a time during which I worked daily with chemicals in textile design—bleach, dyes, paints, photochemicals—and promiscuously took antibiotics for acne and colds. When I went to a group of specialists in Los Angeles, competent doctors who pressed and probed, took blood and urine samples, tested my thyroid, my liver enzymes, my uric acid, my EBV antibody, I was surprised that they nodded their heads, telling me that nothing was wrong. At first I stared at them in amazement, too stunned for irony, my arms loose at my sides. But why should I have been surprised? How could you diagnose someone who fainted at the first whiff of perfume, who became mentally confused when the Santa Anas blew their hot, dry breath into the smog-filled air, who had muscle aches and sneezing fits the first thing every morning? What medical category did I fit? What was physiological and what psychological in this confusing arena of dysfunction?

When finally I was diagnosed with allergies and given traditional treatment (shots, decongestants, and then the more potent prednisone), I was frankly relieved. *See, I do have something physiological*, symptoms that could be converted to tests, prescriptions, and a regimen of treatment. And yet even with the shots and medications, I grew steadily weaker, moving from an active life into the realm of a sedentary hermit, realizing for the first time my own tenuous hold on health. I'd thought health was my birthright, my reward for surviving erythroblastosis. After all, I had been a miracle child, expected to die, but miraculously cured. Now I stood at a new frontier—or was it an abyss?—and like Tolstoy's Ivan Ilyich, I believed that "something new and dreadful was happening" to me.[1] I wanted desperately for someone to fix me, to deliver me from this mess, but recovery was not such a simple package.

For a long time I didn't know what recovery might mean. I believed that recovery was a state of return, a springboard back to the safe shores of the past, the place where I ran freely down the dirt roads of Alabama and swam in the Gulf of Mexico, navigating through life with the self-assurance of youth and health. My body had been a home I paid attention to only when it defaulted, a lapse that was always temporary, something to be treated and restored. Only after I became chronically ill did I have to brood over my body and my stifling ignorance of its rages; only then did I have to reconsider who I might become in a geography I had neither imagined nor desired.

And yet there is a story I can tell of the day I had a glimpse of what recovery might be, a day that began with my driving five and a half hours from Iowa City to Minneapolis to see a new doctor. I had moved to Iowa City in 1994 and was anxious but hopeful about this doctor, as prepared as I knew how to be, with a typed summary of symptoms and questions, and a basket of food (baked chicken, carrot juice, and two quart bottles of spring water; having been placed on a candida diet, I could eat at few restaurants along the way). All I saw before me on this early

1. Tolstoy, Leo. *The Death of Ivan Ilyich.* Translated by Lynn Solotaroff. New York: Bantam Classic edition, 1981, p. 80.

December morning was a gray ribbon of highway and a blanket of snow-covered fields. The land was treeless, a prairie so calm and tractable I drove for two hours in a dreamfog until a mass of snow fell suddenly from the sky. As I squinted into that white glare, I was at first hypnotized by the windblown drifts shifting across the road, the flakes swirling and dancing as if in a riot. Snow pelted the windshield, quickly swallowing the left lane of the interstate before piling into thick, sensuous drifts. I could barely see the road in front of me, and it required all of my attention to stare at the occasional gray patch of highway. In ten minutes, my attention was so exquisite, I saw a blue haze around each flake. I was gliding through this no-man's-land with eyes and forehead strained as if, given no other strength, I could will my way through. And yet inside the pockets of my alertness, a drunkenness took hold, luring me deceitfully toward a restful sleep. I bit my lips, slapped my thighs just to stay awake. There was so little to hold on to, my mind blurred the distinction between snow and road, gray and white. I forgot about the doctor, about treatment, about cure. I trusted only in moving slowly down the road.

By the time I reached Minneapolis, I was so weary I could barely stand up. Eyes red with strain, stomach empty, head throbbing, I made my way into the doctor's office. More than anything I now wanted my doctor to be a shaman, to have new tricks up his sleeve, to deliver me from chaos, from my sad, hungry need. The snowstorm seemed just one more hurdle I'd endured for health, and in return I expected compensation, the restoration of my body. Hadn't I suffered enough? Hadn't I proved my determination? Of course, I was still working on a reciprocal model (if I give you X, you should give me Y): suffering and dedication to be rewarded with the rich warmth of grace. In this game, I had no use for paradox or irony, for the caprice and imbalance of nature. I was frantic, obsessed, and as so often happens to me in this state, what was so desperately desired was denied. That night in my motel room in Minneapolis, I felt sicker than I had ever felt before.

In the early stages of illness I imagined myself earnest but vigilant, moving forward with the applause and approval of doctors and friends. In my vision I was both heroine and model patient. If nothing else, I thought I could will myself into health (a kind of psychic pulling myself up by my bootstraps), that I could outperform, outresearch, outmaneuver whatever disease threw my way. I was ambitious in the only way I knew how to be ambitious, through the language of vigilance and control. What I'd forgotten was that one of the paths of humanity is helplessness, the inevitability that we spend our lives unable to resolve, complete, or define what exists at the center of our beings.

Driving home from Minneapolis the next day on those snowbanked highways, I had plenty of time for reflection. The snowstorm, I realized, had been an apt metaphor for the journey I'd been traveling, one in which I could see neither to the left nor the right but was forced to continue, moving faithfully forward on an unfamiliar road. The quiet was immense, as if a veil had been thrown over the world and I was caught inside its web. I began to think more clearly about my life than I had in the past few years. What would happen, I wondered, if I tried to relax a bit, if, instead of demanding "cure," I allowed myself to live within illness, focusing on how my interior self could reach deep into the dark mystery of illness and see what was there? I'd assumed, as my culture had taught me, that illness was strictly a private prison, unworthy of anything but regret. And though I didn't want illness, I wondered if instead of repudiating it so fiercely, I might learn something from inside its tight grip.

This was such a revolutionary thought, I sat up straighter, more alert than I'd been in days. I needed to think about how illness had changed me, and the first thing that came to mind was how much I'd tried to hide it from the world, attempting to appear normal, a healthy woman, all worries and obsessions locked out of sight, while inside I wore the posture of battle fatigue. The effort of subterfuge had been exhausting, distracting.

I'd developed the habit, I realized, of looking away from people, staring off into the distance as if I were contemplating blowing up a bridge or simply thinking hard about clearing my throat. I often had the sensation of not being quite *there*, but since I worried lest a colleague or friend notice my mental absence, I talked too much, my voice a rush of furtive anxiety. Being wary took an enormous amount of energy, all that watching and waiting to be condemned. "You know, she's not herself," I imagined people saying. "She's not what we expected." I had the uncanny sense of being unreal.

Of course what had made me work so hard at this deceit was understandable, for I lived in a culture that respected—in fact, exalted—autonomy and rigor while the most disturbing aspect of my condition was memory loss and fatigue. To admit my memory was often evasive (what my husband and I call "sludge days") would mean to leave myself vulnerable to rejection and pity. Inevitably, I preferred hiding, rushing around with the ambitious busyness that suggested a successful life. And yet during this time my body had been telling me to stop, to quiet down, to look at the sky, the earth, the cold clean flakes of snow. What was happening around me? What had I missed?

That night after my return from Minneapolis, I walked outside into the crisp winter air. Above me, tree branches drooped with snow. The ice on the ground sparkled like glitter. I could see my neighbor's hammock floating white and clear above the ground like a loose, drifting cloud, and as I focused on the natural environment, the place that has always calmed me, it occurred to me that I could make a radical shift in consciousness, respecting rather than denying my fears of illness, the limitations of the journey. It would mean saying no to many things, respecting the needs of my body before the demands of my culture, and yet what seemed essential to me now was this clarity of being, a desire to dignify my acts with the truth of my fears. There was no getting around it, I was still afraid of never getting well, and more afraid of what I'd become if I didn't. But this, I realized, was the real business of recovery, discovering who I was inside that dark tunnel of vulnerability.

When Mary Swander and I first talked about this book, we were curious how other people caught in chronic illness, in a catastrophic accident, or in the despairing cycle of depression had reclaimed a sense of self. Since recovery, for most of us, involves not only the treatment of physical or emotional symptoms, but also a reassessment of the meaning of suffering in our society, we wanted to know how others had learned strategies—both imaginative and pragmatic—to endure suffering. When I asked Mary how she'd found the strength to face the radical changes required first by environmental illness and then by a ruptured cervical disc and myelitis, she said that the most important lessons in coping had come to her through models. "Like my grandmother," she said, telling me about this woman who had been one of the original Iowa homesteaders, the only daughter in a family of ten children. "She just plowed through hardship," Mary continued, sitting before me, strapped in a harness rigged up with a weight and pulley system to relieve the pressure on her neck. "She survived two economic depressions and buried all of her family before she died. She never shed a tear. Only on her deathbed did she say flatly, *I've had a hard life*, and we couldn't help it, we all broke up with laughter." Mary laughed now as she remembered, but then the amusement left her face as she told me she'd needed both the stoicism of her grandmother and the mindfulness of the mystics who chose a life of renunciation in order to reach a new consciousness. "My situation was a little different," Mary said. "I had to change my consciousness in order to survive. It was almost inevitable that I learned mindfulness because I had to pay attention to everything. Now I look at nuances, at subtleties, at the shadows of the fan in my writing room, the antics of my goats and ducks in the backyard."

Like Mary, I grew up within a tradition of stoicism, a sense that suffering and pain were admitted only to doctors, treated, and then forgotten. Anything beyond that was narcissistic, indulgent. When I cried after a shot, my father said, "Hush," and I did. And yet today I find myself walking a border, caught within an illness that has no such easy solutions, where to be merely an obedient patient is to be ignored. I remember lying in bed one night listening to the crickets buzzing, the frogs croaking, seeing the darkness descend in shades of purple and black. As I pulled the white cotton sheet up to my chest, I felt a secret longing to be well. Not the longing I presented to doctors, that carefully prepared script of symptoms and complaints, but a longing that was intrinsic, of the spirit, a longing to overcome myself, to lift my body, as if from voicelessness into speech. I wanted to be Lazarus, to pick up my bed and walk. That miracle still lies inside me, a tiny seed, while I walk this border between sickness and health.

What does it mean, I wonder now, to live in two worlds, the community of the sick and the community of the well? From the stories of the contributors in this book I see that, in many ways, we're people who are "passing," adapting as we go, the camouflage of remission allowing us entrance to the healthy stratosphere where work and busyness, family and friends can claim us. We stay in this realm for as long as we can, often thinking our lives are more or less normal until the familiar downswing, which sends us back to the doctor, the clinic, the regimen of repair. For a day, a week, a month, I cross over into the land of health, running beneath a serene blue sky, my legs strong, my lungs breathing the soft summer air. I think suddenly that I must run until I reach the end of the earth, and for the moment I believe that I can. Having experienced illness, a week of good health feels like a vacation, a sacred generosity. I remember my husband pulling me playfully into the shower, splashing me, dousing my head as he washes my hair. I remember falling into a mud puddle, sliding in the snow, diving deep into the Gulf of Mexico, surfing on the crest of a wave. And when I turn toward home, I begin laughing, the sounds floating effortlessly toward the sun. In the fat pride of health, I can't imagine being selfish, self-absorbed, certainly never dismissive, for I'm connected to a world of intrigue and desire, to the intimate stories of a life. Yet when the tide shifts, illness pulling me down like an undertow, I understand the precariousness of my affinities.

What I've learned is often quite different from what others expect me to learn, for it's of the mind as well as the body, the terrain of self-acceptance, of reconciliation with my limitations. The art of recovery has most often been a revision of the idealized view of myself as a woman of radical simplicity and perfect health. This ideal is luminous, a self who is ambitious and purposeful, whereas the real self is raw, jarring, often arbitrary and blind. The real self is more vulnerable than I've ever wanted to admit.

Often I dream that I'm another woman, a young girl at the bottom of the sea, swimming toward the surface. It's dark where I begin, the water an indigo blue, full of seaweed and sand. I swim with a lightness that is new to me as I move toward the aquamarine waves at the shore. I cannot see the surface, but I trust that it's there. In my dream, I'm waiting for the moment when I will burst into the air, my body half-submerged, half-exposed, my heart racing, my lungs clear. And yet all I have as I glide through darkness is this belief, my body painting a path through water, each stroke an act of faith.

In 1948, my mother rode with me in the ambulance to the hospital in Mobile. It was late evening, the sky dull, cloudy, the bay as flat as a sheet of steel. Like the water, I was pale, my hemoglobin hovering at 20. When we arrived at the hospital, the pediatrician had already asked the staff (mostly Catholic sisters) to stay late in the evening so that I could have my first transfusion.

Because the outcome was so precarious, my mother wasn't allowed in the treatment room, but was sent to the nurses' residence hall to wait for the results. She walked toward the door, distraught, fearful, my life now in medical hands. It's here that the sister in charge of pediatrics stopped her, placing a hand on her arm. "Your baby's got grit," she said softly. "She held on to my finger as we took her in." She told Mother to go into the chapel and that if the transfusion went well she would call the nurses' residence hall. Mother dutifully went into the tiny chapel lit only by candles. She prayed that I would get well, that I would grow up to be strong and healthy, and that I would never know the terror of my birth. As the night lengthened, she listened to the muffled sounds of the nurses moving down the residence hall, the soft scrape of doors closing, the creak of cabinets opening, the night sounds of crickets buzzing in the trees. On the altar the candles flickered; the room grew small and close. Perhaps it was really years later that she heard the phone ringing, that sound no louder than the tinkling of bells. But it was here that she first listened to my voice: in that tiny chapel she imagined she heard me cry.

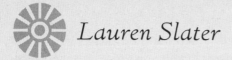 *Lauren Slater*

BLUE BABY

When I was a girl I loved fevers and flus and the muzzy feeling of a head cold, all these states carrying with them the special accoutrements of illness, the thermometer with its lovely line of red mercury, the coolness of ice chips pressed to a sweaty forehead, and best of all, a distant mother coming to your bedside with tea. In illness the world went wonderfully warped, high temperatures turning your pillow to a dune of snow and bringing the night sky, with its daisy-sized stars, so close to your bed you could touch it, and taste the moon.

I loved my illnesses. I loved my regal mother bending to the mandates of biology, allowing me to rest and watch TV. She even read me stories, sitting by my bedside. In the dim room, her wedding ring twinkled like the eye of an elf, and her hands brushed stray strands of hair from my face.

Illness was a temporary respite, a release from the demands of an alienating world. In my world, women had hair as hard as crash helmets. In my world, girls did not play. They practiced: the piano, the flute, French, manners so refined they made all speech stiff. Illness was not stiff. You went kaput. Fluids rushed in and rushed out, your nose got gummy, and frogs hopped around in your chest. Getting better was a grief. One morning you woke up, and your fever had fled. Your throat felt depressingly fine. You looked across your orange carpet and saw your black patent dancing shoes, your child-sized golf clubs. You saw your French and Hebrew workbooks, with all those verbs you would have to conjugate before dinner tonight. You wanted to weep.

Prozac, too, made me want to weep. Prozac, too, was a grief, because it returned me to the regular world with consequences I never expected. For the first few days on the medication I vomited a lot, and I got headaches. Dr. Stanley told me these were normal side effects in the early stages, before the body has adjusted to its new companion.

At first I didn't think much of the stuff. I was as obsessive as ever, and a jitteriness took hold of me. I did notice I was sleeping a bit better, although my dreams were jagged and relentless, filled with images of tide pools and the sounds of shouts. Waking each morning after a few hours of rest, I still felt exhausted.

And then one morning, about five days after I'd first started the Prozac, I no longer felt so exhausted. I opened my eyes and my clock read eight a.m. I'd turned out my light at midnight, which meant I'd gotten, for the first time in I don't know how many months, a seamless eight hours of uninterrupted rest. It was a Saturday, this I remember clearly, and stripes of sun were on my walls. I sat up.

Something was different. I looked at my hand. It was the same hand. I touched my face—nose, cheeks, chin, all there. I rubbed my eyes and went into the kitchen.

The kitchen, too, was the same—table, two pine chairs, gray linoleum buckled and cracked along the floor. The sink still dripped. The grass moved against my window ledge. All the same, all different. What was it?

A piano tuner used to come to our house when I was young.

He was a blind man, his eyes burned-out holes in his head, his body all bent. I remember how strange he looked against the grandeur of our lives, how he stooped over that massive multi-toothed instrument and tweaked its tones. The piano never looked any different after he'd worked on it, but when I pressed a C key, or the black bar of an F minor, the note sprung out richer.

This was what was different. It was as though I'd been visited by a blind piano tuner who had crept into my apartment at night, who had tweaked the ivory bones of my body, the taut strings in my skull, and now, when I pressed on myself, the same notes, but with a mellower, fuller sound, sprang out.

This is what was different—tempo, tone. Not sight, for everything looked the same. Not smell, for everything smelled the same. Not pitch, for the vibrations of the world were just as they'd always been. To describe the subtle but potent shift caused by Prozac is to tussle with failing words, sensations that seep beyond language. But that doesn't make it any less miraculous. Doctors assure the public that psychotropic drugs don't get a patient high; rather, such drugs, supposedly, return the patient to a normal state of functioning. But what happens if such a patient, say myself for instance, has rarely if ever experienced a normal state of functioning? What happens if such a patient has spent much of her life in mental hospitals, both pursuing and pursued by one illness after another? What happens if "regular life" to such a person has always meant cutting one's arms, or gagging? If this is the case, then the "normal state" of functioning that Prozac ushers in is an experience in the surreal, Dali's dripping clock, a disorientation so deep and sweet you spin. A soaring high. For this very reason, Prozac, make no mistake about it, blissed me out and freaked me out and later on, when the full force of health hit me, sometimes stunned me with grief.

I want to describe it. I'm sorry, for there is nothing that bores me quite so much as people who regale me with tales of their acid trips, how the walls breathed and the unity in the world became palpably apparent. Still, descriptions of acid trips, relentless as they may sometimes be, are a staple of sixties literature, characterize the mood of an entire generation. My generation, of course, is the Prozac generation, and no generation can be complete without a record of the substances that have irrevocably altered it.

Don't let anyone tell you differently. If you have been sick for a long, long time, Prozac may make you high. It probably won't make you high the way pot does or acid does; it will make you high by returning you to a world you've forgotten or never quite managed to be a part of, but a world, nevertheless, that you at first fit into with the precision of a key to a lock, or a transmitter to its receptor.

For me, as I've said, it was a question of tempo and tone. Everything seemed to be moving according to a different rhythm, 4/4 now 2/2, a smoothing out or slowing down. It was, to date, the single most stunning experience of my life, although later it would unfold with ever more complexity, even danger. But at that moment, standing in my kitchen on an early Saturday morning, I soaked in it. A cat loped by. Clouds meandered in the sky. But best, absolutely best of all, were the surfaces. Quite simply, they no longer compelled me—to touch, knock, tap, the relentless obsessive itch that had plagued me for months, that had gotten me fired from my job and almost put me back behind the bars of a hospital. I walked around my apartment, curious to see what would happen. Yes, a streak of grease on the window. Yes, the prongs of a plug. I noticed it all, and didn't seem to quite care. Somehow, my attention had become flexible, swiveling left, now right, with such ease it made me giddy.

I don't recall precisely how I spent the next few hours. I dimly remember, now, years later, running my hands over a lot of things to test the medicine's power. I remember standing at my sink and fiddling with the faucets, turning them on and then off, but not completely, so the washers still dripped. It was okay. There would be no punishing flood. God was good. I turned the stove on, watched the blue ring of fire flare at the base of the burner, watched it recede as I swiveled the dial down, down, heat sucked back into blackness. Without checking, I trusted what I saw: The stove was off. God was good. Picking up my transistor radio, I gauged its little ridged dials. I heard bells and violins, settled back on my bed to listen to what I thought might be Bach. In my blissed-out state it took me many moments to realize that what was entering my mind was not Bach, but the simpler mass market stuff called Muzak.

I dozed off to the Muzak and when I woke up again it was nearing noon. Upon opening my eyes the second time that day, I had real misgivings. Was this a fluke? How long would it last? Had the obsessive-compulsive disorder really vanished? Just like that? Was I purely propelled by a chemical? I thought about these things for a while, in a happy, good-natured sort of way, lying back on my bed with my arms crossed, and then I decided to stop thinking and get on with it.

I pulled my schedule out from the night table drawer, the one I'd made upon leaving Mount Vernon, the one I'd been unable to follow for months because of the disabling OCD. My schedule suggested lunch: a scoop of tuna with low-cal mayonnaise, four unsalted rice cakes, a glass of skim milk, and two vanilla wafers for dessert. I'd been eating this meal, or meals just like it, for great spans of time. I couldn't quite believe that. Low-cal mayonnaise? Vanilla wafers? I wanted something richer, something whipped and frozen.

I went to the next item on my schedule, an afternoon workout. I felt too calm for the rigors of a run. Well, then, what could I do? What could I do? Now that my mind was clear, maybe I could return to reading, fifty pages a day, the requirement I'd always set for myself.

I went over to my bookshelves, makeshift boards on bricks. I had a lot of books, most of them nonfiction, because I'd always felt that in nonfiction, specifically in the disciplines of psychology, philosophy, and theology, I might find clues about ways to live my life. I scanned the spines, saw titles like *The Denial of Death* and *Death in Life* and *Man's Search for Meaning,* Sartre's *Being and Nothingness* and Kierkegaard's *Fear and Trembling.* I had always loved these sort of books, loved untangling the dense mats of seaweedlike sentences, underlining and starring meaningful passages that I took in as a kind of elite self-help, which is probably what all this stuff really amounts to anyway. But now, well, now I stood by my bookshelves a little lost. They were full of death and anxiety, the spines seeming to exude cold clouds. I had no desire to read Kierkegaard. Maybe something a little lighter, like Frankl. I picked up *Man's Search for Meaning* and skimmed through the thumbed pages. I read my many beloved Frankl sentences, such as, "A man who for years had thought he had reached the absolute limit of all possible suffering now found that suffering has no limits, and that he could suffer still more, and more intensely still." I spent a long time staring at that sentence. Over and over in my life it had brought me comfort, for Frankl, along with other existentialists, is devoted to the meaning and dignity of pain. I had lived my life by these kinds of banners, only now, searching the sentence, I found little in it that really resonated deep in my bones. I had a cerebral sort of appreciation for the sentence, or, perhaps, an appreciation based in memory, the way one remembers with fondness a past partner, whom one no longer loves.

I slipped the book back among its companions. *Whom one no longer loves.* Herein lay the problem. A new kind of anxiety started to sprout in me, a duller, more distant anxiety, but anxiety nonetheless. For the world as I had known it my whole life did not seem to exist. Not only had Prozac—thank all the good gods in the world—removed the disabling obsessive symptoms; it seemed, as well, to have tweaked the deeper proclivities of my personality. Who was I? Where was I? Everything seemed less relevant, my sacred schedule, my gustatory habits, the narratives that had had so much meaning for me. Diminished. And in their place? Ice cream.

I went outside to get it. The ice-cream truck had chugged up my street, paused by the curb, playing its carnival tunes. A Saturday in deep summer, children swarmed, sweaty money in their little fists. I joined them, the only adult in sight. I felt foolish, my breasts too big, stubble of dark hair on my legs. Now I think I made an apt choice to join the children, for I was a child myself in some significant ways, unschooled in the habits of health. I scanned the menu board—rocket cones, Malibu bars, grape pops. When it was my turn, I ordered something called an orange freeze. I sat on the front stoop of my apartment building to eat it, tearing the paper off, holding the wooden stick, biting down on the bar's bright tip, while, from its center, cream came out.

There are a lot of flukes in the world, sudden synchronicities that appear out of nowhere and fade back. One day you meet your long-lost and very best first-grade friend on a street in Sri Lanka, where you both just happen to be touring. Or you find, in your city's trash pile, the precise tin tile, with its pressed flower medallion and beveled edges, that is missing from your ceiling in an otherwise perfect period home. These are the brief, blessed moments that charm our lives, and we know better than to count on them.

At first I figured, wisely so, that this Prozac business was a fluke. The OCD could not have vanished like that. My overall mood would plummet at any moment. I mentioned the change to no one. This was at a time when no one knew of Prozac, when books and articles had not yet appeared because the medication was brand-new. My aloneness in the experience only added to my awe, my shock. I tiptoed around for the next few days, looking left, then right, pausing to consider. Was I still feeling okay? I touched my head, my eyes. I stroked the lobe of my ear, feeling the skin almost impossibly soft there.

When, after four more days had passed and I still felt so shockingly fine, I called the Prozac doctor. I pictured him high in the eaves of McLean. In my mind his teeth had grown whiter, his hair blacker, and light leaped out from his wooden desk. I believed he had saved me. He loomed large.

"I'm well," I told him.

"Not yet," he said. "You've only started nine days ago. It may take up to a month, or even more, to build up a therapeutic blood level."

"No," I said. "I'm well." I felt a rushing joy as I spoke. "I've . . . I've actually never felt better."

A pause on the line. "I'm not sure that's possible, so fast," he said.

So fast.

Still today, in writing this, I doubt the accuracy of my memory. Research seems to support the notion that Prozac is a slow-acting agent, over weeks or months peeling away the thick skin of illness. My sister, Tracy, who is also on Prozac, tells me I've misrepresented the drug, at least according to her experience, which was much more along the lines of researched case studies, a gradual lifting of a dusty curtain. However, my friends Karen and Veronica—also, alas, on Prozac—say they, like me, recall a very specific and stunning moment when, for the first time, "the world seemed right."

I wonder if my sister Tracy objects to my miracle-tinged description of the drug because it smacks of the illicit, puts one, maybe, in mind of heroin, which "hits" suddenly, or acid, which is often described as having a very definitive moment of onset. Perhaps we are uncomfortable thinking that Prozac may have properties similar to those "bad" drugs, for Prozac is supposedly not "bad," and it is not illicit, and those who take it, myself included, may dislike descriptions that suggest how close and complex is the relationship between prescribed, socially legitimized substance use and its underbelly, the syringes and tabs and little silver snifters.

Also, the effects of Prozac are probably as various as the people who ingest it. Thus, my sister's misgivings, while perhaps defensive, are also quite valid, because for her and many others, Prozac, when it works at all, works more slowly and far less dramatically. I have a hunch, completely untested but a hunch nevertheless, that the initial effects of Prozac are sometimes in direct proportion to the subjective distress of the consumer. I, the consumer in this case, had experienced my OCD as a devastating and life-threatening condition, nothing less. Prior to the OCD, my deviant and hospitalizable behaviors presented formidable and painful impediments to a productive life. So it should come as no surprise that the remission of my symptoms was a blessing, pure and simple; no, not a blessing, a redemption, both bright and blinding, heaven opening up, letting me in. The world.

If I had time, I think, to adjust more slowly to the changes in my world, then maybe the story would have played out more smoothly. As it happened, though, I went from being wracked with a dense array of symptoms to feeling nearly completely happy. This was especially surprising because I had not been prescribed Prozac—as later would become popular—to increase a general sense of well-being, but to combat an acute and discrete episode of obsessive behavior, that touching, that tapping. I was shocked to find that, in eradicating the OCD, it also did away with my chronic angst, an angst so embedded in my sense of self that it had felt inscribed in my skin like a fossil footprint in stone.

When a week went by, suspicion and surprise started to give way to curiosity. Lying in bed at night, I felt, for the first time since I could remember, the press of possibilities all around me. I felt it as physical, the presence of planets in the sky, the stretch of the earth's acres, plants everywhere beneath me, plants nosing up, pursed roses, the blue and white wheels of morning glories.

Whereas before, in the OCD, there had been a thousand and one imperatives to follow, I now felt a thousand and one interests to pursue. I, a long-term mental patient in my mid-twenties, had never been to a rock concert, had, with few exceptions and great displeasure, rarely left New England for more than a day, had never been swimming at Walden Pond, had not in years eaten a meal without anxiety, or taken a walk for no reason, or allowed myself to sleep late, lounging in the yellow light of late morning, or casually dated a man, or, in short, just played.

Now I would play, in some ways simply, in other ways more dangerously. The simple play involved a lot of browsing. I developed an interest in real estate magazines, especially the freebies stacked in stands along the streets. *Harmon Homes, Bremis's Better Buys, Century 21, Country Cottages by Val.* Back in my apartment I read them avidly, each abbreviated description— lvly gambrel with sunken l/r flr and e/I kitch, C/A, C/Alrm, come see the charm!—providing a porthole through which I swam into new spaces. I could feel the cool air circulating inside that gambrel, and light the color of candy poured through the leaded glass windows. There were gardens, for sure, and they contained beautiful flowers, flowers I could smell and see, whose names both proposed and fulfilled the most sensual of possibilities—climax marigolds and false dragonhead, meadowsweet and hollyhocks, pink baby's breath growing side by side with slender spikes of salvia, which, before blooming, issued a froth of sticky white bubbles under the little leaves.

I spent hours imagining myself inside the plethora of houses the world suddenly made available to me. I started going to open houses, pretending I was a buyer. I saw gold chandeliers sprouting down through intricate ceiling medallions, old gas lamps, and blue vases on cream-colored windowsills. In bathrooms I opened the double doors of medicine cabinets and found evidence of sour stomachs and stress headaches, everyday pains. I observed kitchens where foods had been cooked, and I touched double beds with pale yellow stains on otherwise perfectly white pillows. At night I even dreamed of houses, expansive and gorgeous dreams, room opening onto room, old marble garden tables, stone cupids, quilts and spiraling staircases, huge glass walls and vaulted ceilings where, from the shadows, loons and peacocks called.

In the month that followed, I ranged farther and wider, hungry from all the time I'd lost to illness. I went out nights, prowling around by myself until two or three in the morning, standing by the edge of the city river and admiring the waxy sheen of light on the water, or exploring the alleys of Boston, where broken things glittered. I felt invulnerable, or, perhaps, propelled by an unquenchable curiosity, a twenty-five-year-old with the judgment of an early adolescent. I was especially fond of Faneuil Hall, where men and food thrived side by side. I floated up and down the cobblestoned corridors, too nervous to approach anyone, but certainly not too nervous to eat. I had never before not cared about food, and now I reveled in my relaxed attitude. I didn't know when to stop. While I had not been clinically anorexic in many years, allowing myself to eat more or less normally, I had always fretted about my weight, sometimes more, sometimes less intensely. Years of this had left me alienated from my stomach's signals, and I was unaware of what it meant to be full. I remember wandering from stall to stall eating jelly beans in a sack, and dots—little sugary pastilles of pale yellow and pink and blue stuck on long strips of virginal white paper—black and red licorice, malted milk balls and gelati so light it felt like foam in my throat. I tried lemon ices and Sacher tortes and wedges of cake blistered with nuts. I bought a frozen piña colada at an outdoor bar—the first time I'd ever ordered from a bar—and, feeling supremely sophisticated, I toted the drink around, delicately sipping the frothed concoction through a crinkled straw. The glass was cold, and at one point I remember stopping and pressing it to my cheeks, my forehead, the way my mother had a long time ago, when I was ill and needed to be brought down.

And indeed, sometimes in the midst of this newness, this rampant exploration, my body tanked on sugar and dough, I felt I wanted to cry. I often, inexplicably, felt I wanted to cry while watching the Faneuil Hall magician night after night, a brilliant performer with straw-blond hair and a black top hat, whom I fell immediately in love with. This was a magician who knew his craft, who could make flowers blossom from silk swatches and birds flock from his fist. Night after night I watched him, his acts, and as the summer went by they got increasingly complex and wonderful and bizarre, drawing crowds ever larger. One night when I went to see him he had a female assistant with him, and he put her in a box. He brandished a sword, its blade red in the lamplight. The female assistant's head jutted out one end of the box, her feet out the other. She was wearing tiny black pumps, and her hair poured onto the pavement. He cut her in half, very slowly, very lovingly, smiling down at her while she smiled up at him. He separated her parts, walked between them to underscore their bifurcation, and then, with a flourish and a whoop, jammed her back together so she jumped out of the box, whole and unharmed. They kissed. I watched, mesmerized. The crowd clapped and clapped. I clapped, too, but I was not sure what for. When I looked up, the lights of the marketplace were spinning; the odors of hot dogs and pizza were strong, too strong.

He had a kitten with him then, this magician, a little tiger-striped thing that he dangled by the scruff of its neck and plunged into a tub of water. The crowd gasped and fell silent. We could see the animal struggling, or, rather, see his hand holding something frantic down, and down, and down. I felt myself falling. Two minutes passed. Then three. Then four. The struggling stopped. He whooped again, and pulled the same kitten, completely dry and thrivingly alive, from the bucket of water. The world, apparently, was full of illusion, and what was real was not real. I was lost and found, and in the finding still more lost.

"Now," he said, "for my finest act." He scanned the crowd, which had grown, by now, to hundreds. "I need a volunteer," he said.

No one volunteered.

"Contrary to all appearances," he said, "I am a loving man. I won't hurt you. The whole point of my show is to demonstrate the illusory nature of evil. You see?" He smiled. He had a charming smile, and some people popped up their hands, most of them girls with blond or brown ponytails and perfect summer tans.

"I cannot choose," he said, "from such a small sample. I need a genuine response, lots of volunteers. Put up your hands, people. Put up your hands."

"Put up your hands, people, put up your hands," the female assistant called, clapping her own tiny white hands with painted nails. Some men, now, put up their hands, and then a field of hands flourished.

The magician looked around. I did not put up my hand, which is probably why he chose me. Or perhaps he had seen me standing there, night after night, a girl/woman on the edge of awkwardness and excitement. "You," he said to me. "You are the one."

I put my hand to my chest and mouthed, *Me?*

"Yes, you," he said. "I can see you have the mystical sort of temperament this act needs in order to, shall we say, fly. Come into the center now. Come, come," he said, beckoning me.

I went into the center and he placed a light bulb in my hand. His female assistant walked around, with a silver snuffer dousing all the gas lamps and candles surrounding his pavement stage. "Hold your palm very still," he said to me. "Hold your palm very still and think of what it is you most want."

I closed my eyes and thought. I held my palm as still as I could. What was it I wanted? The press of possibilities. The planets, so many, too many, strewn in the sky. The openness of new space, new skin, me and not me, foreign and frightening, lost and found. Where was I? Who was I? I did not know what I wanted.

I heard a drawn-out "Oooh" from the crowd. I felt something lift from my palm. "And open your eyes," the magician whispered, leaning down close to me, his lips at my ear.

I opened my eyes and saw the light bulb maybe five feet above me, lit up, a detached and glowing yellow sphere, a lost and lovely shape hovering. It was a head without a body, an unmoored mind. "You've done it," he said. "She's done it," he shouted, and it was a few moments before I realized the crowd, that crowd, clapped for me.

At home, later on that night, I took off my clothes and looked at myself. My skin had browned from the summer sun. My eyes were clear as newly washed windows. I was the picture of health, as though I had finally come into the body meant for me, the body that had been with me even before birth, its shape hovering in the unformed fetus, fleshing out, fleshing out.

I felt at home in this body. The curiosities and energies that had always been rightfully mine were finally taking their place. This must be what people mean when they say, "Prozac helped me become the person I was meant to be."

And yet for me it was not that simple. My personality, yes, had always consisted of suppressed energies and curiosities, but also of depressions, echoing intensities, drivenness that tipped into pain. With the exception of the OCD, which I was only too happy to be rid of, I missed these things, or parts of them anyway, for they were as familiar to me as dense fog and drizzle, which has its own sort of lonely beauty, as does a desert, or the most mournful of music.

Looking in the mirror, I touched my bronzed shoulders and

nose with its sunny saddle of freckles on it. I thought of the light bulb, loosed, and when I pictured it, it was floating still, far from the magician's black bag, floating over a dark field and then the moving marble of the Atlantic Ocean, searching for its socket, pulsing with a brightness it could not comprehend.

In the past, I had always recorded images that were odd or moving to me in my journal. My methods, perhaps, were a bit odd. When I wrote, it was not from "me," but from the eight people I pictured living inside of me, eight people who had kept me company for more years than I can remember—three men who taunted me, three ten-year-olds with confidence and feistiness, a girl trapped in a glass case, and a blue baby, sometimes dead, sometimes dying. Taken together, these eight beings comprised the core of my personality, providing me with focal points. I knew myself by knowing them, the blue baby's craving for comfort, the glassed-in girl's high-pitched anxiety, her desire for freedom clashing with her need for the airless perfection of a crystal world.

The blue baby was the one who usually had the most interesting things to say to me. When it spoke, I went into a light trance, my pen moving as if of its own accord, and when it was finished speaking, I felt as though I'd visited a place too intense to be anything but real.

Now I picked up my pen and opened my journal. I closed my eyes, hunched over the page, and waited. I said *Yes* to myself, which in the past had been the signals for the baby to emerge and speak with me. Now I heard silence.

Yes. Hello.

Nothing.

Yes, hello.

Maybe a slight stir, a quickening that faded fast.

I kept my eyes closed. And then I could see them all down there, the blue baby curled, the girl in the glass case biting at her nails. And then I could hear them down there, snatches of sentences I transcribed on paper, but the words felt dull, dead. A bright blue layer separated me from them, and as I sensed correctly at the time, the bright blue barrier would remain as a perpetual part of my Prozac career. That night I tried again, and again, my room dark, street lamps shining like candles. Calling. Shhh. Calling. Shhh. The air swirled. Something flapped and faded. The page—I—whiteness. Both blank.

I finally fell into a troubled sleep and I woke with fear. Monday morning. Writing had always been essential to me, not the academic stuff of school, but the looser and loftier stuff of stories, poems. That day, I called the Prozac doctor again.

"I feel weird," I said.

"Weird," he repeated. "Like how?"

I paused, struggling to find the words. "I'm worried," I said.

"Of course you're worried," he said. "You're an obsessive. Obsessives worry."

"No," I said. "I'm not obsessively worrying. I'm worrying unobsessively about the medication. Do you think it can take away your creativity?"

"There have been no studies on that question," the Prozac doctor said. "But I doubt it. I certainly wouldn't worry about it."

"I don't feel like me," I said. "I mean, I feel more like me in some ways and less like me in others. I'm scared. I'm really worried," I said, my voice rising, the memory of silence, company I could not reach.

"I hear that," he said. "Your worry indicates the presence of pathology. We should think about upping your dose."

He told me to take three capsules a day instead of two, which, at first, I didn't do. In fact, I was thinking of stopping the Prozac altogether, torn between my desire for my old self and my enthusiasm for the new. I don't think this conflict indicated the presence of pathology. I was concerned that Prozac, and the health it spawned, could take away not only my "creativity," but my very identity. And the answer to that—although there had been "no studies"—was a resounding yes. I was definitely a different person now, both more and less like me, a burgeoning mystery fulfilling one destiny while swerving from another. There is loss in that swerving. And my experience on Prozac showed me how few there are who understand that loss or are prepared for its expression.

The work of the psychiatrist Arthur Kleinman focuses on the subjective meanings of illness. He calls illness, or suffering, a narrative that, at its best, concatenates a coherent story of self. Symptoms and pain take on value as they become symbols referring to something larger than themselves. The cancer patient must make of her pain *this* or *that*. The schizophrenic sees his pain, perhaps, as stories sent by gods and devils, and, as such, the stories are rich in reverberations. Illness, according to Kleinman, is more than a set of symptoms, over the long term transforming itself into the hows and whys and ways of being.

Having lived with chronic depression, a high-pitched panic, and a host of other psychiatric problems since my earliest years, I had made for myself an illness identity, a story of self that had illness as its main motive. I did not sleep well because I was ill. I cut myself because I was ill. Illness, for me, had been the explanatory model on which my being was based. Having spent much time in mental hospitals, illness had also been something I'd learned, like a skill, like spelling. From Rosie and Katie I acquired ever new and niftier ways of cutting myself, admiring the ruby zippers that tracked these girls' arms. From Ann I'd learned anxiety's different positions and sounds, its jagged breaths and sweat. I knew medication's spectrum, vermillion liquid Thorazine, the melted sky of Stelazine, lavender Halcyons and Ativans scattered like snowflakes on a steel tray. Illness was language as well as color; I knew a secret special language with words like *sharps* and *checks* and *rounds*, and then the longer, arcane phrases and words that every patient picks up—trichotillomania and *waxy flexibility*, *Munchausens* and *borderlines*, the most mysterious word of all, suggesting the line of the horizon, a flat world, a ship tipping over into star-filled night.

And now, gone. I had tipped over, stepped over the border into health. There was no more depression, which had felt like the stifling yet oddly comforting weight of a woolen blanket, or anxiety, which lent a certain fluorescence to things, or voices, which had always been there, sometimes louder, sometimes softer, some North Star of sound in the night.

A few days later, I had a follow-up appointment with the Prozac doctor. His office was just as I remembered it, large, gracious, a plush rug. Added to his Prozac paraphernalia was now a three-dimensional model of a plastic synapse showing how the drug worked. The synapse, which looked like one of those crazy straws, all looped and bent, was bright pink and its tip ended in a dish, labeled the synaptic cleft, where turquoise liquid, simulating serotonin, pooled. He demonstrated for me. By pushing a button on the right, the synapse twitched like an epileptic insect, sucking up the serotonin at a brisk clip. "The obsessive brain," he said, nodding toward me. When he pushed the button on the left, however, the synapse slowed down its sucking, allowing the serotonin to remain lapping in its gap like a deep blue lake.

"By allowing the serotonin to remain for longer periods of time in the synaptic cleft," he said, "Prozac can alter mood and, it appears, diminish, if not eradicate, OCD."

"But what else," I asked, "does it diminish or eradicate?"

"You are still worried," he said to me, trying to act like a therapist, which was not at all in his nature. Still, I appreciated the effort.

"Yes," I said. I was too embarrassed to tell him about the eight people in me. "I'm still feeling . . . off," I said. "Off in a good way, I think, but—"

"Symptoms," the Prozac doctor said to me. "Let's review your anxiety symptoms. Obsessive thoughts?"

"Very few," I said.

"Would you say a sixty percent reduction?"

"Eighty, ninety, maybe even ninety-five."

"Excellent," the Prozac doctor said. "A marvelous response. Depression?"

"Absolutely none," I said. "Except . . ."

"Except what?" he said. "Are you sleeping well?"

"Yes."

"Concentration?"

"I can read faster than I could before, and my thinking's clear."

"Eating?"

"A lot," I said.

At this he looked concerned. He sat back in his chair and folded his arms across his crisp suit. He knew about my history of eating disorders. "Binging?" he asked.

"No," I said. "I'm not binging. It's not compulsive. I'm just not so afraid of getting fat. I don't think I will get fat, even though I guess I've gained. I'm just sampling a lot of foods I never allowed myself to try before."

"Purging?" he said, looking straight at me.

I shook my head no.

"Well," he said, steepling his fingertips and staring up at the ceiling, "it seems Prozac has made you almost completely symptom free. You have had a beautiful response to it. Consider yourself lucky."

I am lucky, people say, *so long as I have my health and my family*. In church people pray, *God grant me my health and my happiness*. On Rosh Hashanah, the Jewish New Year, people eat apples and honey, in the hopes for a robust twelve months. The Western medical profession, which grew directly out of our Judeo-Christian culture, covets health and eschews sickness as though pain were a failing. The Western medical profession, it seems, though, has taken health even further than the religious traditions, assuming health is not only good, but that it's natural.

After all, when you are sick, there are plenty of places (insurance willing) where you can go to get healed, but when you are healed, are there any places you can go to learn not to be sick? The very idea of having to learn not to be sick, of having to learn health, sounds vaguely ridiculous, so ensconced are so many of us in the notion that health is as natural as grass, in the right conditions growing green and freely.

Freud envisioned the human body as a hydraulic machine, seeking to maintain homeostasis, at all times, a humming equilibrium in which the gears and chimes of bone and brain worked harmoniously. Robert E. Ornstein, a neurobiologist, calls the brain a "health maintenance organization," whose purpose is to keep thriving and balanced all the body's systems. New Age doctors, like Deepak Chopra, have gone even further, or, perhaps, been more explicit, stating that the human brain and body seek health at all costs, and its entire construction is geared to the generation and maintenance of the robust.

But health, at least in my case, was not so natural, and I'm not totally sold on its goodness, either. At the risk of sounding, of being, simplistically nostalgic, I look with favor upon the old convalescent homes of the late eighteenth and early nineteenth centuries, a kind of halfway house where the chronically ill, now recovering, hovered in their tentative health, trying it out, buttoning and unbuttoning, resewing the seams, until at last the new outfit seemed right. The old-fashioned convalescent home, chairs stretched by the salty sea, isolated from the world and yet close on the cusp of it, acknowledged the need for socially sanctioned transition, moving the patient incrementally from an illness-based identity to a health-based identity, out of hospital, not yet home, hovering, stuttering, slowly learning to speak the sanguine alphabet again.

Prozac, at least in my case, did not eliminate worry; rather, it shortened its life span so my bouts of fretting over the drug were rather rapidly replaced by longer bouts of cheer. That evening, after having seen the Prozac doctor, I dressed for my first concert ever. An old high school friend had gotten us tickets to see Michelle Shocked. I had been on the medication, altogether, for not more than two months. I put on black leggings and a black tunic and a choker of red around my neck, and although I intended for this costume to express my adventurousness, now I see it as a sign of the searing I felt inside, the choker shining like a slash on my neck, my clothes the clothes of grief.

Now that I was a Prozac person, I owned a good bit of makeup, which I had bought at the twenty-four-hour CVS at one or two or even three in the morning, standing by mirrors and furtively applying cherry balm and frosty pink. That evening I wore my makeup, too, and I slung an army knapsack over my shoulder.

I had never seen such a crowd in love, and it moved me even further beyond myself, up and out. When Michelle Shocked came onto the stage, thousands surged forward, flicking lighters into the air. All around me bodies moved, and I had to move, too, because I was a part of something larger, a perfect, painful rhythm. Michelle crooned out ballads about ice and red clay roads, about high skies and dead friends, and I trembled. The man next to me trembled. He took my hand and had me move left, now right, now out of the aisle and up close to the stage, the music pouring. And then it was over.

"My name," he said, speaking into the sudden silence, his accent Israeli, "is Yehuda."

Yehuda, I thought, swooning stupidly, Joshua, the name of the biblical boy who fought the lions, the heroic man who overcame evil. Such a man could not hurt me. Such a man could only help me. And he was handsome to boot, dark eyes, dark curly hair, broad in all the right ways.

"Lauren," I said, looking down at the floor.

He was very forward, that Yehuda. He put his hand right under my chin and tipped it up, so I was staring straight into his oh-so-sincere eyes. "I am new to this country," he said. "Visiting for a few weeks. I am planning to move here next year. Will you show me around?"

"Yes," I said. *Moving here,* I thought. *Handsome,* I thought. *Jewish,* I thought.

He pulled a bandanna out of his baggy pants and wiped his forehead. Saturday night, muggy, not too late. "I would like to go swimming," he said. "I have heard there are some very good swimming places, not too far."

My friend, at this point, had found me in the crowd. "Time to go," she said.

"I'll call you later," I said to her. "This is Yehuda. We're going swimming."

She narrowed her eyes and looked at me. "Swimming, huh?" She bent close to me. "You're sure that's what you want?"

Yehuda was staring at us. She looked from him to me. "Swimming, huh?" she said again, her voice full of portent. "Aren't you just getting over strep?"

"I'm fine," I said. And, indeed, I did feel fine, quite confident all would be well. I pulled her aside. "He's actually a friend," I said. "An old cousin of mine," I lied. "It's amazing we met here, old family from Israel."

"Yehuda is your cousin," she repeated. "What other cousins do you have, maybe some from Afghanistan, Egypt, Africa? A real international family."

I had a brief image, then, of the eight people inside me, north of my neck, south of my stomach, a muffled population, a distant planet.

"He's the only cousin I have," I said, and for a second I believed it.

Cousin Yehuda had a nice little rental car, a spiffy red thing with a convertible top. He was very polite, ushering me out of the concert hall ahead of him, suavely opening doors and taking my elbow to cross the street. As soon as we had buckled into his vehicle, though, he announced that the night air had cooled him, and he no longer felt like swimming. From his glove compartment he pulled out a tour book, thumbed through it, and announced he would like to visit Boston's famous deer park.

"Boston's famous deer park?" I repeated. I'd lived in Boston all my life and never heard of such a thing.

He put the tour book in my lap and, sure enough, there it was, in a close-by suburb, opened 'round the clock, in all seasons, described in lush and loving terms, acres of trees, fawns springing over moss while the city skyline glowed in the distance.

"Okay," I said, basically agreeing to drive into a forest with a strange six-foot man, one of my dumber decisions, informed by the off-kilteredness that was health to me.

We arrived there in less than twenty minutes. Evergreens spiked into the air. Through the dense darkness I could see the hovering shapes of the trees, their roots breaking the earth like tendons showing through skin. Something moist and furry brushed my knee. Insects rose from rotting logs. He held my hand, this Joshua who beat the beasts, this king cousin, he took my hand and let me into the wild.

My heart was paddling, half from fear, half from excitement. This was life, yes. Here I was, yes. Something flapped above me, a taut wing with a reddish membrane stretched over piping of bone. "Bats," Yehuda announced calmly.

My eyes adjusting to the darkness, I could see better now. I could see bats soaring beneath the dense foliage of trees. I could see the craggy cliff that was this man's face, jutting nose, rocky chin, the steep slopes of his Sephardic cheeks. I didn't think he would hurt me. After all, he came from Israel and, as he'd told me while we stood on the concert floor, he'd been in the army. To a Jewish girl raised by fiercely Zionist parents, that fact made it all seem safe. He was one of the men I'd watched on television as a child. He had rescued the athletes at Munich; he had personally guarded the Golan heights, folding victims of terrorists' attacks into his warm bulk.

And, like all army men, he was more of a doer than a talker. As soon as we reached a clearing, he didn't waste much time swooping me into his arms like I was a victim myself, laying me down on the forest floor, where the worms were.

"Wait a minute," I said, pushing him off me.

"Okay," he said, sitting up. I guess he took me quite literally. He peered at his watch, and after what seemed like precisely a minute had gone by, he descended again, my cousin Yehuda. He unbuttoned my tunic and managed to finagle a breast.

"No. No. Wait a minute," I said, and this time I scuttled away from him.

"Okay," he said in the same good-natured voice. He held up his hands in a protest of innocence and then casually slung one arm around my shoulder. We sat in silence. I could feel the forest encroaching from all sides, the breaths of a million beasts, insects working the earth, dragging and devouring.

I shuddered and Yehuda pulled me closer, a gesture both threatening and comforting, locking me in. "The moon," he said softly, looking up through the trees, "is complete."

Indeed it was a full moon, large and a little sickly looking. I myself felt a bit sick now, like I might be getting that strep my friend had mentioned.

"I have a sore throat," I announced, a comment that makes such perfect sense, for illness had always been both my escape and my means of seduction, the heat between my mother and me.

The Israeli, as though on cue, turned to me. He looked straight at me, his pupils deep as inkwells. As though he had known me forever, he started to stroke my throat, up and down, up and down, long hypnotizing movements, like a lullaby. He didn't push me down or fumble with my buttons, just stroked and stroked, allowing me to open at my own pace. I kissed him first.

I think he could sense my fear. He made love to me like I was a virgin, very delicately. The whole time, I felt there and not there. I felt waves of fear and pleasure. My body responded, rising like dough to his touch. However, my mind felt detached, and while there was warmth, there was also ice, wedging up between us, within me. I had little experience with sex. My one relationship in college had coincided with my most severe period of anorexia. The last time I'd made love, I'd weighed ninety pounds, a woman without a period, a woman all bone and brain, no flesh. This flesh was new to me. Deep in my body, eggs ripened and dropped. Snakes slid on the ground. I imagined deer came forward, hundreds of them, thousands of them watching us with wet and ghostly eyes. Something moaned. Inside me an organ I'd never felt before reddened and stretched. This was new. Pleasure was new. He was new. I was not making love to one stranger, but to two.

He dropped me off in front of my apartment building, and only once I was inside did I realize I was shaking. What from? What from? A narrow escape? The peak of pleasure? A potential rape? A love?

The image of deer kept coming back to me. We hadn't seen any, but I had felt them, their hot breath and rocking canters, their antlers, covered with fuzz.

And when I peeled off my clothes, I saw scat on the back of them, and three hairs from the finest hide.

Three days passed, my breasts filled, and still my period didn't come. I pressed at my stomach, and whenever liquid slid from me, I rushed to the bathroom to peer. Nothing.

But inside, everything. Inside, things puffed and leaked and ripened in lumps. I felt a little fish swimming, a speckled tadpole turning, and turning again.

Terror. I remembered Yehuda, only now without complexity. Now he was purely bad, a man immersed in bloodied bodies, a man with weapons he'd let loose in me, this baby a blade. As for sex, well, sex was sweet, but clearly dangerous, and you could lose yourself in it, if you had not already lost yourself outside of it, sucking down those plump little green-and-cream-colored spheres.

I let a week go by, and then I took myself to a woman's health clinic in Brookline. I was so convinced I was pregnant that I wanted to schedule an abortion before I'd even had a test. "You're putting the cart before the horse," the assistant said, and wouldn't comply.

In a small room with potholders on stirrups and a picture of Monet's water lilies on the ceiling, which women were meant to stare at while doctors did things to them, I got my blood taken. Then they put my blood into a little blender and whipped it up. I kept having to run to the bathroom, I was so nervous. AIDS had not even crossed my mind, only pregnancy. I figured Israelis didn't have AIDS.

"Okay," the nurse said, motioning me from the waiting room, where they had sent me while the test was brewing. I tipped back into the examining room.

"Negative," the doctor said.

Bliss. I loved the Israeli all over again. And what fun that night now seemed, with all those deer.

"I need some birth control," I said to him. "I need a diaphragm." Actually, I wasn't planning to sleep with anybody. The Israeli had gone back home and was probably right now flying in a sleek jet over the golden grains of the desert. But still. Just in case.

"Let's get you fitted," he said. I liked the idea of a diaphragm. I pictured its small rubber cap snapped over my cervix, containing me, covering me while I exposed my skin.

The doctor, who was Russian and who was, for some strange reason, wearing a name tag that said Boris Yazlovian, put on his gloves and then checked me. His hands in me hurt a bit, that organ reddening and stretching. I winced.

"Hmmm," he said. "Is there pain?"

"Yes," I said. "A little."

I was familiar with that particular pain. Anytime I'd had intercourse there had always been a sting and stretch if the man moved in a certain way. I hadn't thought to check it out, just figured it was one of my womanly perks, like a period. After all, I'd never totally reconciled myself to the idea of someone sticking something inside of me, in my rawest part. Of course, along with pleasure, it should hurt a little.

The doctor lowered his head between my legs, and then there was more pain. "Excuse me," I said.

He bobbed back up. His face was flushed, a man who had just made a mighty discovery. "You . . ." he said in his thick Russian accent, "you are still a virgin."

"Am not," I said, sounding like an eighth-grader. I was offended. After all, since I'd been on Prozac, I was a woman of the world. Light bulbs lifted from me, men entered me, I rode on the ridged backs of stags.

"Yes, you are," he repeated. "Even though you are a sexually active twenty-five-year-old, you are still, medically speaking, a virgin."

And then he explained to me how I had an unusual hymen, O-shaped and still intact, very stretched but not quite clipped. A tough little hymen, he said, a stubborn, grisly circle of skin that would bend but not break, and that was responsible for the occasional pain.

"We should take care of it," he said, and I swear I saw a glint in his eye. "It's a simple medical procedure. A local anesthetic, snip, and the end."

But I was perfectly fine with my hymen the way it was.

"Oh, no," he said. "It's not normal."

I pictured my hymen, a red wedge within me, something, through all my Prozac adventures, that had stayed the same, sealed and safe. Deep in my vagina I had my own little locked hospital room.

"We should cut it open," he said. "It's not feasible for child-birth, and continued pain during intercourse could cause . . ."

He paused.

"Could cause what?" I said.

"Psychological difficulties," he said, lowering his voice. "You are a healthy young woman. No need to take a risk like that."

I smiled to myself. "We wouldn't want psychological difficulties," I said to him. I pictured him cutting, the door opening, blue baby, glassed-in girl, all tumbling out of me, birthed from me, severed and separate.

"In five minutes it will be over," he said, calling in a nurse, not waiting for me to acquiesce. In the name of health, I let him lead. A shot of novocaine, and my insides hummed. The scissors were tiny, like cuticle clippers, and he put them up me. I felt not a thing. I heard a crisp snap. In that moment, the last cords to my old self, my sick self, were cut. I thought of the pictures I'd seen as a child, astronauts floating around a foreign moon, all space silent.

I started to cry. At first I cried lightly, and privately, so the nurse and doctor did not notice. As they wheeled me down the hall, though, I started to cry harder, as though there had been a hymen in my throat as well, and now that it was gone the grief of health rose up and ran out, salty.

The corridor was narrow and cool. White lights burned above. We passed what must have been a vacuum aspirator machine, and it was full of fresh contents, red and glinting, wet and salty. Blue baby.

I closed my eyes. I put my hands over my emptied stomach. The novocaine was wearing off now, and my birth canal buzzed, like there was a bee caught in there, like you sometimes find a bee in an abandoned room, buzzing and buzzing among the dusty furniture.

The nurses in the recovery room, where I was placed, were so kind. The room was full of women in various stages of anesthesia, and all of them, I think, had just had abortions. Some lay with their bruised-looking lids closed; others struggled to sit up; one woman moaned and a nurse held a cup of ginger ale to her lips.

I kept crying, freely now, having finally arrived at a place made just for grief. I thought of the hospital, a nurse named Iris, the luscious look of red medicine in a tiny plastic cup, the grayness of depression, the intensity of anxiety, both of which had given me my voice, the people I'd lost, hovering inside me, all my cords cut. "It's okay, dear," a nurse said to me, coming over to stroke my hair. I'm sure she thought I was recovering from an abortion myself, and in a way she was right. Girl gone. Blue baby gone. "It will all seem better soon," she crooned. "We won't have you leave until you're ready."

Until I was ready. No one, in my Prozac career, had yet said that to me. I had arrived at my convalescent home, this brief respite in a recovery room. I lay back in the seat. I let her hand smooth my brow. She had pale pink lipstick on, and she had beautiful skin. The sun coming in through the window sifted through her hair, making the blondness glow gold. Maybe this mother, she would read me a story. Maybe she would bring me tea and toast. Maybe she would stay until the heat passed, and then—I could see it—she would help me stand.

Patricia Stevens

LOST HIP JOINTS AND OTHER THINGS I CAN T LET GO OF

I

For years, one of my life plans was that once I'd turned the big Five-O and both my sons, whom I'd raised alone for more than a decade, were launched from my care, I would find a way to do more walking. I would hike a chunk of the Appalachian Trail or descend a wall of the Grand Canyon, a couple of mere strolls for experienced hikers, but anticipated celebration for a single parent turned fifty, a healthy woman who did not want to waste time contemplating the onset of hot flashes and empty-nest syndrome. Though it was well worth the effort, I traded in a few dreams to see that two young boys grew into fine young men, so fifty would be one huge mile marker: I would take care of me again—find a new place to live, a new job, new adventures, maybe even a new man, most certainly more time to walk. But then I was ambushed, waylaid by having to take on two bionic hips. The ball joints of my old hips, the ones I was born with, were sawn off, replaced with ones made of titanium, and now ride in brand-new polymer sockets.

II

I didn't walk until I was eighteen months old. It was the end of the war and my father was out in the Pacific, drafted into the navy to sit in a ship's belly and stare at a radar screen. Of course, my mother worried about everything: a Japanese torpedo sinking my father's ship; my brother leaving the basement door open. Fearing that I might tumble headfirst down the stairs, she kept me in the playpen, where I grew into a fat baby with a double chin and triple-roll thighs, eighteen months old and not yet walking. The conventional wisdom at the time said I was a "late walker" because I was thus penned, and that theory may have been partially true, because I did walk soon after my father got home and I was let out of the cage to roam free.

Later, I was told that I was double-jointed, a source of pride. As a kid, I could sit on the floor all afternoon playing Chutes and Ladders or dressing my paper dolls, with my legs splayed out like a frog behind me. The other kids were in awe.

Though I'd been told many times over, for as long as I can remember, by scores of different people that "you have an odd walk," and I was sensitive about it, I have never stopped thinking of myself as a walker. Despite my slow start, I took up the practice as soon as I was old enough to cross the busiest street in our working-class, suburban, south-of-Pittsburgh neighborhood. Walking was an escape from the crowded tiny red-brick house where there was usually some form of tension percolating. My walking always had a purpose, which was never mere exercise. As an eight- or nine-year-old I was the one in the family who would volunteer to make the trip from our house to the only store within walking distance: small, dark, all-purpose, family-run Russell's. My mother complained that their prices for milk and bread were robbery, but Kroger's was miles away and she didn't drive. I welcomed the chance to flee. Though I had a turquoise-blue Schwinn, I preferred to have my own two legs carry me so that I would have more time to be out with the sun searing the part in my hair, cooking up the thoughts and images in my head. Even in the house, I lived in my head, but somehow, once I got outside, whatever I kept running around inside my skull was better, more alive, more hopeful.

By high school, the best time of day was the afternoon hike from where the bus let us off at the very bottom of Rockhill Road. It didn't matter what the weather was—the walk was a transitional time and space zone, a necessary brain and lung cleansing that took me from one inside world to another. As time passed I kept on walking: to classes, fast-paced across the table-flat campus at Bowling Green in Ohio; then along the streets of Boston from my apartment to the work I barely tolerated as an employment interviewer for a large insurance company. A few years later, as a married mom in California, I looked forward to my late morning trek down the hill with two little boys—one riding in the stroller, one riding in the apple-green pack on my back—across the Carmel River, and up the other hill to the cozy, one-room library, where the kids were allowed to crawl around on the carpeted floor.

One summer, long after California, when I was in my late forties and my sons were in their teens and back West with their father for two months, I traveled from Iowa City to meet up with a volunteer group in Guatemala. There, I walked up the side of a volcano. With my feet sinking near ankle deep in the volcanic ash that sanded away the leather on my new white Reeboks, I almost gave up on the last few hundred yards. But in the end, with encouragement from one of our young, wiry, machete-carrying Guatemalan guides, I made it, and sat at the summit only to be showered with sparks from the adjoining peak, where the volcano erupted every few minutes. *I could die here*, I thought, unaware that my hip joints were about to fail me. It was frightfully exhilarating.

III

Today, beyond this computer screen, there is a gorgeous eastern Iowa day—sunny, near sixty, the first real break from the long winter's snow, ice, record-breaking low temps, and gloom—and I'm certain it's a day I'd be out in. I'd be fast-walking downtown to do errands, see a movie, maybe stop at the library, or I'd be hiking several miles in the other direction, away from town, just to get my heart pumping, suck the pre-spring air into my lungs, feel the sun on my face, let the bad-sad that's been floating around in my head half the winter transform itself into good-mood fluff. Instead, I'm inside, just a few days short of three weeks since the second surgery. I had the first hip—the left hip, the "bad" hip—replaced five months ago. Then the right one, which had to do all the supporting for the bad left one, abandoned me, too.

From the gene pool, I just happened to draw hip dysplasia, most frequently a first-daughter condition, and in my case not severe enough to be detected during my childhood. ("Hip dysplasia. As in German shepherds and golden retrievers," I say before anyone has a chance to ask, "You mean like *dogs?*") Off and on for almost two decades, I'd had episodes, meteors of pain—sometimes lasting for days at a time—shooting down my legs. All on my own, and not connecting it with my "double-jointedness," I came up with two plausible conditions: sciatica and having let a couple of babies ride around on my hip on teething days. Nothing to be done about that, especially when I did not have health insurance to cover outpatient care and prided myself on never having to visit a doctor.

Over the years, the hip dysplasia set off bouts of osteoarthritis, which then gradually chewed away the cushion of cartilage in the joints. As the damage progressed, the pain spells grew closer together and longer in duration until finally there was just pain. I tried the chiropractor, but when I finally admitted that my condition was only getting worse, I sought help from a rheumatologist and got the diagnosis: The arthritis I didn't even know I'd had, had devoured most of the cartilage in my left hip so that I was just about down to bone scraping on bone; my right hip joint was only slightly better looking. I sat in the rheumatologist's office, staring up at the X rays while the doctor pointed at the partial skeleton hanging there. "See this," she said. It was a nickel-sized spot on the left side of my pelvic bone. "You already have a cyst." Then she proceeded to draw me a diagram on her prescription pad—a series of slow, meandering switchbacks that eventually got steeper and closer together. "It goes faster at the end stage," she said, pressing harder on her pen, "until you need a replacement."

A ripple of shock was followed by a wave of anger, which was followed by a tsunami of sadness. "I am not about to sit in your office and bawl," I said.

"Why not?" she asked. Then she passed me the Kleenex and prepared a bag full of anti-inflammatory drug samples. Before I left her office, she hugged me and said she was sorry.

I eventually settled on the drug with the fewest side effects, one that gave me the least amount of ringing in my ears but that gnawed at my stomach all day and made me think I was hungry an hour after I ate. Months later, when the pain was chronic again, I went back to the rheumatologist. She upped the dosage. "I'm too young for this," I said, choking back the tears. "I'm too young to have my legs taken away."

"I see the same reaction at eighty," she told me.

"I'm a long way from eighty."

Sympathetic, she spent another half hour with me, and when I asked for it, she wrote out a prescription for an antidepressant. After a few weeks, the antidepressant gave me a bladder infection that wouldn't quit and so I had yet another prescription, this time for an antibiotic. For someone who could only remember a handful of times having to take medication for an illness, having the pharmacist know me by name was a humbling experience.

I stopped the antidepressant, replaced it with mindless TV, and hoped for a miracle. It took me another year after that to admit that no matter how many remedies I tried—borage, primrose oil, fish oil, gelatin, folic acid, vitamin B_{12}, anything the health-food store would sell me—I was not going to make my cartilage grow back.

IV

It's amazing, near miraculous, that researchers and biomedical engineers came up with the bionic parts that would give me the hope of walking without pain again. For my grandmother, who my family now thinks had the same malady I have, the only surgical option was being cut open and having her potato-shaped hip bone sanded round like a banister knob, leaving her to shuffle around, from her mid-fifties on, supported by a couple of polished wooden canes. Later, she acquired a motorized armchair that would slowly lower her from a standing to a seated position, then gently nudge her back onto her feet and canes again.

Knowing that I could have *my* faulty hip replaced left me feeling that I should be grateful. But I could only mourn each of my losses: first giving up long walks, then low-impact aerobics class, then step aerobics with Jane Fonda in my living room, then lawn mowing, then short walks, then even wet mopping the kitchen floor. To get up stairs, I had to pull myself up by the handrailing. I begged anyone who would listen—my friends, my colleagues at work, my doctors—to work some magic on me. "The new hips *are* the miracle," most people said. After that, I started holing up at home, where I knocked back three five-hundred-milligram, kidney- and liver-killing anti-inflammatories a day, vegetated at night in my most comfortable chair with a tumbler of wine and a bag of pretzels in front of the blabbing TV, and talked myself into being mindful that my plight didn't come even close to what cancer patients had to go through (fearful the entire time that I would be struck down with that and every other known illness, too).

Nor did it help that Liza Minnelli, who was at least a whole year younger than I, had had a hip replaced. Or that Liz Taylor, who'd had two replacements, was rich and famous. Or that Bo Jackson was on his second bionic hip, having worn out his first one running the base paths for the Chicago White Sox.

My entire image changed. I had once been able to see myself as tough, tough, tough. And healthy. Someone who never got sick, who could move furniture up and down the stairs with the best of them, who did low-impact aerobics four nights a week, who camped out halfway across the country with two young boys. But as soon as I was aware of my worn-out hip joints, I started to think of myself differently (slower, weaker, less attractive); then I began to look different, too. The lack of exercise and the feelings of hopelessness, along with some help from the arthritis drugs, very quickly turned into pounds. I'd gained some weight at forty after I'd quit smoking cigarettes, but now at fifty I was putting on even more! My lack of activity led to more self-pity, which led to Cherry Garcia ice cream, which led to even more self-pity and chocolate. The thighs I'd had at thirty-five when I could still wear the ripped-off Levi's were in there somewhere—I just couldn't see them anymore! At fifty, I was too young for a limp (my friends were speechless when I referred to myself as a gimp), and every time I went out and saw silver-haired women who were sixty, sixty-five, even seventy striding along the sidewalk, I was overcome with grief and envy.

V

Yesterday, I was reading Scott Fitzgerald's essay "The Crack Up," which begins with, "Of course all life is a process of breaking down." I agree, but I didn't expect to break down so soon. After all, I'm at the forefront of the baby boomers, the perpetual youngsters.

I'm also late in coming to realize that a whole chunk of life is about cutting one's losses. I had a brief awareness of this a few years ago, however, when one TV-channel-surfing evening I lit upon a documentary on centenarians. The filmmaker, curious to find out what kept a person alive for a century or more, set out to interview her subjects in depth, expecting to discover that they had all pampered their bodies in a similar way: diets low in red meat and dairy, lifestyles low in stress, no cigarettes or alcohol, regimented exercise, early to bed, early to rise. To her surprise, she found no such common threads, since one participant still smoked cigars, a few swore by a shot of brandy before they went off to bed, most ate whatever they felt like putting in their mouths. What they did all share, however, were two things: work or activity that they loved, and the ability to grieve their losses quickly and move forward. After a hundred or more years of living, they'd all had innumerable painful losses—the worst of which, after the loss of parents, spouses, siblings, and all their closest friends, was their children. One woman of 102 had lost just weeks before the filming her only daughter and only living relative, a woman of seventy-eight. Like any mother, she ached for her child, but despite all the sadness over her daughter's death, she was already marching forward in her own life.

At only half the centenarian's age, I am clearly not forging ahead. I am stranded somewhere on the mountain: My life has been a climb and a fall and more climbs and more falls, and somehow I've made it to this particular elevation. Here I am, alone, more than halfway to the top, taking in the panorama below, and suddenly I notice that I'm on a precipice, stranded by my own self-pity.

Perched precariously at this high altitude, I am indulging myself in tears. Since my surgery, this lack of restraint has become part of my early routine. After a good long cry, I can slide my body out of bed, hop into the kitchen on my crutches, feed the cat by blobbing her food on a paper plate and letting the plate drop straight to the floor, make my tea in a lidded plastic mug, put my granola in a lidded piece of tupperware, slide the tea, the Tupperware, and a spoon into the deep pockets of my borrowed apron, hike on the crutches into the living room, back myself (with my right leg jutting forward so as not to dislocate the new hip) into my armchair (which is now elevated on bricks), grab the remote, and turn on the morning news programs.

Repelled as I am by the faces on the TV (as well as by this rutted routine), I was at it again this morning, flicking between the *Today* show, *Good Morning America,* and *The CBS Morning News* with Paula and Harry. It was there, with Paula, that I took in a five-minute clip on the latest arthritis remedy, a natural substance called glucosamine. "It took away ninety percent of my pain," said one doctor who'd been using it on himself. "And is thought to reverse joint damage," said Paula. Several patients, including a skinny, white-haired guy with an arthritic S-shaped spine, spoke of how it changed their lives. A researcher in Missouri is studying glucosamine's effects right now—on hip-dysplastic German shepherds.

I looked down at where my legs meet my torso, envisioned that shiny metal/polymer combo inside, and bawled yet again. Each time I sneak a peek at the foot-long pink zippers that run a slow curve up the outside of each thigh before veering off to each side of my butt, I try to imagine exactly what those titanium joints look like inside of me—how the metal stakes that connect to the metal balls have been pounded down into the hollows in my leg bones. The day after the first operation, my surgeon said, "You have plenty of bone; I had trouble getting the joint in there." I know I'm supposed to be grateful—both for the technology and for all the calcium I must have ingested as a kid—but I'm furious. I've seen my X rays with those foreign parts in my body; during my first pre-op session, I was shown a video and even given a bionic joint to hold in my hand; but when I look at where my legs are hooked up to the rest of my body, I can't bear to envision the metal where just bone and tissue used to be. The metal screams at me, like ice cream on a brand-new tooth filling.

I've given up my hip joints, but I want them back so I can try some of the miracle substance I'd spent almost two years looking for. Never mind that there are thus far no conclusive tests on glucosamine. And while I'm grieving my long-gone joints—thrown into the incinerator with the other "hospital waste"—I'm grieving every other loss I've ever suffered.

Now that I'm past life's midpoint, I'm starting to see that living may mean always being in some state of grieving. Not that there can't be a lot of joy tossed in at irregular intervals, but every day we're older is another day lost. When I was twenty, or thirty, or even forty, I didn't see any decision I'd made as irrevocable. But turning fifty and losing my hip joints has opened the floodgates on a torrent of regret: Where did all those years go? Tens of thousands of hours in my twenties and thirties stoned on marijuana—I want them back. That ugly divorce that heaped mountains of pain on those precious, innocent little boys and took away their childhoods, and there's no way to do it over and make it right. The time that I spent stressed and depressed and shouting at my children when I should have been organizing rounds of silliness and laughter and board games around the dining room table. Gone. A couple of good men I let go because they were steady and they listened and they took a genuine interest in me. Where are they now?

I've been deceived by the perennial youth culture into believing that there would always be endless doors open to me. Now that I'm past fifty, there's near panic as I watch the gates bolting from behind.

VI

Both times, the surgery itself went well. I opted not to have general anesthesia. Instead, I chose the spinal and a heavy dose of some Valium derivatives. I was warned that I might hear the surgeon and his resident minions using their power saws on my bones, but I didn't, either time. I heard voices in the room, and though I couldn't make out a word, I had complete trust in both the orthopedic surgeon and the anesthesiologist—both give doctors a good name. A short time after the operation, I was wheeled back to my hospital room, ready for long-distance phone calls and some *Larry King Live*.

But the next day when I endured several rounds of vomiting from the morphine and couldn't pee after they pulled the catheter out, and the day after that when my mouth was so dry from the painkillers that my taste buds were cracking open, and the day after that when I watched in Demerol-disbelief as my substitute physical therapist's hand slid (purposely?) under my breast instead of my elbow, I knew that these were surely not the best of times.

I had roommates, though, which helped pass the hours. Not more than forty minutes after my first roomie, Lydia, a young mother of three who'd come to have a rod and a metal plate put in her leg, was discharged, and not more than fifteen minutes after housekeeping had sanitized the bed, did Frances arrive. I soon learned that she'd fallen earlier in the day as she was on her way to have her hair fixed at her local beauty shop. Her boot hit a patch of ice on the sidewalk and Frances went down, shattering her elbow. When her younger sister and her niece arrived a few hours later and the doctor showed up, I was right there in the next bed eavesdropping. At eighty-one, according to the doctor, Frances had two options: to have surgery and a pin put in the elbow, or to let the elbow set the way it was; the latter option, she was told, would leave her with about half her normal motion. The orthopedist, a good-looking, gray-at-the-temples guy about my age, then rocked his left elbow a few times, showing Frances what her limited range of motion would look like. She might have opted for the surgery, but there was a catch: Frances had been diagnosed with diabetes a few years earlier, when she'd had surgery on her pancreas; she was an eighty-one-year-old with dwindling bone mass; and when she'd hit the ground in Fairfield, she'd powdered a good portion of her elbow. "There's a risk doing the surgery, and the pin might not hold," the handsome-in-that-middle-aged-way surgeon said. "If you were my mom, I'd tell you to let it heal the way it is." Frances, her sister, and her niece held a short family council, then took the doc's advice.

As it turned out, Frances didn't go right home. Since she would need some help, especially with her insulin shots, she stayed on as my roommate until the arrangements for a visiting nurse and meals-on-wheels were made. I could tell right away that she didn't like the idea of being dependent on outsiders, but her sister convinced her that she could fire them all if she later discovered she didn't need the help.

In spite of the trauma, Frances's sense of humor was intact. After her family left, she looked over at me and said, "Too bad it had to happen *before* I got to the beauty parlor." She ran her fingers through a rather thick head of gray permed hair. "I look like a bush," she said, laughing. "I look like I've just been plugged in."

The next day we laughed over dueling Oprahs as we watched our separate TVs, which sat on shelves high above our beds. It was about this time that we first heard Vern. Although we never did see the guy, Vern was in a room somewhere close to our ortho-pod at the end of the corridor, and every time one of the nurses went into his room to do something to or for him (we had no idea what was wrong with the old guy), he would start screaming at her. "Get away from me, you whore. You slut. You fumbling bitch."

"Now, Vern. Be nice," one of the nurses, Janice, always tried. But Vern would go on like a broken record, several times a day, for as much as fifteen or twenty minutes or until the particular nurse was fortunate enough to finish with the procedure and leave the room. At these moments, I would lie in my bed thinking what a pig Vern must have been in his younger days and realizing that when the troika of male residents made their rounds every morning and afternoon, Vern never issued a peep. During dinner one night, when Vern was carrying on at quite a clip and I was imagining that if I had been Vern's nurse he'd have been permanently anesthetized, Frances glanced up from her hospital meatloaf, pointed toward Vern's room, and said, "He's the entertainment."

Frances had a way of looking on the light side—a gift I did not seem to be blessed with. The Thursday following her accident, she was supposed to have flown to Atlanta, where she would spend what remained of our never-ending Iowa winter with her only son and daughter-in-law. She mentioned the trip twice, talked about how she'd been looking forward to it, how she'd have to cancel her plans. "But I'll get there," she told me. "It just can't be now." Two times she recounted her loss, and that was it; she was over it. I lay in my bed thinking that she was like the centenarians, who grieved their losses quickly and moved on. Frances was already moving forward with her shattered elbow, telling me how, if someone prepared the insulin, she'd have no problem giving herself her daily injection.

The next day she talked about the rest of her family: her three grandchildren and her three great-grandchildren. "I've got to get down to Kentucky to see those kids. I've got a lot more living to do," she said, looking down at her splinted arm.

When I got home from the hospital I started thinking about Frances and, in turn, how some people seem to be able to find comfort knowing there's one feather in a bed of stones, when I'm the one who feels the pea under the mattress.

VII

The loss I feel the most is family, and the family stuff is somehow connected to these brand-new titanium joints. As I've already said, I've been self-indulgent. After getting up in the morning following a nightmare in bed—of sweating under the white elastic Ted hose I wear day and night to stave off postsurgical blood clots, of waking up every hour or two to turn from the two positions (my back or my old-incision side) I'm permitted to sleep in—I usually wallow in self-pity for at least half an hour. It is during this time that I hang on like a leech to everything I've lost: the cartilage in my hip joints, the two and a half years I had to spend as a gimp, the "tough" self-image; from there it multiplies to smooth skin, smooth thighs, shiny hair—then to where it's no longer physical. What I most grieve, along with my hip joints, is that I didn't get the mom-pop-two-kid family, that despite the many friends who bring me casseroles for dinner every night, I am out here alone. Not that I want my long-gone marriage back. I want the time back to choose more thoughtfully. I want the time back to get the pop to go along with the mom and the two kids.

Why is it that one big loss connects so intimately in the brain with all the other big losses? Maybe for me it's because as I look down at the places where I was cut open, then stapled back together, I think, *This is irrevocable. You've lost something here and no amount of toughness is going to bring it back.* I think, *You've fought all these years to be strong, independent, show the world that you can raise a couple of kids, work two jobs at a time, learn to write a novel, and what did it get you? A couple of bionic body parts.* I look down at the staple tracks and think, *What man is going to want you now?*

My surgeon all along has had high hopes for my future—that I'll be walking distances again, that with some modifications, I'll be able to step again with Jane Fonda in my living room, that if I'm not terrified of falling and dislocating the joints (forever and ever a risk) I might be cross-country skiing. Still, I can't let go of the real joints, the ones that have already been hacked off and are by now ash at the bottom of the hospital incinerator. The ones that would let me cross my legs or crawl out the window onto the porch roof or run across the street while the light is changing to red, all things I hear the bionic ones won't let me do. What man is going to want me now? Hip replacements don't become me; they're for great-aunts, fat old men, and the Queen Mum.

It's the same thing I said when, almost fifteen years ago, my then-husband packed up his things and walked out the door. My oldest son, who was six at the time, hung on his leg and cried, "If you leave, Papa, I'll hate you."

I got the kids to sleep somehow that night, then I lay on our king-size marriage bed, and thought: *What man is going to want me now?*

The only thing I knew was that I'd messed up big-time and I wanted it back to do all over again. How can you know when you're still in your twenties that one decision, like who you're going to marry, can so profoundly affect the rest of your life? That there are some decisions that alter the course of a life in such a way that they can never be changed? Once the ball joints are sawn away and replaced with metal ones, you can't go back. It's too late for miracles like glucosamine. But I want to take some herbs and reinvent my family. Now that I'm grieving my joints, I want to go back and marry smartly. I want to be fifty-one and celebrating my silver wedding anniversary with this wonderful man who is my best friend. We have proudly raised two children who are well-adjusted, confident, compassionate young men who did not suffer the pain and the indignity of having had to live most of their lives in a single-parent family, and now we, the gleaming parents, will share the rest of our lives together. We are financially secure, which means we have a house nearly paid for and I no longer have to work writing multiple-choice items for reading assessment tests for students who no longer read. This husband and I will travel to exotic places together, knowing that our children are thriving because we did such an outstanding job together. He'll invent a series of jokes about the pink zippers on the sides of my thighs, and when we're in bed he'll tell me they make my body more interesting.

VIII

I got myself out of the hospital in five days when the normal route for a total hip replacement is seven to ten because, despite all the whining I do, I'm stubborn. My incision was still draining and my surgeon was at first reluctant to release me, but I had graduated from physical therapy in just three days, could go up and down a few stairs and get to the bathroom by myself. Now I hop around on crutches and plan to be back to work on my four-week postsurgery anniversary. I'm trying to maintain at least a thread of the tough image. "I'm proud of you," the doc says. In a get-well card, one of my colleagues from work writes, "You're the only woman I know who truly has buns of steel."

And yet, I'm paralyzed. It's all this grief, all this past baggage that I can't seem to let go of. I'm not grieving my losses quickly like the centenarians have done. Maybe I won't even make it to eighty-one, my hospital roommate Frances's age. Eighty-one. That's thirty more years. Whatever will I do with those thirty years now that my kids are raised and I can't go back to my regular low-impact aerobics class? Now that I'm past fifty (having once agreed never to trust anyone over thirty) and I have a pink zipper on each side of my body and no man to joke about it? I'm at the front end of the pack of baby boomers and I'm supposed to be liberated. From what? From being like someone in Frances's generation?

We boomers were supposed to be more honest, straightforward, let-it-all-hang-out types, but where did it get us? Every day I put it out there and now I'm wallowing in it. It ain't a pretty sight and I have to stop. *Buck up. Just. Buck. Up.* There are terrible stories all around me: half a family gone in a car accident, hit by a drunk head-on; a thirty-year-old who is in her last days unless she gets a new heart; a nineteen-year-old hemophiliac with full-blown AIDS; a farmer with his arm caught in the auger; a family who lost one child to leukemia and now, five years later, is facing the same thing with a second child. *So buck up.*

IX

I try to push the self-pity aside by midmorning because just before noon my friend Anne drops by after teaching her freshman rhetoric class at the university. We have lunch together— peanut butter on toasted English muffins, apple slices, and chocolate graham crackers. Our conversation usually begins with something that has happened in Anne's class that morning and usually ends with something that has happened in one of the books either of us is reading. This is always a relief—to focus on something other than me.

After Anne drives off, I situate myself lengthwise on the couch and escape into reading. Today, it is *Shooting the Boh: A Woman's Voyage Down the Wildest River in Borneo*. Forty-five minutes after opening the book, I am ready for my nap, a long, luxurious, two-hour siesta, the highlight of my postsurgery life.

During the preceding twenty child-rearing years (the last thirteen as a single parent), nap time has been at a premium, but now that rest is a prerequisite to my recovery, I can nap guilt-free. Minutes after the Borneo river trip starts to blur over the page, I am transported to that unworried, untroubled, tranquil zone between waking and sleep. When my sons were nursing infants, I used to love to watch them drift into this very state. Their eyelids would flutter, every muscle in their bodies would relax, and at the corners of their pink, rosebud mouths the hint of a contented smile would form. Their bellies full, their heads securely resting in the crook of my arm, they were completely at peace with the world they'd just entered.

I am rediscovering just how restorative a midday rest can be. When I open my eyes to consciousness after today's nap, I feel as protected as an infant. In a couple of hours, my friend Linda will be stopping by. The day I went into the hospital, she gave me seven personal notes attached to the top of seven carefully wrapped gifts, and I was to open one each postsurgery day. As if that weren't enough, she's insisted on bringing me dinner a couple of times a week. I have a troupe of friends—from my writers' group, from work, from up the street—who have offered to cook for me. I have two sons who have taken time from their busy college-student lives to come home to do my laundry, take out the garbage, and vacuum the living room rug.

Most of my loyal friends have come into my life since the last time I had to realign myself, which was thirteen years ago. Then, I moved halfway across the country with two little boys into a house I'd rented sight unseen. I was starting over. I'd taken a wrong path and was trying to right myself again.

I tell my sons, "Life's an adventure," and yet each time I'm faced with another chapter I cannot go into it without a kicking-and-screaming, all-out fight. But today the battle seems to be coming to an end. Of course, I will be defeated, so I guess I have no choice but to start reinventing myself: A fifty-one-year-old, stubborn, independent, says-what's-on-her-mind, long-divorced mother of two, with titanium/polymer hip joints and good friends, is starting page one of the next chapter. As she rises up off the couch to balance on one leg and two aluminum crutches, she is making the effort to head out once again—forward, though no longer running, across the busy street, for another loaf of bread.

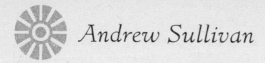

Andrew Sullivan

WHEN PLAGUES END

Notes on the Twilight of an Epidemic

I

First, the things I resist remembering, the things that make the good news almost as unbearable as the bad.

I arrived late at the hospital, fresh off the plane. It was around 8:30 in the evening and there had been no light on in my friend Patrick's apartment, so I went straight to the intensive-care unit. When I arrived, my friend Chris's eyes were a reddened blear of fright, the hospital mask slipped down under his chin. I went into the room. Pat was lying on his back, his body contorted so his neck twisted away and his arms splayed out, his hands palms upward, showing the intravenous tubes in his wrists. Blood mingled with sweat in the creases of his neck; his chest heaved up and down grotesquely with the pumping of the respirator that was feeding him oxygen through a huge plastic tube forced down his throat. His greenish-blue feet poked out from under the bedspread, as if separate from the rest of his body. For the first time in all of his illnesses, his dignity had been completely removed from him. He was an instrument of the instruments keeping him alive.

The week before, celebrating his thirty-first birthday in his hometown on the Gulf Coast of Florida, we swam together in the dark, warm waters that he had already decided would one day contain his ashes. It was clear that he knew something was about to happen. One afternoon on the beach, he got up to take a walk with his newly acquired beagle and glanced back at me a second before he left. All I can say is that, somehow, the glance conveyed a complete sense of finality, the subtlest but clearest sign that it was, as far as he was concerned, over. Within the space of three days, a massive fungal infection overtook his lungs, and at midnight on the fourth day his vital signs began to plummet.

I was in the hall outside the intensive-care room when a sudden rush of people moved backward out of it. Pat's brother motioned to me and others to run, and we sped toward him. Pat's heart had stopped beating, and after one attempt was made to restart it, we intuitively acquiesced, surrounded him and prayed: his mother and father and three brothers, his boyfriend, ex-boyfriend and a handful of close friends. When the priest arrived, each of us received communion.

I remember that I slumped back against the wall at the moment of his dying, reaching out for all the consolation I had been used to reaching for—the knowledge that the final agony was yet to come, the memory of pain that had been overcome in the past—but since it was happening *now,* and now had never felt so unavoidable, no relief was possible. Perhaps this is why so many of us find it hard to accept that this ordeal as a whole may be over. Because it means that we may now be required to relent from our clenching against the future and remember—and give meaning to—the past.

II

Most official statements about AIDS—the statements by responsible scientists, by advocate organizations, by doctors—do not, of course, concede that this plague is over. And, in one sense, obviously, it is not. Someone today will be infected with H.I.V. The vast majority of H.I.V.-positive people in the world, and a significant minority in America, will not have access to the expensive and effective new drug treatments now available. And many Americans—especially blacks and Latinos—will still die. Nothing I am saying here is meant to deny that fact, or to mitigate its awfulness. But it is also true—and in a way that most people in the middle of this plague privately recognize—that something profound has occurred these last few months. The power of the newest drugs, called protease inhibitors, and the even greater power of those now in the pipeline, is such that a diagnosis of H.I.V. infection is not just different in degree today than, say, five years ago. It is different in kind. It no longer signifies death. It merely signifies illness.

The reality finally sank in for me at a meeting in Manhattan this summer of the Treatment Action Group, an AIDS advocacy organization. TAG lives and breathes skepticism; a few of its members had lambasted me only nine months before for so much as voicing optimism about the plague. But as soon as I arrived at the meeting—held to discuss the data presented at the just-completed AIDS conference in Vancouver, British Columbia—I could sense something had changed. Even at 8:00 P.M., there was a big crowd—much larger, one of the organizers told me, than at the regular meetings. In the middle sat Dr. David Ho, a pioneering AIDS researcher, and Dr. Martin Markowitz, who presided over recent clinical trials of the new treatments. The meeting began with Ho and Markowitz revisiting the data. They detailed how, in some trials of patients taking the new protease inhibitors used in combination with AZT and another drug called 3TC, the amount of virus in the bloodstream was reduced on average a hundred- to a thousandfold. To put it another way: Most people with H.I.V. can have anywhere between 5,000 and a few million viral particles per milliliter of their blood. After being treated for a few weeks with the new drugs, and being subjected to the most sensitive tests available, many patients had undetectable levels of the virus in their bloodstreams. That is, no virus could be found. And, so far, the results were holding up.

When Ho finished speaking, the questions followed like firecrackers. How long did it take for the virus to clear from the bloodstream? Was it possible that the virus might still be hiding in the brain or the testes? What could be done for the people who weren't responding to the new drugs? Was there resistance to the new therapy? Could a new, even more lethal viral strain be leaking into the population? The answers that came from Ho and Markowitz were just as insistent. No, this was not a "cure." But the disappearance of the virus from the bloodstream went beyond the expectations of even the most optimistic of researchers. There was likely to be some effect on the virus, although less profound, in the brain or testes, and new drugs were able to reach those areas better. The good news was that H.I.V. seemed primarily to infect cells that have a short half-life, which means that if the virus is suppressed completely for two years or so, the body might have time to regenerate tissue that was "aviremic." And since the impact of the drugs was so powerful, it was hard for resistance to develop because resistance is what happens when the virus mutates in the presence of the drugs—and *there was no virus detectable in the presence of the drugs*.

The crowd palpably adjusted itself, and a few chairs squeaked. These are the hard-core skeptics, I remember thinking to myself, and even they can't disguise what is going through their minds. There were caveats, of course. The latest drugs were very new, and large studies had yet to be done. There was already clinical evidence that a small minority of patients, especially those in late-stage disease, were not responding as well to the new drugs and were experiencing a "breakout" of the virus after a few weeks or months. Although some people's immune systems seemed to improve, others' seemed damaged for good. The long-term toxicity of the drugs themselves—their impact on the liver, for example—could mean that patients might undergo a miraculous recovery at the start, only to die from the effects of treatment in later life. And the drugs were often debilitating. I tested positive in 1993, and I have been on combination therapy ever since. When I added the protease inhibitors in March, the nausea, diarrhea and constant fatigue had, at first, been overwhelming.

Still, after the meeting, a slightly heady feeling wafted unmistakably over the crowd. As we spilled out into the street, a few groups headed off for a late dinner, others to take their protease drugs quickly on empty stomachs, others still to bed. It was after 10:00, and I found myself wandering aimlessly into a bar, where late-evening men in suits gazed up at muscle-boy videos, their tired faces and occasional cruising glances a weirdly comforting return to normalcy. But as I checked my notebook at the door, and returned to the bar to order a drink, something a longtime AIDS advocate said to me earlier that day began to reverberate in my mind. He had been talking about the sense of purpose and destiny he had once felt upon learning he was positive. "It must be hard to find out you're positive now," he had said darkly. "It's like you really missed the party."

III

Second, the resistance to memory.

At 6 o'clock in the morning in the Roseland Ballroom in Manhattan on a Sunday last spring the crowds were still thick. I had arrived four hours earlier, after a failed attempt to sleep. A chaotic throng of men crammed the downstairs lobby, trying to check coats. There were no lines as such, merely a subterranean, almost stationary mosh-pit, stiflingly hot, full of lean, muscular bodies glacially drifting toward the coat-check windows. This was, for some, the high point of the year's gay male social calendar. It's called the Black Party, one of a number of theme parties held year-round by a large, informal group of affluent, mainly white, gay men and several thousand admirers. It's part of what's been dubbed the "circuit," a series of vast dance parties held in various cities across the country and now a central feature of an emergent post-AIDS gay "life style."

When people feared that the ebbing of AIDS would lead to a new burst of promiscuity, to a return to the 1970s in some joyous celebration of old times, they were, it turns out, only half-right. Although some bathhouses have revived, their centrality to gay life has all but disappeared. What has replaced sex is the idea of sex; what has replaced promiscuity is the idea of promiscuity, masked, in the increasing numbers of circuit parties around the country, by the ecstatic drug-enhanced high of dance music. These are not mass celebrations at the dawn of a new era; they are raves built upon the need for amnesia.

Almost nothing has been written in the mainstream media about these parties, except when they have jutted their way into controversy. A new circuit party, called Cherry Jubilee in Washington, incurred the wrath of Representative Robert Dornan because drugs had been used in a Federal building leased for the event. The annual Morning Party in August on Fire Island, held to raise money for Gay Men's Health Crisis in New York, was criticized on similar grounds by many homosexuals themselves. But in general, these parties have grown in number with a remarkable secrecy, reminiscent of the old, closeted era when completely bifurcated gay lives were the norm. But their explosion on the scene—there are now at least two a month, involving tens of thousands of gay men in cities as diverse as Pittsburgh and Atlanta—is interesting for more than their insight into party culture.

The events are made possible by a variety of chemicals: steroids, which began as therapy for men wasting from AIDS and recently spawned yet another growing sub-subculture of huge body builders; and psychotherapeutic designer drugs, primarily Ecstasy, which creates feelings of euphoria and emotional bonding, and ketamine, an animal anesthetic that disconnects the conscious thought process from the sensory body. On the surface the parties would be taken for a mass of men in superb shape merely enjoying an opportunity to let off steam. But underneath, masked by the drugs, there is an air of strain, of sexual danger translated into sexual objectification, the unspoken withering of the human body transformed into a reassuring inflation of muscular body mass.

As the morning stretched on, my friends and I stood in the recess of a bar as the parade of bodies passed relentlessly by. Beyond, a sea of men danced the early morning through, strobe lights occasionally glinting off the assorted deltoids, traps, lats and other muscles gay men have come to fetishize. At the party's peak—around 5:00 A.M.—there must have been about 6,000 men in the room, some parading on a distant stage, others locked in a cluster of rotating pecs, embracing one another in a drug-induced emotional high.

For a group of men who have witnessed a scale of loss historically visited only upon war generations, it was a curious spectacle. For some, I'm sure, the drugs helped release emotions they could hardly address alone or sober; for others, perhaps, the ritual was a way of defying their own infections, their sense of fragility or their guilt at survival. For others still, including myself, it was a puzzle of impulses. The need to find some solidarity among the loss, to assert some crazed physicality against the threat of sickness, to release some of the toxins built up over a decade of constant anxiety. Beyond everything, the desire to banish the memories that will not be banished; to shuck off—if only till the morning—the maturity that plague had brutally imposed.

IV

I talk about this as a quintessentially homosexual experience, not because AIDS is a quintessentially homosexual experience. Across the world, it has affected far, far more heterosexuals than homosexuals; in America, it has killed half as many intravenous drug users as gay men. And its impact has probably been as profound on many heterosexual family members and friends as it has been on the gay men at ground zero of the epidemic. But at the same time, AIDS was and is inextricable from the question of homosexuality in the psyche of America because it struck homosexuals first and from then on became unalterably woven into the deeper and older question of homosexual integration.

In so many ways it was a bizarre turn of events. In the past, plagues were often marked by their lack of discrimination, by the way in which they laid low vast swaths of the population with little regard for station or wealth or sex or religion. But AIDS was different from the beginning. It immediately presented a *political* as much as a public-health problem. Before homosexuals had even been acknowledged as a central presence in American life, they were suddenly at the heart of a health crisis as profound as any in modern American history. It was always possible, of course, that, with such a lack of societal preparation, America might have responded the way many Latin American and Asian countries responded—with almost complete silence and denial—or that the gay world itself might have collapsed under the strain of its own immolation. But over the long run something somewhat different happened. AIDS and its onslaught imposed a form of social integration that may never have taken place otherwise. Forced to choose between complete abandonment of the gay subculture and an awkward first encounter, America, for the most part, chose the latter. A small step, perhaps, but an enormous catalyst in the renegotiation of the gay-straight social contract.

And an enormous shift in our understanding of homosexuality itself. Too much has been made of the analogy between AIDS and the Jewish Holocaust, and they are, indeed, deeply distinct phenomena. One was an act of calculated human evil, designed to obliterate an entire people from the center of Europe. The other is a natural calamity, singling out a group of despised outsiders by virtue of a freak of nature, and a disease that remained asymptomatic long enough to wipe out thousands before anyone knew what was happening. But in so far as each catastrophe changed forever the way a minority group was viewed by the world, the two have eerie parallels.

The hostility to homosexuals, after all, has far more in common with anti-Semitism than it does with racism. Homosexuals, like Jews, are not, in the psychology of group hatred, despised because they are deemed to be weak or inferior, but precisely because they are neither. Jews and homosexuals appear in the hater's mind as small, cliquish and very powerful groups, antipathetic to majority values, harboring secret contempt for the rest of society and sustaining a ghetto code of furtiveness and disguise. Even the details resonate. The old libel against Jews—that they would drink the blood of Christian children—has an echo today in the bigot's insistence that he has nothing against homosexuals per se, but doesn't want them allowed near his kids. The loathing for each group is closely linked to fear—and the fear is fanned, in many ways, by the distortion of a particular strain in Christian theology.

But that fear was abated, in both cases, by extraordinarily contingent historic events. The Holocaust did many things to the structure of anti-Semitism, but in one hideous swoop it helped destroy the myth that Jews were somehow all powerful. The mounds of bodies, the piles of artifacts and the grotesque physical torture that the Jews of Europe suffered did not exactly indicate power. Out of that powerlessness, of course, came a new form of power, in the shape of achieved Zionism. But the idea of

Jewish victimhood seared by mass murder into the Western consciousness was seared indelibly—and it remains one of the strongest weapons against the canards of anti-Semitism today.

Similarly, if on a far smaller scale, AIDS has dramatically altered the psychological structure of homophobia. By visiting death upon so many, so young, AIDS ripped apart the notion of subterranean inviolability that forms such a potent part of the fear of homosexuals. As tens of thousands of sons and uncles and brothers and fathers wasted away in the heart of America, the idea that homosexuals maintained a covert power melted into a surprised form of shock and empathy. For some, the old hatreds endured, of course, but for others an unsought and subtle transformation began to take shape. What had once been a strong fear of homosexual difference, disguising a mostly silent awareness of homosexual humanity, became the opposite. The humanity slowly trumped the difference. Death, it turned out, was a powerfully universalizing experience. Suddenly, acquiescence in gay-baiting and gay-bashing became, even in its strongholds, inappropriate at a moment of tragedy. The victimization of gay men by a disease paradoxically undercut their victimization by a culture. There was no longer a need to kick them, when they were already down.

I think this helps explain the change in the American psyche these last 10 years from one of fearful stigmatization of homosexuals to one of awkward acceptance. And it's revealing that the same thing did not really happen to the many other victims of the plague. With inner-city blacks and Latinos, with intravenous drug users, there was no similar cultural transformation, no acceleration of social change. And that was because with these groups, there had never been a myth of power. They had always been, in the majority psyche, a series of unknowable victims. AIDS merely perpetuated what was already understood and, in some ways, intensified it. With gay men, in contrast, a social revolution had been initiated. Once invisible, they were now unavoidable; once powerful subversives, they were now dying sons.

AIDS, then, was an integrator. If the virus separated, death united. But there was a twist to this tale. As the straight world found itself at a moment of awkward reconciliation, the gay world discovered something else entirely. At a time when the integration of homosexuals into heterosexual life had never been so necessary or so profound, the experience of AIDS as a homosexual experience created bonds and loyalties and solidarities that homosexuals had never experienced before. As it forced gay men out into the world, it also intensified the bonds among them; as it accelerated an integration, it forged an even deeper separation. The old question of assimilation versus separatism became strangely moot. Now, both were happening at once— and feeding off the same psychological roots.

I remember the first time I used the word "we" in print in reference to gay men. It was in an article I was writing as I witnessed my first AIDS death—of a stranger I had volunteered to help out in his final months. He was thirty-two years old when I got to know him, back in 1990. Without AIDS, we would never have met, and the experience changed my sense of gay identity for good. Before then, although I had carefully denied it, I had quietly distanced myself from much of what I thought of as "gay culture." Tom helped to change this.

He was the stereotype in so many ways—the '70s mustache, the Alcoholics Anonymous theology, the Miss America Pageant fan, the college swim coach. But he was also dying. His skin was clammy and pale. His apartment smelled of Maxwell House coffee and disinfectant and the gray liquid that was his constant diarrhea. I remember one day lying down on top of him to restrain him as his brittle, burning body shook uncontrollably with the convulsions of fever. I had never done such a thing to a grown man before, and as I did, the defenses I had put up between us, the categories that until then had helped me make sense of my life and his, these defenses began to crumble into something more like solidarity.

For others, the shift was more dramatic. Their own incipient deaths unleashed the unfiltered rage of the late 1980s, as decades of euphemism and self-loathing exploded into one dark, memorable flash of activism. The fire behind Act-Up was by its very nature so combustible that it soon burned out. But its articulation of a common identity—the unsustainable starkness of its definition of homosexuality—left a residue behind.

And I began to understand the pull of this identity more instinctively. Suddenly, it seemed, as my twenties merged into my thirties, everyone was infected. Faces you had got used to seeing in the gym kept turning up on the obit pages. New friends took you aside to tell you they had just tested positive. Old flames suddenly were absent from the bars. I remember thinking that a new term was needed for something that was happening to me with increasing frequency: I would be walking along a street and see an old man coming toward me whom I vaguely recognized. And then I would realize that it wasn't an old man; it was someone I knew who had just gone through some bout with pneumonia or some intestinal parasite. Like Scott, a soldier I had got to know as a 220-pound, 6-foot-3-inch, blue-eyed, blond-haired bundle of energy. During the gays-in-the-military affair early in the Clinton Administration, I had urged him to come out to his commanders and troops, sure that the new President would protect him. He told me I had to be out of my mind, and, of course, as it turned out, I was. And then, a few weeks later, he bumped into me on the street and confided the real reason he didn't want to confront anyone. He was H.I.V.-positive and needed the Army's support. He told me with genuine anguish, as if the knowledge of his disease demanded a courage his disease would also have punished.

Then, a mere year later, I saw him with a cane (literally), his spirit completely broken, his body shrunk to 140 pounds, his breath gone after the shortest walk, his eyes welling with the bitterness of physical pain and isolation. His lover of several years somehow endured the ordeal, nursing him every inch of the way, until Scott became a 90-pound skeletal wreck, unable to walk, his hair weak and gray and glassy, his eyes sunken miserably into a scaly face. Scott never fully reconciled with his family. And after Scott died, his lover told me that his last words had been, "Tell my mother I hate her."

When I would tell my straight friends, or my work colleagues or my family, about these things, it wasn't that they didn't sympathize. They tried hard enough. It was just that they sensed that the experience was slowly and profoundly alienating me from them. And they sensed that it was more than just a cultural difference. The awareness of the deaths of one's peers and the sadness evoked and the pain you are forced to witness—not just the physical pain, but all the psychological fear and shame that AIDS unleashed—all this was slowly building a kind of solidarity that eventually eliminated my straight friends from the most meaningful part of my life. There comes a point at which the experience goes so deep that it becomes almost futile to communicate it. And as you communicate less and less and experience more and more, you find yourself gravitating to the people who have undergone the same experiences, the ones who know instinctively, the people to whom you do not have to explain.

I remember the moment when my friend Patrick told me he had AIDS. We had been friends for a long time, yet the meaning of that friendship had never been fully clear to us. But at that moment we were able to look each other in the eye and tell each other we would be there for each other, whatever it took and however hard it became. I don't think I had ever made such a commitment before—to anyone. It survived watching him waste away, seeing him buckled over on the floor, thumping the ground from the pain of his infections; it survived him messing himself in panic as he fumbled with his IV; it survived his bloody-minded resistance to risky treatments that might have helped him; it survived the horrifying last hours in the intensive-care unit and the awkward silences with his family a year after he passed away. It survives still, as does the need to find a way to give it meaning in his absence.

For a long time I never broke down or cried about any of this—the dozens of acquaintances who have died, the handful of friends I have mourned or resisted mourning, the sudden flashes of panic at the thought of my own mortality. But late one night I caught sight of Senator Bob Kerrey on *Nightline*. He was speaking haltingly of his relationship with Lewis Puller, the paralyzed Vietnam veteran who had survived the war, only to ultimately succumb to depression, alcoholism and, finally, suicide. There was in Kerrey's bitter, poignant farewell a sense that only he and a few others would fully understand Puller's anguish. Kerrey grasped, because he had experienced, what it was to face extreme danger and witness in the most graphic way possible the deaths of his closest friends and colleagues, only to come home and find those experiences denied or ignored or simply not understood. And as he spoke, I felt something break inside me. Kerrey knew, as Mark Helprin expressed so beautifully in his novel "A Soldier of the Great War," what almost every gay man, in a subtler, quieter way, has also learned: "The war was still in him, and it would be in him for a long time to come, for soldiers who have been blooded are soldiers forever. They never fit in. . . . That they cannot forget, that they do not forget, that they will never allow themselves to heal completely, is their way of expressing their love for friends who have perished. And they will not change because they have become what they have become to keep the fallen alive."

At the time of this writing, almost three times as many young Americans have died of AIDS as died in the entire Vietnam War.

V

In Camus's novel *The Plague*, the description of how plagues end is particularly masterful. We expect a catharsis, but we find merely a transition; we long for euphoria, but we discover only relief tinged with, in some cases, regret and depression. For some, there is a zeal that comes with the awareness of unsought liberation, and the need to turn such arbitrary freedom into meaningful creation. For many more, there is even—with good reason—a resistance to the good news itself because "the terrible months they had lived through had taught them prudence." The reactions to the news, Camus notes, are "diverse to the point of incoherence." Many refuse to believe that there is any hope at all, burned by dashed expectations one time too many, "imbued with a skepticism so thorough that it was now a second nature." Others found the possibility of an end too nerve-racking to bear and almost dared the plague to kill them before it was too late.

And even now, among friends, there are those who refuse to be tested for a virus that, thanks to the new treatments, might be eliminated from the bloodstream. And there are those who are H.I.V.-positive who are still waiting to take the drugs and are somehow unable to relinquish the notion that being positive is a death sentence that they can endure only alone. And there are those many who, having taken all the drugs they can, have found that for some reason the drugs will not work for them and watch as their friends recover while they still sink into the morass of sickness made all the more bitter by the good news around them. And those more who, sensing an abatement of the pressure, have returned, almost manically, to unsafe sexual behavior, as if terrified by the thought that they might actually survive, that the plague might end and with it the solidarity that made it endurable.

You can already feel, beneath the surface, the fraying of the bonds. A friend in New York, H.I.V.-positive for ten years, contemplates breaking up with his boyfriend because he suddenly realizes he is going to live. "I felt safe where I was," he tells me. "But now I feel like an attractive person again. It's more what you're radiating inside—the feeling that, finally, you're not a potential burden. I mean, maybe I'm *not* a potential burden." Another positive friend, this one an AIDS advocate of hardened credentials, feels the meaning of his life slipping away. "At some point, you just have to go on," he says. "You say that was a great period in your life, but it's a big world and at some point you have to find a way to slip back into it and try and be a happy citizen. What I want is a boyfriend I love, a job that doesn't make me crazy and good friends."

But normalcy, of course, is problematic for gay America. The "normalcy" of gay life before AIDS is something few can contemplate and fewer remember. There are ways (the circuit parties) in which that history is repeated as farce, and ways (like the small revival of sex clubs) in which it is harder and harder to sustain. For the first time, serious resentment is brewing among H.I.V.-positive men about the way in which AIDS has slowly retreated from the forefront of gay politics. And among the longest-term survivors, there is a depressing sense that a whole new generation of post-AIDS gay men have no understanding of the profundity with which their own lives have become suffused.

Take John Dugdale, a thirty-six-year-old photographer living in New York, tall and chiseled, with dark hair and even darker eyes. But when Dugdale looks at you these days, he merely looks toward you. Some time ago, he became almost blind from an AIDS-related virus. He took the new drugs, experienced euphoria as they obliterated the virus from his blood, crashed again a few months later as the virus returned, then experienced yet another high as his health improved once more. He knows his own survival is tenuous and is depressed by the shallowness of a culture that is clearly beginning to move on. As we chatted recently, he recalled with not a little edge a particular moment at the Black Party in New York earlier this year. It concerned a friend of his with AIDS, a body builder who still prized himself on being able to consort with the best of the competition. There was one problem: he had lesions on his body, lesions he refused to have treated. And when he took his shirt off that night to dance with the throng, the lesions were all too visible. Not so long ago, they might have been viewed as war medals. Now, they're something different. "This guy came up to him," Dugdale recalled, "and said: 'Would you please put your shirt on? You're ruining it for everybody else.' "

For some, of course, the ebbing of AIDS could mean that the old divisions between H.I.V.-positive and H.I.V.-negative men could heal. With a less catastrophic diagnosis, the difference in life span—and self-definition—between negative and positive men might narrow. But there is also another possibility: that with a smaller and smaller percentage of gay men having H.I.V., the isolation of those infected will actually increase, and that those with full-blown AIDS could feel more intensely alone than before.

Even at the showing of the AIDS Memorial Quilt in Washington this year, the divides were subtly present. There were those who went to see the quilt itself or went to the candlelight vigil and those who went only to the many parties that filled the weekend. (In truth, many went to all.) And the internal tensions were palpable. It is as if many H.I.V.-positive men have emerged from transformingly deep spiritual experiences only to re-enter a culture that seems, at least in part, to be returning to the superficial. And the lifting of the veil of terror has served, paradoxically, only to isolate them still further in a subculture that has less time and less energy to sympathize or understand. The good news from the laboratory has robbed them not simply of the drama and intensity of their existence but also of the recognition of that drama and intensity. And even among their own kind.

VI

A difference between the end of AIDS and the end of many other plagues: for the first time in history, a large proportion of the survivors will not simply be those who escaped infection, or were immune to the virus, but those who contracted the illness, contemplated their own deaths *and still survived.* If for some, this leads to bitterness, for others it suggests something else entirely. It is not so much survivor guilt as survivor responsibility. It is the view of the world that comes from having confronted and defeated the most terrifying prospect imaginable and having survived. It is a view of the world that has encompassed the darkest possibilities for homosexual—and heterosexual—existence and now envisions the opposite: the chance that such categories could be set aside, that the humanity of each could inform the humanity of the other.

Greg Scott is a Washingtonian I've known for years. We're both in our early thirties, and as the plague has unfolded over the last decade it has affected us in different ways. Greg is from a traditional Southern family, and when he was thrown out of the Navy for being a homosexual, he threw himself into years of furious activism. When I first came to know him, he was renowned in D.C. for hanging around bars and staring wildly at passers-by as a prelude to either lecturing or seducing them. For a short period of time, he would follow me around D.C. screaming "Collaborator!" to punish me for the sin of writing or voicing politically incorrect views. But we both knew, at some level, that we were in the epidemic together, and so when I saw him slowly declining over the last two years, I felt a part of myself declining as well. My friend Pat once described Greg as "hanging by the same length of rope" as he was, so for some time I half-expected to see Greg's face in the crowded obituary columns of the local gay paper along with the dozens of other faces I had known or seen over the years. When I wrote an op-ed piece a year ago hail-ing the latest breakthroughs in AIDS research, Greg came up to me in a bar and regaled me. "This is *not* a survivable disease!" he yelled over the music. "What do you know about it, anyway?"

So I learned to avoid Greg as far as I could. I never relished our meetings. Since he didn't know I was positive, too, our conversations had this false air about them. The solidarity I felt was one I could not fully express, and it ate away at me. I occasionally spotted him walking his dog in the neighborhood, his body, always thin, now skeletal, his large, staring eyes disfigured by lesions, his gait that of a 60-year-old. When my parents visited, I pointed him out from a distance on the street, in some doomed attempt to help them understand: "See. That's my friend Greg." Read: "See. That's my friend, Greg. *Do you see what this is doing to us?*" Last fall, Greg was taking morphine twice a day. He was on a regime of 60 pills a day and was virtually bedridden. So when I caught sight of him five months ago, I literally jumped.

I had grown used to the shock of seeing someone I knew suddenly age twenty or thirty years in a few months; now I had to adjust to the reverse. People I had seen hobbling along, their cheekbones poking out of their skin, their eyes deadened and looking down, were suddenly restored into some strange spectacle of health, gazing around as amazed as I was to see them alive. Or you'd see them in the gym, skin infections still lingering, but their muscles slowly growing back, their skull-faces beginning to put on some newly acquired flesh. This is what Greg now looked like, his round blue eyes almost tiny in his wide, pudgy face, his frame larger than I remembered it: bulky, lumbering, heavy.

In one of those bizarre coincidences, I bumped into him the day I quit my job as editor of *The New Republic*. He was one of the first people I was able to tell, and from the minute I spoke to him, I could tell he was changed. The anger was somehow gone; a calm had replaced it. He seemed to understand intuitively why I might want to take time to rethink my life. As we parted, we hugged awkwardly. This was a new kind of solidarity—not one of painful necessity, but of something far more elusive. Hope, perhaps? Or merely the shared memory of hopelessness?

Since then, I've become used to Greg's describing the contours of what he calls his "second life." And he describes its emergence in a way that is shared by more people than just him. The successive physical and material losses of his illness stripped him, he recalls, of everything he once had, and allowed him, in a way that's unique to the terminally ill, to rebuild himself from scratch. "There were times I was willing to accept that it was over," he says. "But things were never fully tied up. There were too many things I had done wrong, things I wanted to amend, things I still wanted to do. I was hanging on tenaciously out of some moral judgment of myself because I knew I hadn't got it right the first time."

In his progressive illness, Greg had lost first his energy, then his ability to digest food, then his job, then his best friend and then most of his possessions, as he sold them off to pay for medications. But he hung on. "In the early days," he remembers, "I couldn't imagine going through all that to stay alive. My friend Dennis would say that I'd never go that far. But then he died. Looking back, it's absurd the lengths I went to. I'd never realized I cared so much about myself." (Greg's story brings to mind that of another friend: his illness finally threatened his sight, and he had to decide whether to pursue a treatment that involved an injection of a liquid directly into the eyeball. In other words, he had to watch as the needle came closer and closer and finally penetrated his eye. I remember asking him how on earth he could go through with it. "But I want to see," he told me.)

"When you're in bed all day, you're forced to consider what really matters to you," Greg elaborates. "When the most important thing you do in a day is your bowel movement, you learn to value every single source of energy. You go into yourself and you feel different from other people, permanently different." Some gains are subtle. "It sparked a new relationship with my grandmother. Like me, she was suddenly finding she couldn't drive her car anymore, so we bonded in a way we'd never bonded before. You suddenly see how people are valuable. I mean, if you're healthy, who has time for this old lady? And suddenly this old lady and I have so much in common. And I still have that. That's a gain. I have an appreciation and love for her that I never fully had before." Some gains are even more profound. "My grandfather would say, 'You don't squeak under the bottom wire unless you're meant to.' And I feel that there's this enormous responsibility on me that I've never felt before. And it's a pleasant responsibility. I mean, lay it on me."

Responsibility is, perhaps, an unusual word for Greg to be using, and until AIDS it was not one usually associated with homosexuality. Before AIDS, gay life—rightly or wrongly—was identified with freedom from responsibility, rather than with its opposite. Gay liberation was most commonly understood as liberation from the constraints of traditional norms, almost a dispensation that permitted homosexuals the absence of responsibility in return for an acquiescence in second-class citizenship. This was the Faustian bargain of the pre-AIDS closet: straights gave homosexuals a certain amount of freedom; in return, homosexuals gave away their self-respect. But with AIDS, responsibility became a central, imposing feature of gay life. Without it, lovers would die alone or without proper care. Without it, friends would contract a fatal disease because of lack of education. Without it, nothing would be done to stem the epidemic's wrath. In some ways, even the seemingly irresponsible outrages of Act-Up were the ultimate act of responsibility. They came from a conviction that someone had to lead, to connect the ghetto to the center of the possibilities of living. I realized I could do what I wanted to do, write what I wanted to write, be with the people I wanted to be with. So I wrote a book with a calm I had never felt before about a truth I had only belatedly come to believe. The date I inscribed in its preface was two years to the day since my diagnosis: a first weapon against the virus and a homage to its powers of persuasion.

And for a precious short time, like so many other positive people, I also sensed that the key to living was not a concentration on fighting the mechanics of the disease (although that was essential) or fighting the mechanics of life (although that is inevitable), but an indifference to both of their imponderables. In order to survive mentally, I had to find a place within myself where plague couldn't get me, where success or failure in such a battle were of equal consequence. This was not an easy task. It required resisting the emotional satisfaction of being cured and the emotional closure of death itself. But in that, of course, it resembled merely what we all go through every day. Living, I discovered for the second, but really the first, time, is not about resolution; it is about the place where plague can't get you.

Only once or twice did I find that place, but now I live in the knowledge of its existence.

So will an entire generation.

(1996)

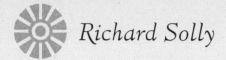

Richard Solly

THE WORLD INSIDE

I was lying toward the middle of the bed the morning I first swooned over Annie, my home care nurse. When she was cutting bandages on the dresser, I noticed her long, thin neck, blond hair, and blue eyes. She always wore slacks, kept her hair cut short, and thankfully never wore perfume. I was acutely sensitive to smells and disliked any strong odor. For months, Annie had been coming every day to my house, except on weekends, when another nurse would come in her place. For the first few weeks after my discharge from the hospital, Annie, always punctual, came twice a day, once in the morning and once in the late afternoon. Normally when she was ready to clean my abdominal wound and change its dressings, she stood alongside my bed, leaning over me, which strained her lower back. The surgeons had left my abdomen open in order for the infection to drain, and there were no plans to close the wound for quite some time. That morning, after Annie approached me with the gauzes in her hand, she suddenly sat down. Though it made sense to do so while she untied the Montgomery straps, she hadn't until then. No doubt she was instructed never to sit on the bed of a male patient at his home. "If you don't mind," she said, "it will be a lot easier for me."

She swung one leg up onto the bed and began untying the straps. My legs stretched out behind her and pressed against her buttocks and thigh. Though I was emaciated and pale, with a gaping wound in my belly, I suddenly felt handsome. For the first time, I didn't see a drawn face and sunken cheeks in the mirror above the bureau, but a healthier, younger self. I imagined that she, too, found me attractive. But so what if she didn't? That I *felt* attractive was what mattered.

After that morning, she always sat on the bed while dressing the wound. She became more alluring to me than ever and in some odd way more vulnerable. Her eyes looked more brightly blue and seemed to gaze at me longer. Now she rested her hand on my arm. I felt trusted. For the first time in months, I was at peace.

During those five months I had spent in the hospital for Crohn's disease, everything was an electrical storm with only flashes of memory. Pain sent jolts of current through me. Shuttled from one bed to another, I was wheeled out of operating rooms and elevators into intensive care. Sheets were pulled over me and kicked off, needles were stuck in my arms, catheters inserted up my penis and through my jugular vein. Green tubes, like the tentacles of an alien inside my body, came out of my nose, throat, and abdomen. I lost track of how many machines I was hooked to, how many operations I had, how high my fever reached before I went into septic shock. Every cubic millimeter of my body and blood was infected. I awoke and saw one friend at my bedside, fell back asleep, and woke up to another. They stood silently around my bed while I unhooked from reality and traveled farther and farther away from my body.

All sensations existed out of any context or environment: the cold in the operating room, a bright light unhinged from the ceiling and floating in the air above me, a transportable bed where I lay blissfully in a long hall, the metallic sound of wheels rolling over floor tile, oxygen masks that cut into the bridge of my nose, a hand making the sign of the cross over my body, carts wheeling past, a crack of light under the door. For days, the sound of an ambulance siren blared in my hospital room, where I imagined myself lying in mud. Rainwater splashed under the black boots of Civil War soldiers running past. I'd wake up, soaked with urine. Voices questioned me. I was rolled onto my side and back again. Three nurses sat me up, forced me to stand and take a step. I didn't know why.

Finally I abandoned my body, hooked to a respirator, on a bed in a snake nest of tubes. I floated up to a brilliantly lit room, colored white like alabaster, ivory, or eggshell, but nothing then needed a name. A milky stream of light flowed over my feet and what must have been a floor, though nothing was above or below. There was a single window with its shade pulled, and though I couldn't see the door, there was one that opened both ways, depending on whether I entered or left. I couldn't explain how, but I was atomized in pure being. This was a place where I didn't need legs to walk, hands to wave, a voice to call out "Dad."

There, in the room with me, were my dead father and sister, Louise. He was wearing blue trousers and a white shirt with his sleeves rolled up, and she a long yellow nightgown with a white lace collar. Only my father spoke: "If you cross over, we will meet you." Hearing his voice, soft-spoken and confident, and seeing my sister's calm presence, I relaxed and felt at peace. I returned to my body, the hospital bed, my friend sitting alongside, and whispered, to my friend's bewilderment, "I'm not who I used to be."

Days later, I was taken off the respirator, wheeled out of intensive care to another unit, where I awoke to masked surgeons and nurses leaning over me. Their knuckles gleamed under the tight rubber covering their hands. The surgeon's stare over the edge of his mask frightened me, and I raised my head from the pillow to look. A nurse was holding bandages over a basin. I glanced down at my abdomen and saw pink and red tissue. I closed my eyes. "We had to leave your abdomen open to drain," the surgeon said, his voice muffled.

The abdominal wound exposed viscera, pink intestine slowly turning red from granulation and exposure to air. Thick, tough fascia tissue and muscles were parted like drapes. Inside the wound, holes burrowed deeper into dark abdominal space. I thought I saw steam curling out of them. When nurses rolled me over in bed to prevent bed sores, I worried that my intestines would spill out onto the sheet. Not even morphine could stop the pain.

When nurses and surgeons came into my hospital room each morning to clean and irrigate the wound with a tube, I pulled my hospital gown up over my head so that I wouldn't have to look inside my own body and see what no one should ever see. A nurse chuckled, seeing a grown man hiding under a sheet pretending to disappear. I didn't care. Underneath the gown, I felt secure, like a child again lying on the carpeted floor between two chairs draped by a bedsheet. Then the sheet was a white sky, a starched roof, a cool cave that sheltered me from the sight of my dying sister, Louise, hobbling through the room on crutches, a scarf covering her bald head. No one, not my father, mother, brothers, or sisters, insisted that I come out.

"You have to look," a nurse commanded, just before covering the wound with new bandages. She tugged at my gown.

"No, I don't," I replied. I wanted this refuge from the wound and wet gauzes, their gloved hands inside my body. "I'll look when I have to," I said. Had I known then that the wound would remain open for over a year, I might have let myself die.

The nurse wrote in my chart: "Patient is in denial and will not look at wound. Covers his head with a sheet." She implemented a behavioral modification program, requiring me to take incremental peeks at the wound. First I was to peer at the wound through the gown, then the next day lie in bed without covering my face, though I wouldn't have to look. She hoped one day I'd catch sight of the glistening intestine in my peripheral vision and be ready to face reality.

But I thought denial was sometimes God's way of giving a person a good night's sleep or time to prepare for the unimaginable—the navel no longer at the center of the body but off to the right, halfway to the hip, as if it were pasted there, and the stoma, an end of intestine brought through an abdominal hole where a plastic ostomy bag was hung by black magic.

One day a nurse, unfamiliar with my behavioral program, stood alongside my bed. She watched me struggling to yank the gown out from under me and pull it up over my head. "Here, this might be easier," she said, handing me a towel to cover my face. My eyes moistened. I was so grateful that finally a nurse would help me accomplish what I wanted instead of what she thought best. Soon afterward, I stopped covering my head and simply gazed up at the ceiling while they cleaned my abdominal cavity.

By the time I was discharged and Annie was assigned to my care at home, I was looking at the wound, but reluctantly. It seemed to me that my wound was deeper than flesh, deeper than what the eye could see. Though the doctors had given me a diagnosis of Crohn's, a chronic inflammatory bowel disease of the gastrointestinal tract usually affecting the lower part of the small intestine and the colon, the label didn't make my suffering more comprehensible or offer an explanation for the cause of an illness that escaped even the surgeons. Then, as a result of intense pain and drugs, I could not think rationally about my body any longer. In my imagination, I considered my abdomen much like an ancient might who had no medical illustrations or textbooks to explain logically the body's pain. The word *abdomen* itself comes from an archaic Greek word of undetermined origin meaning "hidden" or "occult." Strangely, I considered my own abdomen as containing not only my colon, liver, and small intestines, but my soul, a hidden universe. Inside were not just my bowels but the bowels of the earth itself—the primordial ooze of this planet, the mud out of which *Homo sapiens* arose, the swamp of the unconscious and its instincts. While in a deep trancelike state induced by morphine, I imagined my own dreams originating there. They sprang out of abdominal dark waters and swam through intestines, against the flow of blood and gravity itself, which threatened to pull them back down into the abdominal swamp. To peer inside the abdomen, which sheltered the essence of my primordial being, seemed forbidden, sacrilegious, a desecration of the human body, temple of the soul. Because the abdomen concealed this primitive life, I could believe surgeon and author Richard Selzer, who wrote that when he first looked inside a patient's abdomen, he expected to see buffalo drawings on its wall.

In my mid-twenties, as a college student, I voraciously read D. H. Lawrence's books and espoused his belief in a consciousness rooted in body, not mind. If Lawrence claimed that primal consciousness existed in the abdominal cavity of the solar plexus, I also claimed it. I disliked the same intellectual man Lawrence did—the one who lacked emotion and feared the physicality of sexuality. I took literature classes to understand what the abdomen and body meant in his beliefs. I underlined favorite phrases in all his books, starred some of them: "In the devouring whirlpool beneath the navel . . . the universal lotus really blossoms in the abdomen." How could anyone, I wondered as I lay in the hospital bed, look into the abdomen, the place of birth for the child and—as Lawrence believed—human consciousness itself? He could not have appreciated body as a source of primal consciousness had he not known how people lived in their bodies, and how they lived in elemental relation to the earth, to the coal mines, to animals, to each other as sexual partners, and as I would now add, to pain itself. Understanding Lawrence was not the intellectual exercise I took it to be as an eager young poet and student.

For Tibetan Buddhists, the ferocious wind of the Himalayas was also one of three humors or elements that resided in the abdomen. Tibetan healers will lay their heads on a person's body to listen to the Wind inside. When my abdomen was opened during my surgeries, the holy Wind of the Tibetan mountains must have blown furiously from the intrusion of mortals into its canyon. Though surgeons saved my life, their scalpels seemed to incise and defile what was sacred in me. I was horrified that their hands muddled my abdominal cavity, squeezing and cutting intestine, untangling coils from infected abscesses, while the Wind whirled madly through me.

Had I lifted my head and peered inside the wound, doing what the nurses asked of me, I would have seen the coil of the occult, the primordial ooze of the earth, the seat of the Wind and primal consciousness, the stars of the universe, the swamp of the nether life. And most frighteningly, the Sepulcher housing my own death. I could not look.

When I was discharged from the hospital, I was no longer Richard the softball player and runner—strong, handsome, and healthy—but an emaciated weakling who couldn't get up from his wheelchair without help. The person I used to be was unraveled by pain. How could I manage the simple details of wound care at home like Annie wanted me to when I was lost in these primal forces? But if I didn't, I would die.

It was Annie who encouraged me to see the wound more medically and less mystically. "You have to look at your wound more like a doctor rather than like the poet you are," she told me in my bedroom on our first meeting. She reminded me that I would never lose my lyrical gifts, but I would lose my life if I continued mystifying my wound. "You need to accept it as simple tissue and intestine that requires constant care," she said.

Annie was not into New Age healing through prayers, meditation, visualization, or even acupuncture. For her, healing would be accomplished only by putting on surgical gloves, cutting bandages, peeling away the soiled gauzes, letting air into the wound, rinsing the wound with saline solution, inserting six-inch Q-Tips into abdominal holes. Before applying new bandages, she connected a hose to a small portable machine kept on the nightstand alongside my bed. The machine operated like a vacuum cleaner, whirring and clacking as it sucked saline and infection out of my wound into a small canister that was emptied when she finished. Annie often made diagrams on scratch paper to explain the location of viscera in my abdomen. After she'd leave, I'd lie in bed looking at her drawings. Her pencil never shaded in primordial ooze, the embryo of primal consciousness, the Tibetan Wind, the River Styx.

Each morning, promptly at nine, she rang the front doorbell and then let herself in. I often left the door unlocked for her, since walking downstairs to open it would have been too painful. Though having the door unlocked all night left me vulnerable, I decided it was the cost of avoiding pain on some mornings. As she shut the door behind her, she hollered, "It's me!"

"Come on up!" I yelled. I appreciated her shout. She didn't, like many hospital staff had, take liberties with me and intrude unannounced.

If I was feeling well, I would meet her at the top of the stairs. On days when my damaged Achilles tendons and bone spurs caused too much pain to take even a few steps, I would lie in bed, listening to the rhythmic creak of oak under her feet as she walked up the stairs and down the hallway.

Sometimes I scolded myself for lying in bed like a corpse when she came. "At least you could have gotten up and shaved, you bag of bones," I said to myself. It was true. I rarely shaved and weighed only 105, having lost nearly sixty pounds. None of my clothes fit anymore. I could count my ribs in the mirror. The first concession I made was to push myself up in bed, swing my legs off the side, and sit on the edge.

Later, as I grew stronger, I was often standing at the dresser organizing the medical equipment when she came in. I would lay out two surgical gloves, open each package of Q-Tips, uncap the saline solution, and cut the bandages, gauzes, and Montgomery straps, wide adhesive strips to be secured on my hips. Cloth strings that looped through holes at the ends of the straps were tied over four layers of bandages to hold them in place. I'd tie the strings into a bow over my wound like a ribbon on a present.

Each morning began with some chatting about her children or my daughter, but always came her proclamation, "Okay. Let's get started." Then I girded myself with determination. I lay back in bed, untied my bathrobe, wiggled my underwear down to my knees, pulled the sheet up over my genitals, and lay perfectly still as she untied the Montgomery straps. Before she gingerly lifted the gauzes out of the wound, she'd pause, look directly at me, and ask, "Are you ready?"

"No," I often said during the first few weeks with her. Unlike some of the nurses in the hospital who walked out of the room whenever I showed any resistance, Annie was more patient. She'd wait for me to collect myself and return my attention to the bandages she was about to peel off.

"Now?" she would ask again. Annie waited for however long it took me to compose myself.

"I'll never be ready, but go on," I said.

"Try to relax. Everything about the body is good," she said. Her hands never shook like mine, but demonstrated her acceptance of the body. Her two fingers gently pulled the wet bandages out of the wound. Sometimes gauze would stick and new tissue peeled off or bled. The red granulated tissue often quivered, as if it were recoiling from our sight or the sunlight in the bedroom.

"It's only peristalsis," she said in a matter-of-fact tone. "It is always occurring, even when the wound is covered."

In the middle of the wound, a fistula, a growth of intestine that had pushed through the peritoneal sac, pulsated. "It's ugly," I said to her. "A red worm!"

Annie wouldn't argue. "Yes, I know," she said. "But it's more than that, too." She explained how a fistula released infection, and it did no harm in pushing through the wall of an organ. The explanation didn't make the fistula appear any less grotesque, but I appreciated Annie's insistence that every part of the human body was beautiful and natural. I felt less like a freak.

I was infatuated with Annie and felt more attractive. When I smelled her hair when she leaned over me, I felt the heat in my face as it reddened. I don't know how I was able to fantasize about her. I hardly had the energy for that! When sick, libido evaporates like a drop of water on a hot plate. An erection could only be raised with Herculean strength, which I didn't have. Sexuality didn't induce health, but was induced by health. Libido didn't restore me, but my recovery was restoring my libido. For a brief moment, I could imagine Aphrodite herself occupying Annie's body as she prepared the dressings and galvanized my recovery with primal energy, but for Annie our relationship required hard work, patience, and medical expertise, not fantasy. My nurse could have been a man and the relationship I had with him could have been equally restorative and healing. The healing happened in the daily tasks between Annie and me. Now I would work as hard as she was teaching me to get well.

During the first six weeks, I made remarkable progress with my wound care, but when Annie inserted extra-long Q-Tips into abdominal holes I had to look away, up to the ceiling to find plaster cracks to connect like a dot-to-dot drawing. I'd draw imaginary lines connecting the chipped plaster and cracks to make a kite with a tail of bows that my father once showed me how to fly. "Please," Annie said, insisting on my attention. "Watch me. Today I want you to try this yourself."

She held the Q-Tip like a baton, and I half-expected to hear a dramatic drumroll. She then inserted it into a tiny tunnel that burrowed deep into my body until the stick nearly disappeared. In her hand, the Q-Tip inserted five inches into my abdomen didn't hurt nearly as much as I imagined it would in my hand. I looked up at the kite in the ceiling sky. "Like this," she said, drawing my attention back to her fingers, twirling the Q-Tip to gather infection from inside the hole. When she finished and took her hand out of my body, she said just what my father had said when, after the kite was flying, he handed me the string: "Now it's your turn."

One morning she announced that we would discontinue irrigating the wound with the machine. Instead, she would help me into a chair placed in the bathtub so I could rinse the wound out myself with a shower hose attached to the water faucet.

While in the hospital, I was often naked in front of nurses who showed no interest in me as a man, not even out of the corner of their eyes. When a nurse routinely changed the bed linen, my gown, and bathed me each morning, I automatically slid my legs up the sheet for her to wash under them. When I was too sick to move, nurses washed my groin area as well. Then they disrobed me, wiped my rectum and genitals, carefully swabbing the tip of the penis where a catheter was inserted, and patted me dry with towels. No part of my body was left untouched. Sometimes they forgot to close the door to my room or pull the curtain around my bed, and a visitor passing by would peek in. Though I was deathly ill and the nurses' hands were necessary to my survival, I still felt stripped of my manhood, like an anatomically correct mannequin stored away in room 4021. But with Annie, I never felt objectified.

Now every morning we walked down the hallway together to the bathroom. There, she unfolded the chair, set it in the tub, and connected the hose to the spigot. The bath towel was always close at hand, usually on the sink. Annie leaned over the tub and adjusted the water flow and its temperature. Joint pain is common for people with Crohn's disease, and because I had severe bursitis in my shoulder, Annie always offered to help me out of my bathrobe. As I untied my robe, she stood behind me, helped me lift my one arm out of a sleeve, then slipped the robe off the other. When my robe slid off my shoulders and down my back, I shuddered.

She laid the robe over her arm and extended the other for me to hold as I stepped over the rim of the tub and onto the chair. Though I was in a hopelessly dependent situation, Annie's touch never felt demeaning. When I held Annie's arm, emotion in her body seemed to tingle under my fingers.

"Are you cold?" she asked, after hanging my bathrobe on the door hook. Without waiting for an answer, she laid the towel over me, briefly letting her hands rest on my shoulders. Though sitting in a chair in the tub with a towel over me to keep me warm, I still felt like a man, not a sick, sexless body. It was her hands on my shoulders that somehow enlivened and invigorated me.

While I washed, Annie often sat on the toilet lid talking to me about her husband. By then, she would tell me about his habits that irritated her. He was quiet and withdrawn in the morning. Unlike her, he wouldn't talk at the breakfast table. And he often complained about her leaving lights on in the house. I enjoyed these confidences that helped balance our relationship.

As weeks went by, I grew more and more efficient at wound care. Once, when I commented on how magically the wound seemed to be healing, Annie said emphatically, "No. Nature and your hard work heal the wound." I nodded and smiled. Yes, I had to demystify the body and possibly face my own death by placing my hand in the wound, touching the crusted intestine and moist fistulas, and sopping up my fear of the ooze with bandages. The unknown and alien loomed too large. The force of primitive life frightened me with its inexplicable swelling and quivering. By peeling away soiled bandages, irrigating the infection, and replacing old dressings with new ones day after day, I rid myself of my illusions and fears about the body. I had to suspend for the moment, like Annie said, beliefs I borrowed from literature and philosophy and, by looking into the turgid infection of the wound, see for myself how resourceful the human body is.

One morning, in the bathroom, she was especially quiet, intensely watching me clean the wound. "It looks like you don't need me anymore," she said. "You can do all the wound care yourself."

I shut off the water and said emphatically, "No, I can't do it myself. You have to keep coming."

"Yes, you can," she said. "You do almost all the wound care now." For the first time, I felt angry with Annie. I stood up in the tub and took the towel from the sink without waiting for her to give it to me. How could she abandon me while I still depended on her? That morning I wouldn't take her hand as I stepped out of the tub.

She was right, of course. I was perfectly capable then to remove the dressings, twirl the Q-Tip inside the holes, pour cold saline solution into the wound, and rinse it out in the bathtub. In fact, I no longer needed her to help me onto the chair in the tub. Though she always gave me her arm to balance myself when I stepped in and out, her gesture of support was more from courtesy than necessity, like someone opening a door for me. Still, I didn't want to face the day when she stopped coming to my house. Who would ring my doorbell every morning? Who would sit on the edge of my bed and talk with me?

I don't know what changed her mind, but on the way downstairs she said, "Okay. I'll see if I can convince the insurance people to let me keep coming."

*　　*　　*

Annie did convince them to allow her to come another two weeks until early August, nearly four months after her first visit. On her last visit, I was shaved, dressed in a clean white shirt and slacks. I met her at the front door. Instead of heading upstairs, I invited her into the kitchen for coffee. I had already cleaned the wound.

Upstairs, the bandages were put away, the rug vacuumed, no gauzes left on the floor, the waste basket emptied, and with my medical supplies in a drawer, the top of my bureau was clear enough for family pictures. I was taking care of myself now.

Annie hadn't taught me complicated medical care techniques that I couldn't have learned from anyone. No, from her I learned something more intangible—to have confidence in myself and trust in natural physical processes. The bow I tied over the bandages each morning was much like the ones I tied rags into for a kite tail, and Annie helped me remember racing across the grassy field at Cranwood Park, tugging the string, yanking the kite up higher until, looking back over my shoulder, I saw it lifted it seemed by my own hand into the sky. Of course its flight depended on the wind, perhaps the Tibetan one, but I had learned to tie the rags, to run hard and yank the string, to steer the kite away from treetops. There was work to do if I wanted to see myself in the sky again.

Before Annie left, I gave her flowers that I had bought for her the day before. At the door, we hugged good-bye. I would never see her again.

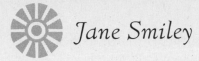

Jane Smiley

TWO PLATES, FIFTEEN SCREWS

I. Having a Broken Leg

Immediately after I got myself ensconced in my hospital bed in the dining room, I began to read *A Leg to Stand On,* by Oliver Sacks. What better preparation for six weeks, eight weeks, twelve weeks (I wasn't really listening) on crutches than a little research, especially if the author in question had impeccable scientific and literary credentials? Ah, but as I read, I realized with growing alarm that Sacks was no model for ME. He reacted to his leg injury first with heroism (doing the crab walk down an isolated mountainside in Norway after his injury), but later with hysteria (losing touch with his leg, then, apparently, with reality altogether). And his leg wasn't even broken! He had screws, no plates. I felt a little superior, not only in the severity of my injury, but also in the rationality of my response to it. I was cheerful. I was realistic. I was undemanding. I was an ideal patient, and all I needed was an audience for my patience. Unfortunately, my family wasn't cooperating. My three-year-old son avoided me entirely, my daughters had other things to do, and my husband, who had to now do all the family business while I lolled in the dining room, didn't have a lot of free time. So be it. I settled down to appreciating myself.

I appreciated how brave I had been after the accident. A fall from a horse, a tall horse, on hard ground. A good fall, loose, with my head tucked and my arms out. No other part of my body was even bruised, even tender. It was just that heel coming down last, whiplashing into the hard ground. Bam, and my fibula was powder. (The doctor enjoyed pointing this out to me, as a way of getting me to admire his handiwork, but I refused to listen, because I didn't want to be intimidated by the seriousness of my injury.) Had the ground been soft, I would have gotten up and walked away. I told this to everyone who asked what happened, to get partial credit—even though my leg *was* broken, it didn't *have* to be. It was almost not broken. I found this very comforting. I'd known it was broken, too. Fate was playing no tricks on me. I saw it hit, I rolled over and told my trainer to pull off my very expensive boot before the thing swelled up. And it didn't hurt, either. And the break was about as far from my neck as it could possibly be. In the year of Christopher Reeve, who fell from his horse and broke his neck at the first and second vertebrae, a broken ankle was a happy injury, almost no injury at all. All of these details were virtues that belonged to me, that spoke well of me. In such pleasant circumstances, Sacks-like hysteria was obviously not even an issue.

Except that I lost twenty-five pounds in the hospital, I cried all the time, I couldn't stop talking, I hated my doctor, and I couldn't look at my crutches.

My mind viewed the injury as purely mechanical, a break in the framing, nothing like illness, nothing like an attack on the whole system by alien invaders. My mind's opinion of what was happening was corroborated by the general lack of pain at the site. I was keeping my weight off the leg mostly because that jerk the doctor said to and I was a good follower of instructions.

("The plates," he intoned, "are a weight *sharing* device, not a weight *bearing* device." Okay, I heard you the first time.)

My body was in a panic. I was exhausted and weak. I went in twelve hours from the sort of person who drove horse trailers, rode two big horses in a morning, and carried heavy equipment to a layabout who couldn't even make dinner in the evening, could hardly tolerate standing up. One cold sore followed another. Two or three bites of food, any food, and my appetite failed. My hair was dirty. My hip, flexed so that The Ankle could be elevated, throbbed and ached. The hair on my good leg, which had gone unnoticed for forty-five years, began driving me crazy.

Puggh! I hated the word *healing*. *Healing* was for cancer, despair, the invisible hurts stemming from childhood trauma, spiritual debility. *Fixing* was for bones. I also hated the idea of learning a lesson. What lesson was there to learn? I fell off the horse. I was already trying to learn to ride better. I already recognized that I was a little oversubscribed, a little distracted, needed a break. What terrified me was the Christopher Reeve lesson—no horses at all. That was the lesson the doctor and my mother thought I should learn. Then there was, or might be, the lesson of age. I was forty-five, soon to be forty-six. Old bones and all that. The doctor, a man of maybe thirty-five, loved to talk about this. What he would do if healing didn't take place—more operations, bone grafts from the hip. These were the penalties of not knowing how old you were and how careful you should be. No sign of osteoporosis (when the jerk joined together my bones, he checked out their density), but that didn't mean I was in the clear, knitting-wise. He could tell me stories. . . .

Everyone told me stories. The scariest one involved two years of crutches and no healing at all. The woman's body took a "What, me worry?" attitude and only intervention after intervention persuaded it to take hold and get going. I sternly informed my body that such behavior wouldn't be tolerated, but who knew? The ankle was mute inside its cast, the bones keeping mum. Every night, I stared at the whole apparatus and ommmmed, but for all I knew I was broadcasting into empty space. My husband laid on his hands every night, too, and told me he felt the energy—a ball of light hopping back and forth between his palms—but speaking of palms, I suspected he was just palming me off.

I began doing more, going to work, cooking dinner, getting out, driving again. I looked independentlike, though of course that was only a facade. I went to see the horse. My new way of moving and my crutches disturbed him, so he turned his haunches to me and hardly even took his carrots.

I became depressed. This is what they said. Not to mention irritable and hard to get along with. Nobody dared to suggest that. In the first place, there was no reason to become irritable, depressed, and hard to get along with, because a break in the ankle is very far from the brain and a purely mechanical failure. In the second place, my aim was to be the best patient ever— that was all I had to do with my time, after all. Even so, I stared at my crutches. They began accreting symbolic power. Rather than helping me, they represented me now, told strangers all about me. I didn't want to take them out in public, but then I didn't want to sequester myself, either. A friend of mine, who uses a cane, was superhumanly sympathetic with my whining. In my journal, I weighed the rights and wrongs of being depressed, and decided I was both a fool and a knave for being depressed. Look at Christopher Reeve! Right there on Barbara Walters, he was as happy as could be! I began crying more at night rather than less.

I got a lot of work done.

I spent more time with my family—since I was in the dining room, they couldn't avoid me.

The time passed, my healing was not miraculous, but I did not become one of those stories that my doctor would frighten his future patients with.

Two weeks before I got off the crutches, I got back on the horse. We walked, halted, trotted. The experience of being upright and moving stepwise rather than crutchwise was exhilarating beyond belief and erased four months of the blues.

II. Not Having a Broken Leg

So I said to the physical therapist, "Why does the bottom of my foot hurt more than the break ever did?"

She said, "Oh, that's your fat pads. They haven't touched the ground in four and a half months."

My fat pads—who had ever heard of them?—were screaming. Just to save myself a little pain, I started crawling from room to room, but then my ankle would ache. "Stress to the bones helps them heal," said the doctor. "Keep walking." My ankle, swollen and hot and red, seemed worse than ever. I would take two Advil every night at bedtime, but it was no use. By four a.m. they had worn off and my ankle was throbbing with the buildup of lactic acid. After three weeks of Advil, I started to get rebound headaches. And then there were my riding lessons.

I had vowed to go slowly—walk for a month, trot for a month, only then try a canter. I was riding without stirrups and there we were, trotting along nicely, and I just gave in to temptation. I inched my heel back and gave the old boy the signal for the canter. Oh, delight! Oh, perfection! Oh, the single best sensation of 1996 as he rocked beneath me and my hips and torso swayed to his rhythm. Two days later, my trainer said, "You can't ride without stirrups." A day after that, she said, "They need to be shorter." And she cranked them up two holes. I posted to the trot. My ankle flexed. My fat pads howled. When I got off, I could barely walk. The pain in my ankle augmented by the minute. I was crippled by bedtime, couldn't sleep. The next day was worse. And then, thirty-six hours after she cranked up my stirrups, the pain dissipated, the ankle flexed like a baby's ankle. "Oh," said the physical therapist, "you must have broken out some adhesions. My brother did that when he ran out of the house with his kids in his arms during an earthquake. Sometimes works."

What worked was posting to the trot. Up, down, heels down. "What," said my trainer, "is your heel doing? It's coming up!"

"That's my broken leg."

"So what?"

So what, indeed.

I wasn't afraid of falling off, but of the horse falling, tempting me to launch myself and land awkwardly on the ankle. Don't think about it.

I discarded the cane. The fat pads shut up. I began mounting from the proper side, which meant putting my broken ankle into the stirrup and swinging the other leg over.

Sometimes I limped from pain, sometimes from stiffness that wasn't real pain, sometimes from habit. I limped uphill, went slowly downhill, always held the banister, was extremely wary of tufts of grass. Only on the horse was I just about normal.

Meanwhile, the horse was having problems with his left hock, that is, his "ankle" joint, exactly analogous to my ankle joint. His hock had a bone spur, was stiff and painful, and the pain was moving into his back muscles. He was moving, for a horse, just like I was—instead of stepping forward with his leg, he would swing his whole back end to the left. And then there was Nureyev, the most expensive sire in Kentucky. On a tour of horse farms, I was shown Nureyev's compound—his own octagonal breeding palace, an entryway, and a huge stall knee-deep in straw, every surface covered with satiny gold oak paneling. He makes six million a year in stud fees. He broke his left leg just about where I broke mine, and has lots of screws holding him together. I felt a kinship. Nothing like comparative anatomy. I pondered ordering my ankle therapies from vet catalogues.

My broken ankle became a chapter in our half-humorous family lore about things that have happened to Mom over the years. Remember the time I got novocaine in my mandibular joint, and then couldn't open my mouth for three weeks? God, Mom, you looked so funny. Remember my frozen shoulder? God, Mom, I can't believe you didn't realize that you couldn't raise your arm more than twenty-five degrees until you went to the doctor! Remember the broken leg? God, Mom, my boyfriend wouldn't even come in the house, because you were lying in bed in the *dining room*! And it was hot, and you didn't have very many *clothes* on!

III. And Yet, It Changed My Life

Every accident is particular. When I was watching Christopher Reeve on *20-20*, I recognized the analytical passion he brought to the question of why he didn't put his arms out to break his fall (his hands got caught in the reins). I felt that, too. Somehow, it seemed that if I figured out the precise physics of the injury, then that was a charm against its ever happening again, even against its having happened the first time. This illusion was very hard to break, and yet the lesson of the accident was clear—every one is a fluke full of specificities. Another entirely particular accident could easily happen. Nonetheless, I haven't brought myself to jump the horse again, yet—every injury is, at the very least, a significant inconvenience.

Every accident breaks up your routine. I hate this. Agenda-setting is my forte, and I like to set the agenda a long time in advance. I hadn't planned to lie in bed for weeks, I hadn't planned to take painkillers, I hadn't planned to sojourn in the realm of old age. But, you know, I hadn't planned to spend so much time with my daughters, either, and to have our conversations blossom so pleasantly into time-filling confidences. I hadn't planned to read so many books and so quickly find a subject and an approach that could work for a new novel. I hadn't planned to subscribe to the *Thoroughbred Times*, get interested in bloodlines, and end up breeding horses. I hadn't planned to be disappointed in *The Adventures of Huckleberry Finn* and get embroiled in a literary controversy. I hadn't planned to ponder my bones and their density, test their healing powers, stack my luck against Christopher Reeve's. I hadn't planned to learn that one of the things that makes life worth living is the thought that whatever it is that happened, it could have been worse.

I hadn't planned to regard myself with such fixity for so long. This effect seems to be the inescapable result of injury and recovery. One's injury powerfully attracts one's own attention. I can't say that I have made good use of this opportunity by drawing important conclusions, self-knowledge-wise. But the very experience was an interesting one, somehow, an exercise in focus when I was visualizing those bones and ommming to them. I was ashamed of this self-regard at the time, as if it weren't polite, as if my leg, not being my neck, wasn't worth it. I noticed a similar sense of self-effacement in Mr. Reeve, as if his neck, not being his life, wasn't quite important enough to warrant the attention paid. Well, sir, it is, if only for the sake of particularity.

A person with an injury has the same challenge as a person telling dreams—trying to experience the self while connecting with others. It's not, I think, that an injury shows you who you are, or even that it makes you who you become, it's more that an injury reminds you that you are precisely and exactly yourself. What has happened to you is distinctly yours and how you deal with it is idiosyncratic, too. Flukes are all, flukes are us.

And one last lesson—while I would never recommend a broken ankle, I do now think that any able-bodied person who parks in a handicapped spot for even one second should be sentenced to three months on crutches, to be served during an icy winter.

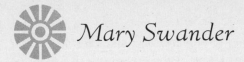 *Mary Swander*

THE FIFTH CHAIR

On an early February Saturday morning, the temperature thirty-five degrees below zero, a howling wind driving snow against my windowpanes, I woke up unable to move. Pain shot down my neck, through every vertebra in my back, and out my tailbone. Pain pulsated through my shoulders, elbows, and hips. My knees, swollen twice their size, throbbed with an excruciating rhythm of their own, and the nerves running down my calves to my big toes felt like piano wires tightening tauter and tauter. I tried to raise my legs, but couldn't. I tried to twist my torso, but couldn't. I'd been ill and alone before but had always been able to hop, stagger, or crawl to the bathroom. This was different. Overnight, I'd become a Kafkaesque cockroach, stuck on my back, incapable of righting myself.

The previous day I had felt a stabbing pain in my right knee. But what was new? I've walked around in pain since age fifteen when I had suffered a severe neck injury in an automobile accident. I had tried various forms of physical therapy with various results. When the injury finally manifested itself as fibromyalgia, a rheumatoid condition, the doctors simply advised: Learn to live with it. A Midwesterner to the core, I masked my daily discomfort, bullying my way through the days, trying to focus on other things, trying not to complain. Thirteen years before, I'd also made a comeback from a near-death experience from Environmental Illness and had lived a very restricted, controlled, and isolated life in response to that disease. So what was a little knee pain?

There I was at six a.m. unable to turn my head, wiggle my toes, or even reach up and scratch my nose. I was living in rural Iowa, fifteen miles from town, in the heart of the heart of the country, on the coldest night of the coldest month of the year, of the decade, of my lifetime. I lay in the darkness and tried to think, the pitch of the pain rising higher and higher. Fortunately, the phone was right beside my bed and I could bend my elbow just enough to get it up to my ear.

My nearest neighbors worked nights and wouldn't be home until around eight. Then they went straight to bed, turned on their answering machine, and slept through any disturbance. I would try to catch them just before they slept, asking them to feed my animals and help me get to the bathroom. After that, I had no plans. All I wanted to do was pee, and somehow then I thought everything would be fine. I waited, moaning to the beat of the pain zinging down my leg, and listened for the sound of their car, the slam of their door.

"Sure, sure. I'll feed the critters and Donna'll be right over to help you," my neighbor Stu said.

Quickly, Donna appeared, lifting me up off of my futon, pulling down my pajama bottoms and plopping me on the toilet. Soon she maneuvered me into my wing-backed chair, clicked on the radio, put the phone in my hand, and after having been up all night, went back to her house to sleep.

I sat in the chair. One hour passed, then another, the pain becoming more and more intense, the piano wires underscoring a whole symphony orchestra. On the radio, the Click and Clack

Brothers gave tips on how to fix the electrical system of a used car, then Michael Feldman asked, *"Whad'ya know?"* and the audience replied, *"Not much. And you?"*

I considered who to call next. I kept thinking that I didn't want to impose on anyone. With the extreme cold, most cars were dead or needed a jump start. Furnaces were going out, pipes freezing. People had their own troubles. For some reason, it didn't occur to me to try and call an ambulance. Then, one right after another, I received a series of phone calls from friends.

"Are you warm enough?" James asked.

"Yes, but I can't move. I have pain in every joint."

"Weird," he said, then went into a long description of how he'd been awake all night listening to the strange popping noises that his house was making, how he had a very busy day ahead without time for anything.

"How are you?" Victoria asked.

"Horrible," I said. "I can't move."

"Bizarre," she said, then talked about her taxes.

I called my literary assistant. We were supposed to meet in town later that morning. "Could you possibly come out here?" I asked. "I have hideous pain in my joints and can't move."

"Oh, yes. I know how that is," she said. "I get this awful pain in my elbow . . ."

I called my gynecologist, who had just put me on hormones for menopause. I thought perhaps those pills had caused a stroke. She said this wasn't her specialty, that she was on her way out of town and would leave me her number.

"I don't have a pad or pencil and can't get up out of this chair to get them." I told her to call back and leave the number on my answering machine. Then I hesitated on the phone.

"What do you want me to do," she asked, "besides come out there and take care of you?"

Years before, through death and divorce, my family of origin had disintegrated. Both my parents were only children, so I had no aunts, uncles, or cousins. I had no spouse, no children of my own. I had my friends and neighbors, thank God, and good ones, too, but for whatever reason—my stoicism, their denial or inability to comprehend the severity of the situation—I could not communicate with them enough to connect during this moment of crisis.

I was Chekhov's taxi driver in his story "Grief." The driver's son dies one morning, then the father spends the rest of the day feebly attempting to tell one passenger, then another, of his agony. Each interrupts him, completely missing the import of his words. All day, he is unable to unburden his sorrow until he returns his horse to its stall at night and, brushing it down, tells the animal his whole, long story.

That Saturday morning my horse was in its stall in the barn wrapped in a blanket, and I was inside the house in my pajamas in the wing-backed chair. The pain had moved from the string section to the kettledrums and clash of cymbals. I could no longer tolerate sitting up. My head wanted to flop to either side, and when it did, the Click and Clack brothers' electrical system shorted out, sending a convulsive shock down my arm. My hands braced on the arms of the chair, I tried to rock myself forward. Nothing budged.

I tried to push up with my feet, but the mere pressure of my toe against my sock sent tears streaming down my face. Finally I let my whole body go limp, slack. Inch by inch, I slithered down out of the chair and spilled onto the floor. I lay there for half an hour, splayed across the hardwood, coldness pressing against my cheek. Then, with my arms stiff at my sides, with a stunted scissors kick, I propelled my body headfirst across the floor to my futon. With the last little ounce of brute force I had, I hoisted my head and torso onto the cushion. My legs had given out. They dangled down onto the floor as if on some muddy river bottom.

Eventually help arrived, and a series of trips to the emergency room followed, where I received a diagnosis of "gout," then was sent home to my own devices. (Over the course of the next four months, the diagnosis progressed from gout, to an exacerbation of my fibromyalgia, to rheumatoid arthritis or lupus. A full ten months later, I finally was found to have a ruptured cervical disc and myelitis, a viral infection of the spinal cord akin to polio.) Home from the ER, I was bedbound and forced again to turn to my neighbors and friends. This time I had to make my needs clear to them, to accept their refusals as well as their help.

Naked, I sat in Chair #2, this one in the shower stall. I stared at my friends Kelly and Katrina, and could not meet their eyes. My right leg stuck out into the room, unbending, foot cold and exposed.

Kelly and Katrina glanced away.

Well, I thought. You could sit here shivering in this chair, or you could get on with it.

Slowly, our heads lifted, eyes met.

Kelly and Katrina rolled up their sleeves and hot water sprayed down over my head and trickled off my back. The women reached in, and at my direction, lathered up my head with shampoo. Water cascaded off their arms and dampened their shoes. Shampoo slithered down my face and my friends tried to keep the suds out of my eyes. They soaped my body and with a washcloth made gentle but clear swipes under my arms, across my back, over my breasts, and between my legs. They rinsed me down and, turning off the water, patted me dry with towels.

So in they came, the neighbors and friends. Thirty-nine different people. Three or four a day for three weeks. From my closest chums to my students and colleagues. Even my electrician signed up for a shift. Every four or five hours, a new pair of hands opened my kitchen drawers, rummaging for utensils. They opened my mail, searching for checks. They opened my closet, hunting for clean clothes. Some steady, some hesitant, some downright shaky, they opened my robe and lifted my neck to change hot packs.

Whish, boom. When they first opened the door, each one of these men and women—old and new friends alike—entered wide-eyed, willing, but unaccustomed to their new caretaker roles. Shedding their coats and hats, they stepped into my bedroom and no longer were just acquaintances and pals. Suddenly they were my nurses, my guardians. I was their patient, their child.

"Welcome to the funhouse," I quipped, trying to ease my nervousness.

To ease theirs, the women chopped onions and carrots and stirred big pots of stew. They sat beside my bed and read me stories. They helped me hobble to the bathroom and turned away their faces until it was time to wipe. Whish, boom. Most of the men were back out the door as soon as they came in, feeding the cats and dog, running after groceries, renting a walker, a commode. Inside, they sat at the kitchen table and sharpened my knives.

"Hey, Mom," I whispered to my friend Sarah, who slept beside me on the sofa one morning. Seven-thirty a.m., I'd been awake since six, needing to urinate. Ashamed of my problem, I hadn't wanted to wake Sarah. I lay there in the darkness, the tick of the clock growing louder and louder, until I finally murmured, "Can you get me up?"

Sarah roused herself and stood beside my bed, swallowing hard.

Tentatively, she put one hand under my neck and wrapped the other around my waist, as I had coached her. Then, cradling me in her arms, she pulled my body upward and we abandoned ourselves to the primitive intimacy of the moment. Awkward though we were in our newfound tie, we were kin.

A few minutes later, she sat me down at the kitchen table. Immobile, I was like a child in a high chair, a voyeur at my own feeding. I directed her to the freezer compartment of the refrigerator in search of a bag of cherries. She pawed through cold packs and hunks of frozen meat until she found the fruit, which she began warming in a pan on the stove. My stomach growling, mouth watering, I watched her slowly stir the fruit, steam rising from the pan. Sarah tied a napkin around my chin. I opened my mouth wide.

"Coming in for a landing," she said, buzzing the spoon through the air and dishing up a bright red cherry.

The fruit lodged on my tongue, the juice warm and sweet, pooling in my cheeks, trickling down my throat. Sarah reloaded the spoon and I chewed again and again, one cherry at a time, my teeth breaking through each membrane, sinking down into the flesh. We had both given in.

Shortly, Sarah left for work. I thanked her, wished her a pleasant day, and held back my tears until I heard her car pull out of my drive. Then I let myself cry. I realized I forgot to ask her to put me back in bed and I was stuck in Chair #3 until early afternoon, when someone else was due to arrive. Now I was the baby in her crib, left with a babysitter, bawling her head off when her mother steps out the door. Except there was no babysitter. Now, in the midst of the parade of these genuine caregivers, I'd never felt more alone.

Solitude had always been an important factor in my life. As a child, I was constantly thankful that I had two older brothers who had to share a room and that I was privileged enough to have my own. I would enter my space, an enclosed sleeping porch, shut the door, and play by myself for hours, the wind blowing the elm trees back and forth past my windows, the breeze cooling and slightly raising the hairs at the nape of my neck. Or I would curl up with a book in my bed and read while the squabbles and oversights of the rest of the family brewed all around me.

I devoured books like *The Secret Garden*, *Treasure Island*, *Jane Eyre*, and Oliver Twist's orphanage made the household tensions around me seem manageable. I was the child who abhorred the thought of going away to summer camp, even if we could afford it. Camp seemed like the ultimate orphanage, lacking any kind of privacy. Although I loved sports and the outdoors, the thought of sharing a cabin with ten or twelve other girls terrified me. That was way too much noise and togetherness.

At the same time, I sincerely liked people, liked to laugh, joke, and play team games with them. But at the end of the day, I craved alone time, to gather my thoughts, to be quiet and feel safe emotionally. I was extremely shy. People, although fascinating and fun, were scary, saying and doing unpredictable things that I found difficult to comprehend. I needed the time and space to regroup and reorganize before launching off on another morning.

In my adult life, I have mostly lived alone, again happy to have my own space and time at the end of the day. Self-sufficient, I've always supported myself financially and grown almost all of my own food. Self-entertaining, I have existed without a TV or a VCR. From this single lifestyle has come a para-doxical connection to a large number of people as well as an unblocked passionate outpouring of artistic work.

For several winters in a row, I have been in the habit of getting up early every morning, pulling on my boots, hat, and down coat, and taking a walk down to the local Amish General Store. On the way back I usually pass Gracie, an Amish girl of about fifteen who clerks behind the counter and stocks the shelves full of flannel work gloves and wool socks. Babushka tied under her chin, Gracie walks down to my house every morning and when we cross paths, the sky streaked magenta with the dawn, we often stop for a few seconds and exchange bits of information about the weather or our lives.

Some days, Gracie is the only other human being with whom I interact, and that small exchange is enough to sustain me. Yes, living alone, I do have my spooky nights and frustrations with having to cope with every event and decision myself. I do some-

in Chair #1 has driven me to hang up my skates forever, but it has allowed me to edge closer to the knowledge of the Old Masters. I now understand suffering's "human position" at a deep, visceral level, and know that when we sail by a drowning boy, we fail to take in not only the boy, but something larger, more mythical. When we fail to notice the boy, let alone rescue him, we play right into the hands of the fates. We fail to confront our own attempts at escape from Minos, our own attempts to escape death. In that failure we miss an opportunity to understand how to live more fully, to stay away from the hot rays of the sun that will melt our wings, and to assume our rightful place in the universe.

Chair #2 gets more complex. This is the loneliness of vulnerability. In the bathroom stall dependency becomes real. Whether you have to abandon yourself to thirty-nine people, or to just one, you still must maintain your self-dignity. Chair #2 loneliness can at the same time feel invasive and healing. You acknowledge your difference but must allow yourself to be cared for. While Chair #1 can feel disconnected, Chair #2 is the Great Connector. That is the real beauty of Chair #2.

At least for a moment. After Kelly and Katrina patted me dry that day, they walked out the door and virtually vanished from my life for four or five months. They're busy people, I rationalized, but the pull of our closeness in Chair #2 and the tug of their disappearance saddened me. Finally, well into the summer, Kelly confessed that the Chair #2 scene had completely freaked her out, that she couldn't take it, that it reminded her of her mother's death and that was something she'd never grieved.

At first I was wounded by Kelly's confession. Oh, great, I thought. You have the option to flee, but I don't.

"Our contemporary culture doesn't attend to the sick and dying anymore," my therapist tried to explain. "Just two generations ago, people dressed their own dead and laid them out in their homes. Now we don't even touch them. We pay a stranger to do all that."

"If I could pay a stranger to lay me out right now, I would," I joked.

Ultimately, I was grateful for Kelly's honesty and forgave, remembering what she had done for me. I realized that there were many on my "list" who had probably experienced the same phenomenon. These people said they were "busy" and I knew that was so very true, but now I also know that everyone emotionally distances from the ill, even your nearest and dearest, even the kindest and most compassionate. And some outright abandon. "You were sick and alone, and that's the scariest thing for anybody to face. So many of us ran away from you," one of my friends admitted.

"I just don't know what to do with my emotions when I see these people again. Are we going to pretend like nothing happened?" I asked my therapist.

"Step back and reevaluate the friendship," she said.

"But I'm having to reevaluate almost every friendship."

"That's right," she said. "And if you were partnered, you'd be having this same difficulty with your significant other."

This is the real pain of Chair #2.

Chair #3 is the loneliness of infantalization, of being stuck physically and emotionally. You want to be comforted, to be encouraged, to be held and rocked. You want everything you had, or in most cases didn't have, in your childhood. Chair #3 is primitive, frustrating, shameful, and filled with flashbacks. I sat in Chair #3 that day and all my "stuff" came up, as if I were clicking through the slide show of my life. Tray after tray of images beamed on my interior screen—the good, the bad, the ugly— from the thrill of my first airplane ride and the way the wings dipped and dived over the rolling summer-green Loess Hills near my home, to the fright of my second car accident and the way the automobile spun around uncontrollably on the winter ice. From the gift of my first ice skates one Christmas morning, and later that afternoon my attempts to maneuver their blades across the lagoon, to my wiggling and wobbling attempts to maneuver in and out of relationships in my adult life. From my first splash in academe in second grade with a thoroughly researched A paper on milk, to my first failure and fall from grace weeks later when the teacher hung my artwork upside down.

Months, seasons, and years juxtaposed with each other, reversing and fast-forwarding, collaging, blurring and focusing and blurring again. While Chair #1 is raw trauma, Chair #3 is the confrontation with that trauma. Suddenly you must look at yourself on the screen, with all your strengths and imperfections—the little lines that have formed around your eyes, the extra pounds you've gained. You cannot back away. You cannot sail calmly out of the room. Your own image is blown up larger than life in front of your face. The carousel clicks to my face at four years old, beaming, tongue out, licking the frosting from my fork, one big bite of birthday cake about to go into my mouth. The carousel whirls to the grimace on my lips, tongue out, when I am facing down my playground tormentors when I was eight. The carousel clicks to the powerful arms of the neighbor boy who tried to choke me when I was ten, then the arms of the college boy holding me down on the bed, trying to date-rape me when I was twenty. The carousel clicks to my mother's arms securing the sides of my crib when I was two, then my arms lifting the sides of her hospital bed when I was twenty-two. The carousel clicks and whirls. The carousel spins uncontrollably on thin ice. Chair #3 is the ultimate heart-throb of separation and abandonment and can land you right smack in Chair #4.

I sat in Chair #4, a wheelchair—the fold-up variety—and emotionally everything collapsed around me. On late Wednesday afternoons, the county handicapped bus arrived in my lane. The friendly driver greeted my dog, then tried to maneuver me in my wheelchair down the front steps, over the ice and snow, up onto the lift and into the van. Once I was belted in place, we bounced along in the frigid weather, the driver making conversation, shouting back to me about the songs he had written to perform on his guitar, his voice echoing in the cavernous empty van.

I had been trying to keep teaching my graduate class—one night a week from seven until ten o'clock. We were only two weeks into a fifteen-week semester when I found myself in Chair #1. I needed the money from teaching and knew that my absence would cause the department nightmarish hassles. So each week I crawled out of bed, dressed, and got myself to the university. There I threw myself into the professorial role, taught with cheer and confidence, then returned home, in too much pain to even step out of my clothes, and crawled back under the covers for another week.

And the weeks stretched into a month. With only slight marks of improvement. The parade was long gone, my family of whish-boomers having returned to their extremely active lives. I coped with two hired helpers who each came in four hours a week and a loyal friend who made a weekly pot of soup. Most of the time I was alone. Bare, bald alone. This state was different from the self-imposed exile of my youth. This condition was superimposed, so at first I fought it. I thought about cross-country skiing, about the concerts and plays I was missing. I railed against myself for having to cancel readings and writing assignments from major newspapers. And I longed for company, some steady, quiet, reassuring presence.

"I wish I just had a sister, or cousin, or an aunt, or someone who could come and stay for a few days," I told my friend the soupmaker.

"Nobody has that," she replied. "And even if you were married right now, most spouses would leave a mate in your condition."

The voice of reality. After a few days of squaring myself off with that remark, I finally tried not to think about what could be happening but instead notice what was happening. First the ceiling fan became interesting and I learned to meditate to the tilt and twirl of its blades. Then I began to notice more nuances, how the shape of the clouds could predict the brushstrokes of the sunset, how as we headed toward spring, the days becoming longer and longer, the geese began to venture farther and farther from the neighbor's coop.

I was finally home long enough to peer out the window long enough to figure out how Scruff, one of the pygmy goats, could escape from the pen while Mac and Shenanigan couldn't. At last, I saw Scruff take a running jump from the top of the shed, plant his hoof on the five-foot-high cattle panel, twist and spin in the air, doing a back flip and landing with grace on all fours on the other side of the fence. I was finally home long enough to spot the red fox slinking back toward the ditch in the early morning. As if in one breath, his whole body disappeared into his den, the den I'd never before been able to find.

Above ground, the Hyakutake comet streaked through the sky. While others traveled to observatories and strained to locate the celestial body, its presence filled my window. Its tail, millions of miles long, trailed across my vision through the night and led my thoughts back down to earth where the ground lay frozen and bare. In its dormancy, my garden plot readied itself for spring, for the arrival of my hoe and spade, an expectation I was becoming more and more worried I could not meet.

I was home long enough to meet every UPS delivery and began to recognize the sound of the home health aid's car, its low throaty voice, almost like that of a heavy smoker, when it pulled into the lane. I learned the growl of the mail carrier's Jeep, its wheels spinning in the mud near my box. I learned the whine of the poacher's light pickup truck parked on top of the hill, a rifle poking out the window in hopes of popping off deer running down by Picayune Creek.

When I watched the deer dash through the trees unharmed, when Donna appeared at the door with the first six goose eggs of the new year, when Scruff wiggled his way back into the pen, this time through the tiny crack in the gate, I learned to sit back in that wheelchair and do what those doctors had told me years ago. I learned to live with the pain.

But the pain went on. And the months began marching right toward spring break, a week when many of the whish-boomers fly off to Aspen to ski or to the Caribbean to snorkel along the coral reef. I skied down my own slippery slopes, my mobility improving during the sunlight hours. I was now able to bend over to pull on my socks, to reach up and blow dry my hair. But when darkness descended, my joints locked into place like the brakes of the wheelchair. My pleasure in the nuances of the sunsets disappeared as they began to mark the transition into fitful nights of the Click and Clack Brothers reruns. The terror of Chair #1 revisited me when I woke in three a.m. darkness with a hot flash, sweat streaming down my body. I could not raise my arms or kick my feet to remove my down comforter. I lay there until morning staring into the night.

A huge chasm opened between me and the rest of the world. I looked toward others for support and a cacophony of well-meaning voices rose up to fill the empty spaces. *You're making a joke of everything, taking this too lightly,* some said. *You're making too much of a deal of this,* others said. *You're not asking for enough help. You're asking too much. You need to let me know your needs. I'll pick you up anytime. You live too far out and will have to find your own way. Everyone is really busy. You look good. You look really old. You're so robust it's hard to believe you're sick. If I didn't have Fritz, if I didn't have Gary, if I didn't have Jake, I'd be alone, too. I know what it's like, I had gout for two days. You look good. You look like my grandma. I know what it's like, I had the flu for five days. You must've done something really horrible in your past life to bring this on yourself now. You're such a good person, why's this happening to you? Are you depressed? I'm glad you can be so cheerful. Why don't you move to town? Why don't you go to New York and see your specialist? Why don't you move to New Mexico?*

"Is there anything I can do for you?" a friend from Alabama finally asked one night on the phone. "I feel so frustrated from so far away. Is there anyone I can call?"

"Yes," I said. "Do you have a pen and paper?"

"Shoot. Who is it?"

"Well, I don't know the number, but you can get it from Pontiac, Michigan, information."

"Okay. First name?"

"Jack."

"Jack . . . Last name?"

"It's spelled K-E . . ."

"K-E . . ."

"V-O-R . . ."

"V-O-R . . . No, no, I'm not calling him."

Suicide is actually not in my ethical code. Although I have had suicidal thoughts during bouts of other severe illnesses, I've fought too long and hard to stay alive to prematurely put an end to my existence. Yet this time the three a.m. darkness became a literal state of mind, a black mood I couldn't shake. I was Inanna, the Sumerian goddess of heaven and earth, descending into the underworld. Totally naked by the time she arrived, stripped of her powers and pretenses, Inanna was hung up on a hook and left to die without hope, a putrefying piece of green meat.

I thought about staying forever in the underworld, and then I thought again. No, I didn't really want to call Jack. I just wanted to get drunk. To alter my reality for an hour or two. But since medical restrictions had eliminated alcohol from my diet for the last twenty-five years, booze was out. And wisely so. But what's a good Irish Catholic girl to do? One night, almost as reflex, my lips began moving in prayer. *Hail, Mary*, I began.

Raised a strict Catholic during my youth, but disillusioned by both the structure and strictures of the Church, I have been a "recovering" Catholic most of my adult life. Although I'd lost the format, I had always retained the essence of my faith—that of a deep communal mingling and connection of all spirit and flesh. As I lay awake one night, drifting in and out of sleep, the sky dark and all-enveloping outside my windows, I flashed back to the lives of the saints, that other parade of characters that whish-boomed their stories through my early life.

The martyrs might provide the easiest answers. As a child they at once fascinated and horrified me with their boilings, beatings, and beheadings. Yet in my present state it wasn't the martyrs and their gory ends that gave me solace. Rather, the mystics came to mind with their kinder, gentler acceptance of suffering. The Zen saints, as I liked to think of them: St. Theresa of the Little Flower, St. Theresa of Avila, St. John of the Cross, St. Clare of Assisi, those men and women who had chosen a path of deprivation to reach some higher state of consciousness. The ceiling fan came back into focus, the tilt and twirl leading me to a meditation on how the mystics had each gone through their own kind of hell, how they had allowed their solitude to take them down a different path, where they found an interconnection with all beings, a life of love and giving.

I stopped answering E-mail and the phone. I stopped playing the radio and the stereo. I let the silence fill my room. I read Thomas Merton, Aldous Huxley, Hildegard of Bingen. I read Meister Eckehart, Thomas à Kempis, and the Rule of St. Benedict. I read Walt Whitman, the Book of Job, Lao-tzu, and Mary Baker Eddy. All these people understood the same basic truth: that suffering can either pull you inward, turning you guarded and bitter, leaving you there forever on the meat hook, or it can push you up out of the underworld to another level of consciousness where, as the Buddhists say, we can find the jewel in the lotus of the heart. At its best, suffering opens the heart to others' suffering and produces love and compassion: what we all long for from each other but find so hard to both give and find. The love for our fellow humans seems to inevitably work its way "down" toward all other living creatures and "up" to find its full force in love of God or a higher power.

"What does this mean?" asked Hildegard of Bingen. "No creature is so dull in its nature that it does not know the completeness of its case. What does this mean? The sky has light, the light air, and the air winged creatures. The earth nourishes greenness, the greenness fruit, and the fruit animals. All things bear witness to this order because the strongest of all possible hands ordered these things."

Hildegard as well as the other mystics knew that the spiritual was not found in the grandiose, but in the small growing things and the ordinary moments that previously you may have overlooked or found mundane. The antics of a pygmy goat, the sound of a car in the lane.

The German poet Rainer Maria Rilke understood these same mystical sentiments:

I Find You, Lord, in All Things and in All

I find you, Lord, in all Things and in all
my fellow creatures, pulsing with your life;
as a tiny seed you sleep in what is small
and in the vast you vastly yield yourself.

The wondrous game that power plays with Things
is to move in such submission through the world:
groping in roots and growing thick in trunks
and in treetops like a rising from the dead.

I fixated on the small, the tiny seeds. In my case, the literal seeds of my literal garden. Lying awake in bed at night, I'd worried how I would ever prepare the soil, plant, weed, dig, and harvest. I contemplated making raised beds. I contemplated making trellises. I contemplated not having a garden at all. The covers up to my chin, I stared out at the comet and remembered reading Viktor Frankl's classic *Man's Search for Meaning* my freshman year in college. The book's message flooded back to me. Those who survived the Holocaust held on to a faith in something spiritual, no matter how large or small—be it their God, their memory of family, or the fulfillment of a special talent.

Finally, I got up one morning, clomped down to the basement with my walker, and started my garden seedlings. Two little seeds in each pot. Then back up the steps, one slow foot in front of the other. Four trays in front of the window, the sun streaming in through the glass. I put all my faith in those living plants—tomatoes, peppers, cabbages, Brussels sprouts, and broccoli—even though I had no faith in my ability to garden ever again. I fussed over their temperature, their watering. I misted them with organic fertilizer. I labeled their pots, switched their positions in their trays, and watched their tiny necks struggle up through the soil. "The Ground of God and the Ground of the soul are one and the same," Meister Eckehart said, and I was getting ready to transplant my seedlings into the ground.

The spring began. I still lay awake at night and the fan went around and around but my mind was at rest. Lawrence LaShan, the research and clinical psychologist who works with cancer patients to help them rally their weakened immune systems, asks his clients: If your whole life were designed to carefully and lovingly teach you a lesson, what would that be? *Two little seeds in each pot. Stripped of all connections, it was only then that I could experience the inner-connectiveness of all things.*

"Let's look at it another way," my therapist said one day. "Your illness aside, if you could change your reality or have a different kind of existence, what would it be?"

I looked at her blankly.

"You like your life?"

"Yes."

"Despite the hardships, or because of them, you've carved out a pleasurable life."

No trumpets sounded, no locusts or horses swept across the

land, but now the air was crisp and clear, the stars so bright that I had to pull down the window shades that night to sleep. I began talking to people again and enjoying their company, wanting nothing more than that.

Again, as the Buddhists describe it, I was letting go of desire, the need for support, the need to be understood. In place of desire came a sharpening of intuition. My mind became a kind of caller ID. I began to know who was calling on the phone when I heard the first ring. Old friends came to mind, and there in that day's mail was a letter from them. So many uncanny things happened, so many strong hunches entered my head, yet hard as I tried to go with them, I couldn't quite trust myself.

One afternoon I pulled myself out of bed, got dressed for class, sat in the wheelchair and waited for the county bus. They're not going to come today, I said to myself. Something different is going to happen. That's ridiculous, I thought. The bus was ten minutes late, then twenty, then thirty. The guitar player must have had a heavy schedule, I thought. Or a late night. He'll be here soon. No, he won't, I answered. Then he was forty-five minutes late. I called the dispatcher. No, he said, your name's not on the list. We're shut down for the day. I'm sorry.

"But you pick me up every Wednesday."

"I'm sorry," he said. "We'll do better next week."

I looked at my watch. I needed to leave soon to get to the university on time. Briefly, I thought about calling around trying to find someone to come and get me, but it seemed like a lot to ask at the last minute. And there wasn't much time. I didn't think about canceling the class. I just got up out of Chair #4, took the steps with my walker, and climbed into my car. Carefully, I checked my rearview mirrors, as I couldn't turn my neck. I forced my feet up on the pedals, and in screaming-meemies pain, drove to town.

Home the next day, I began sitting for brief periods in my desk chair to work at the computer. The pain was intense but the wheels on my desk chair took me to a different place altogether. I'd realized that all of the mystics I'd read had found their fulfillment in some kind of creative activity that gave something back to the world—be it the charitable works of Mother Theresa or the contemplative writing of Thomas Merton.

I'd like to say that once I got back to work and started writing again in Chair #5, loneliness was banished forever. I'd like to say that Chair #5 was Nirvana. I'd like to say that when Lady Lazarus got up out of Chair #5, she could walk forever without a brace or a prop or a limp. All I can say is that while Chair #5 is a place of peace and productivity where solitude again reigns, it is also a chair of detachment, an integration of alienation. All I can say is that at the time, I had to go through the distress of Chair #4 to propel me to Chair #5. Life transforms into art. Chair #5 is a moving forward with hope despite the pain, connected wholly and intimately with both the light and shadowy sides of the self.

"You have no intimacy in your life," a friend once told me. The reality was that I had no mate, no sharing of physical affection. This was true. But when one is ill and alone, one is forced into a self-intimacy that can result in a larger, more cosmic closeness with the rest of the world. Sexual intimacy is a wonderful, pleasurable thing, satisfying a basic instinct. But the compassionate care of Kelly and Katrina in the shower stall, of Sarah at the kitchen table, the altruistic giving of care without reward, might be the ultimate intimacy. And you cannot give or receive unless you've stared at yourself in the rearview mirror.

Now, *what do I know?*

Recovery from chronic illness is a looking back. It is similar to recovery from the devastation of a flood, for you don't know exactly when crisis begins and when it ends. The only certainty is that it will surely flood again. I have experienced these five chairs before and I will again. Each time I am surprised by my own pain, how little and much I've learned. For this siege? I am up and around. The comet has long since disappeared from sight.

The garden soil has been prepared, the seedlings planted in the ground. Early each morning, I'm dressed and hobbling down the road again, where I pass Gracie, who smiles and does not mention my long absence. I've learned to walk with a cane, learned when and where to lean. And if some nights I still lie awake in the dark, I know that tomorrow the fan will still be there above me, spinning around and around.

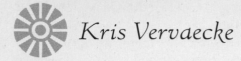

BACK IN THE BODY

We lived then in a cottage on the bank of the Willamette River in Oregon. Rhododendron, azalea, and wild blackberry tangled around the porch and the dense firs. My hospital bed was in the living room next to the woodstove, where I could look out the double-paned glass at the sparkling river, and when I was too tired to be propped up and turn my head, I lay on my back and watched ripples of light undulating across the shiny ivory painted ceiling, reflecting the river's surface. Like anyone who is pulled away and has the fortune to return, for weeks after I was released from the hospital I was overcome by the everyday beauty of the world. When our baby, seven-month-old Ben, was quiet, he, too, was transfixed by the light washing over the ceiling. The moving currents of reflected light were more beautiful than the river itself.

The cottage had been built by Swedish immigrants before the turn of the century. It would have been torn down and replaced by something expensive except that our landlady, Mrs. MacLaughlin, had known Lars and Sophia, and she said she couldn't yet bear to let the cottage go, although she said it was very likely we—Robert and I—would be the last tenants. The faded flowered rugs were those Sophia had brought with her from Sweden, as were the loose-weave, rose-colored curtains, worn to a scrim.

It was obvious that Lars and Sophia had loved each other very much. The kitchen cabinets that Lars had built swung open and stayed shut without a catch, and they had panes of glass in them so that Sophia could see her dishes gleaming there. Lars had paneled the bedroom walls with rubbed and shellacked pine and built a fireplace next to the bed. Before I got sick, I changed Ben's diapers on a table next to that fireplace. I have a photo of freshly diapered Ben arching backward like a sea lion to better see the fire his daddy had made to warm us. Robert had made many repairs to the cottage, cleaned out the stove and chimney, fixed a hole in the wall, and replaced loose wiring. He painted walls and ceilings and hung mobiles he'd made for the baby, fanciful animals he'd sewn from scraps of his old clothes. A large hibiscus tree potted in the corner bloomed profusely after he washed the old windows, their glass thickening at the sills. He chopped wood and laid in a good supply under the eaves for winter, the woodstove being the only source of heat we had.

I have a photo of Robert, all six feet five inches of him, stretched out across our bed. He has one arm folded behind his neck, and with his other hand he's supporting Ben, who is about four months old and can't reliably sit up by himself. Ben is wearing a mint-green terry-cloth sleeper and an expression of deep engrossment, as he is trying to pull red-blond hairs from the thicket on his daddy's chest. Robert is laughing, and because his father's chest is shaking, Ben must concentrate even harder on grasping those glistening hairs. Robert holds him expertly with one hand. If you look closely at his wrist, you can see one line of the hangman's noose that Robert tattooed on himself when he was in reform school at nine.

Before Ben was born, Robert and I worked together taking

care of emotionally disturbed children. Nearly every weekend, we took the kids to the waterfalls at Silver Falls State Park. As we drew close to the park gate, the youngest child, a plump blond five-year-old, Scotty, would begin shivering with anticipation. When the roar of the water reached us, Scotty called out to it in his odd, hoarse voice. Next to the wildly plunging water, drinking in the cascade of light, Scotty danced on the rocks in the fine spray, calling two syllables, "Dee-rah," while Robert, endlessly patient, watched over him. I could see what sort of father Robert would be.

Another photo of Robert has him holding me close as my pregnancy is beginning to show. The hills behind us are lush with forest. As I see his mother approaching with the camera, I'm beginning to pull away, but Robert's hand cups my cheek. He is smiling broadly, telling me not to be silly—I look incredibly beautiful four months pregnant. He's exhilarated, having just announced our news to his parents, standing on this hilltop, breathing in the air, fragrant with pine. Then his mother catches his eye, and for a split second, something solemn slips between them. He's been clean of heroin for three years, finished out his parole that week: For the first time in his adult life, he's full of hope. Now he's got two of us to reassure, but he smiles even wider. She snaps the photo. The certainty in his eyes doesn't waver.

From the time I left high school, I'd flung myself headlong in the direction of what I'd passionately, furiously wanted: to escape my mother's glacial anger; to go to college (which, by my family's standards, was unnecessary for a girl); to leave the economic landscape of Omaha for the ocean and the lush, ancient forests of the Northwest; to work for social justice; to have real love. The year I was twenty, I worked as an ACTION volunteer through a campus VISTA program in Oregon. Rain fell through that fall and winter and beyond the spring, swelling the azalea and rhododendron blossoms until they dropped, like sodden skirts, to the ground. The constant rain made Omaha, where I'd grown up, seem far away, possibly nonexistent; my parents and their decade-long conflict grew shadowy, too, although sometimes when I sat over my bitter teas or improvised soups in my rooming house on Stark Street in southeast Portland, I felt isolated and alone.

Through ACTION, I'd been assigned the job of investigator and organizer for a leftist law collective. That year it was involved in two highly politicized cases: one defending prisoners who claimed to have been organizing against racism, but whom the warden charged with a plot to commit murder; the other the defense of American Indian Movement leaders charged with transporting explosives across state lines. I never knew the reason I'd been placed with the law collective; it's hard to imagine someone more ill-prepared for political work than I was.

I remember a Tuesday night in January 1975, waiting upstairs at the Oregon State Penitentiary to be searched and taken downstairs for a UHURU (Freedom) meeting. I dreaded going back down inside the lockup. Day after day and week after week, I'd been conducting private interviews with prisoners; most recently, I'd had to question the men who'd had their cells burned out—mostly rapists and pedophiles.

From the inside of the upstairs waiting room, I glanced out the window, but glimpsed instead my own face, almost unrecognizable with exhaustion and fear. I was afraid because earlier that day in this waiting room, I'd seen a woman with a badly beaten face and because it was the first time I'd been to the prison at night. I wore a faded skirt and a shapeless, boiled-looking sweater and braided my hair back with deliberate indifference. Trying to shed layers of cultural, class, and sexual accoutrements, of course, I was simply trying on others, but as my physical and psychological pain increased, I was also trying not to *have* a body. Still, I didn't consider refusing an assignment or leaving the collective.

I'd grown up during the King years and had been deeply affected by the civil rights movement, looking to it as a moral center. I felt it would be too cowardly to quit. And, until things grew worse, the daily tension I felt was not unfamiliar. Psychologically, it was not so different from being consumed with making peace between my parents, pushing myself to try harder—something I'd been asked to do since I was a young child.

That night, after the long meeting and the drive back to Portland, in my bed at the rooming house my jaw, wrists, hands, elbows, hips, and knees hurt, keeping me from sleep. It was raining, and the damp cold permeated my body.

I dozed and awoke with the sensation that my body was a fallen tree, slowly petrifying. Through the walls, I heard the chanting of the Krishna devotions again. Most of the other renters were Hare Krishnas, something I hadn't known when I'd taken the room. For a few moments, I couldn't straighten my fingers, or roll over, or get out of bed.

During that year Patty Hearst was filmed robbing a bank with the SLA, and sometimes a prisoner, meaning to pay a compliment, called me "Tania," after the name Donald DeFreeze had given her. I had no interest in street Marxism, guns, or terrorism, but the situations I encountered frequently made me feel frightened, humiliated, and shoved up against my ideas about nonviolence. Over the course of the next year, I received middle-of-the-night threatening phone calls, my car was rammed from behind, flipping it over and sending it skidding upside down along the interstate. Although I wasn't seriously injured, the effects of prolonged stress, exhaustion, and fear wore on my body; my periods ceased, and I had frequent joint pain.

The law collective was disintegrating, overwhelmed with work and mired in irresolvable questions of ideology. All but one of the other workers quit. I would not allow myself to leave until I began running high fevers—104—so that I could not work.

I left the law collective, rested and recuperated for six weeks, then moved to Eugene. I put in a garden and lay in the sun. I had to relearn the habit of sleep, but long hours in the sun helped me relax. Color returned to my face, I began menstruating again, and I gained back some of the weight I'd lost. I got a job caring for the children at the group home. Robert and I fell in love.

The next year, we decided to have a baby. It was a time of tremendous hope for us, and I felt relatively healthy. Much later I would understand that the body produces natural cortisonelike hormones in pregnancy, and many women who have rheumatoid arthritis are virtually symptom-free during that time. After a normal pregnancy, I delivered a healthy eight-pound boy.

I was intensely happy with our baby, but I couldn't regain my strength. In photographs from those months, I appear thin and exhausted, as though I've been partly erased. I attributed my exhaustion and joint pain to the demands of attending to an infant—who wouldn't be tired? But one afternoon when Ben was seven months old, I became abruptly and violently ill, vomiting and soiling myself until I passed out. Just stomach flu, I told myself, but a few nights later I awoke in the middle of the night, in fierce pain and unable to move.

September 1977, a Portland hospital. *Middle of the night. Dinging bells, my ears ringing because of the high doses of anti-inflammatories. I've lost perception of space and depth; my body is huge with pain, a world collapsing into itself.*

Pain is my bed and my body. My fever is 105, and I want to open my mouth to call for help, but my jaw is locked in a fevered cramp. The bed is slightly inclined, so that my head and shoulders are settling into my spine. I want to straighten, to lengthen the space between my vertebrae, but I am powerless to move. Fire the body, brimstone the bed fixing me to its burning.

There is a cord to pull to summon a nurse, but hours before I had despaired of being able to move my arm, grasp the cool thing in my hand, move my thumb to push the button. My sole desire is to straighten on the bed. My joints are compressing, closing like teeth around the soft tissue, grinding, forbidding the mercy of absence of pain. Cartilage as grace intervening in the constant friction of bone.

Every joint in my body is penetrated by pain. Although there must be lengths of unjointed, painless body, I cannot feel them or remember pain's absence; pain is all I can believe in or understand. I think of my baby at home, and he stirs my heart with a longing alien to the sharp pressure at my heart that is costochondritis.

My body is constricting, my fingers curving like claws, every joint shrinking. Please straighten me, lay me out, gently pull me apart.

Every evocation of hell is through the body. Why didn't I understand before? The burning I wanted to save my father from, as a kid crying in bed, praying to Jesus? It was the body I wanted to save him from.

But I'm not thinking, I'm burning, I'm struck dumb and blind with my body incinerating itself. I live only so I can be gently lifted into water, cooling my bones, which are rubbing like sparking sticks.

But no one comes, my pain will last forever. I'm spinning over a fire. The burning skewer through the soles of my feet, my legs twisted around and around, squeezing tighter. My spine and head should explode, but they refuse. If someone would just smooth me to the flat bed. Let my body be the slightest indentation on the silky sand, the tide coming in.

Someone at my bed, a nurse or aide.

"Your meds. Sit up."

I stare at her, trying to open my mouth. I'm lying askew on the sheets, head twisted down on one side. My head is roaring; I'm trying to part my lips. "Help me move," is what I'm trying to say, but I can't unclench my jaw.

"Sit up."

She switches on a light. She is a small, middle-aged woman, no doubt overworked and underpaid. I can see contempt on her face.

Hasn't she read my chart? Can't she see I need help? I feel a grainy wash of humiliation over my powerlessness. I would do anything, abase myself in any possible way, to get her to help me.

"You're wasting my time." She turns off the light, goes away.

An eagle's claw digs deeper into my back, drawing my skin tight. Another claw tears into the skin of my forehead, sinking into bone. I will be devoured, torn apart limb by limb. . . .

But now I feel a presence in the room, a benevolence that has somehow been there all along, like an inaudible murmur, which, when turned up, is the sound of clear, clean water being splashed over those burning bones, the sound of the most lucid words you've ever heard, laughter, a choir singing in a thunderstorm.

I am held in rapture in that presence until morning, when ordinary life resumes, when my fever is down to 104, and the doctors come.

To be ill is to enter, quite unwittingly, the bizarre hierarchy of patientdom. If your lab test results are "off the charts," you get to be a "star" patient. My lab values were wildly abnormal, making it difficult to settle on a diagnosis, but after a week in the hospital, I was told there was a ninety percent chance that I had "acute, atypical rheumatoid arthritis," a ten percent chance that it was systemic lupus, or another disease, often fatal, which my doctor did not name. I had trouble taking in all this good news at once.

My doctor was a kind man, reticent about offering too much by way of prognosis. He did tell me that I had a severe, disabling form of the disease. When I told him that I was not going to be disabled, he simply nodded. When I badgered him about what the various blood tests actually meant, he brought books from his medical library and propped them on trays on my bed, because I could not hold them.

When the nurse came in, I asked her to bring me a phone. She dialed the number for me and tucked the receiver by my ear. As soon as Libby answered the phone, I began sobbing, which must happen to therapists a lot.

She listened to me quietly. Telling her what had happened, simply telling her the story, I began to calm down. Only when I explained rheumatoid arthritis to her, whispering my shameful secret which I would guard from everyone else, *"They say I will be disabled,"* did she interrupt.

"You know that I have rheumatoid arthritis, don't you, dear? You've noticed my hands, haven't you?"

Her hands? I saw Libby sitting across from me in the little breezeway she used as her office, ferns and viney plants ingratiating themselves around our shoulders, seeming to wind the two of us together, Libby's soft brown hair swirled with gray, falling over her pewter-colored sweater, pooling in her lap where her hands rested, pawlike and somehow fierce. I'd known they were unusual, but it had never occurred to me that they were deformed. They seemed powerful, hands which would be used only in well-considered ways. . . .

"It's the ulnar drift," she said briskly.

I saw my fingers twisting away from my palms, slender pieces of driftwood. Silently, I objected, *But you're old, fifty or something, and I'm only twenty-three, too young to be arthritic.*

"It doesn't mean *your* hands are going to look like mine. I'm much, much better than I was during the phase when my hands were crippled."

"How'd you get better?" I whispered.

"I found many ways to heal. I think differently, eat differently, move differently, love differently. I was thorough. If I were angry, angry enough to break a dish, I broke every dish in the house. I sought out the company of people who were good for me, avoided those who weren't. But don't take it all on at once. For right now, just rest, knowing that you will heal."

I told her that I was afraid. As I remember (can this be true, this incredible kindness?) she told me to go to sleep while she stayed on the other end of the telephone; that way, if I couldn't sleep, I could pick up the phone and talk to her.

I did fall asleep and, when I woke up, discovered the nurse had come in and taken away the phone.

The day I finally got to go home from the hospital, my doctor was off-duty and so his son, who was entering his father's practice, saw me. I told him I was grateful that I probably did not have systemic lupus, but rheumatoid arthritis.

"Well, as sick as you are," he said in an offhand way, signing my chart, "I don't think you're any better off with R.A. Lupus can be fatal, but your R.A. is going to be badly crippling."

I was too stunned to reply.

Robert came in the room, carrying Ben. Ben's hair was curling madly, and he wore his royal blue shirt and red corduroys. When he saw me, he began squawking and kicking his legs, as though to launch himself from his daddy's arms into mine. As Robert brought him closer, Ben made an openmouthed, headfirst dive for my face, and only Robert's quick maneuver prevented a collision. Robert held him while Ben delivered his first unsolicited, full-mouth, sucking kiss. He smelled of baby powder and peanut butter toast.

It was raining as Robert lifted me into the backseat of our car so I could ride wrapped around Ben in his car seat. I felt full of joy at being back with my family, even with the doctor's words echoing in my ears.

The hours I spent in awe, yet bathed in love, that night in the hospital, do not belong wholly to this life. They occurred at the deepest point of my journey into the wilderness.

Robert and I had health insurance, which seemed like a miracle, and it paid for everything: all hospital charges, a home health nurse who cooked and cared for me and the baby, rental of a hospital bed and wheelchair, and physical and occupational therapy. I saw the doctor three times a week. My friends organized, with Robert, a schedule of round-the-clock care for the evenings and nights when he was working and the nurse wasn't on duty. I was not able to lift Ben or even hold him, but he took his naps next to me on the bed. With someone else holding him, I could talk and play with my baby until I tired.

The system began to break down when the winter rains came, making my pain and stiffness worse. The sun did not show itself; the house seemed gloomy, and I was always cold. The woodstove heated the living room, but the bedroom, kitchen, and bathroom never got warmer than forty-five degrees. If the nurse or a friend who was there to help did not respond to Ben's crying, I was filled with panic and then rage that I could not go pick him up and comfort him myself. I still could not grasp things in my hands, wash or comb my hair, clip my nails, or walk more than a short distance.

Robert's energy was flagging under the burden of care and worry. We were short of money. Fissures in our relationship were cracking open under the strain of my illness and the humiliation of my helplessness. I could see him struggling to manage everything, but he was growing silent when once he would have talked with me freely. His mother commented to him, within my earshot, that if she ever became a burden to others, she would shoot herself.

We were distressed by leaning on our friends for so much and so long. Once deterioration had set in, it seemed impossible to halt: Someone tracked a tarish substance over one of Sophia's rugs. The hibiscus tree died, either from neglect or the severe pruning my mother had administered when she'd flown out to see me while I was in the hospital. What I loved—the lush foliage outside, our flourishing houseplants—my mother found depressing, and certain it couldn't be good for me, she'd reduced the tree to a quivering twig.

One weeknight in early December when Robert was working, Bill, a friend who'd agreed to fix supper and care for Ben and me, had to wash every dish and pot we owned before he could begin cooking. Then, poking around in the refrigerator, he found only celery and milk. Undaunted, he made an exquisite creamed celery over rice, but before he could take a bite of the supper he'd made, Ben began crying. Bill brought him over to me, and I tried to comfort him. Ben's sleeper needed to be changed, his nose was cold and running, and he smelled of sour milk. I felt enraged that I couldn't bathe him myself. Bill walked with him back and forth across the floor to no avail. We agreed that it was chilly and that the fire needed to be stoked. Bill put Ben in the playpen, where he screamed miserably while Bill went outside to get wood, which turned out to be wet and produced more smoke than heat.

That evening I called my mother and asked if Ben and I could come to her house. It had been ten weeks since I'd been released from the hospital, and I was little improved. My mother had offered to take care of Ben and me in Wahoo, Nebraska, where she'd moved with her new husband. I knew that my mother, who loved babies, would take exquisite care of Ben.

After I made the phone call to my mother, I felt as I had when I was five years old, high up in the air on a teeter-totter, anchored on the other end by nine-year-old Donny Henderson. Donny had kept me up in the air a long time, lulling me, raising me up and floating me down a mere foot or two, then lifting me back up. When he jumped off his end, plunging me to the ground so that I smashed the ankle I'd curled underneath my seat, there was too much to feel all at once: vertigo, the sickening thud resounding through my bones up to my head, the throbbing pain, the grown-ups rushing over in excitement, the questions, Donny's mother slipping off her Keds to paddle Donny, my protests. *No, I didn't want to go to the hospital, no, don't spank Donny, no, go away and leave me alone.* It was too distracting from what I felt, where I needed to linger, back up in that cornflower sky, the sun on my face, where I could see out to the lake, where I floated like a puff of cotton from the cottonwood trees. I was crying because I wanted to go back up. I hadn't known that you could fall so abruptly from one world to another, no matter how tightly you hung on.

Robert had to remain in Portland because of his job. As he tucked me into the airplane seat, having arranged for someone to help me with the baby during the flight, we told each other I'd be back soon, when I was well, certainly by spring.

My body's story is one of naïveté. As a child I had puzzled over the problems my body posed, the chasm between my yearnings, which my soul told me to believe in, and the attention claimed by my flesh, which could be made miserable by mosquitoes. So how would I manage under torture? If I were that Vietnamese girl trying to flee my burning flesh, offered a chance to slip back into my cool skin . . . would I betray my own mother? God, I didn't want it to be so. At ten, I'd looked at my mother—my diminutive mother, folding my ribbed undershirts and underpants, fresh-smelling and still warm from the dryer, and felt my skin shrink as I tried to compress my ungainly bones and my mutinous desires.

In the hospital, I had drawn close to what seemed like the end of my life, and as I began healing, I returned to something like its beginning. Wahoo, Nebraska, turned out to be an actual town (I discovered it before David Letterman did), my stepfather's house a small, weather-tight brick the wolf could not blow down in a thousand years. As snow gritted the windows, I listened to the wind howl down the stovepipe as I sat in my mother's kitchen with a neighbor, Mrs. Hammerstead, who had popped in to talk to Mom, still at the beauty shop. To Mrs. Hammerstead, I was a curiosity: the black sheep daughter, the one who'd been living in Oregon in a shack with no heat except from a woodstove, the one who'd been working with prisoners and Indians and God knows what else, the one who had a baby without being married. Ben was asleep in the bedroom; Mrs. Hammerstead had tiptoed in to see him, and I'd had my Midwestern moment of compliments on his beauty, which, in all truth, could not be overstated.

Across the table, Mrs. Hammerstead leaned toward me, adjusted her glasses, and asked, as though sympathetically, "Kris, has your mother told you about Eleanor Nice? Up at the care center on the hill? Eleanor has a very bad case of rheumatoid.

The poor dear can't bathe or feed herself. She has to be lifted in a harness and lowered to the toilet seat."

Here Mrs. Hammerstead paused to acknowledge the indelicacy of Eleanor's condition.

"But you just can't find a sweeter soul anywhere," she finished. "And she never, ever complains."

Sweat popped out on the back of my neck under my long, curly hair, itched at my armpits, evidence of my gross corporeality that my mother's toiletries could not mask, but I kept quiet because I didn't want to further embarrass my mother. I'd become accustomed to being like Eleanor, the grotesque, the object of fascinated horror, the standard by which others console themselves. *Oh, you're "it," too*, was what Mrs. Hammerstead meant when she told me about Eleanor Nice. *You've drawn the black mark on the card. It's too bad, but there must be some reason for it. Let us instruct you in being "it."*

To be ill is to be fitted into others' stories, to be pressed for reassurance by the healthy that there is significance in your being ill and their being well. In Wahoo, the story was either a perversion of Christian martyrdom or a staple of my childhood, Old Testament punishment. In hipper Portland, the story had been a perverted version of karma. These stories *are* seductive in their way, preferable to the chaos of corporeal anguish, because they impose a sense of meaning and time on the experience. But they do not correspond to what I lived.

I had not for a moment accepted the black mark on the card, not if it meant resigning myself to being sweetly passive and physically helpless. Since I had been ill, I'd fallen in love with movement. I recalled with longing every fluid motion my body used to make. As I lay in bed, I sent my body up and down trails, my thighs and calves tightening with the effort, my knees buoyant, unswollen. I imagined Ben in my backpack, my legs strong enough to carry the two of us forever. Or I danced, danced late into the smoky night, my back, arms, and legs slippery with sweat, languid with a pleasant tiredness. I ran across the meadow by the Platte where I played as a child, swirling like the grasses in the wind. As I ran and leaped, spun and fell, I could smell the earth again, the sweet alfalfa, the rough mint. On top of my mother's stiff, freshly laundered sheets, I recovered every moment I could remember of my body, I moved until I felt spent, and as I drifted off to sleep, I imagined that I was swimming in the Willamette, floating on those endless, glimmering currents of light.

And at this moment hope cinched me so tightly I could not breathe, hope because I realized, in the strength of my desire, that I was ever so slightly better.

So, I simply raised my eyebrows at Mrs. Hammerstead—a gesture that did not require movement from any of my joints—knowing I would someday have the health and strength to leave.

Of the flight to Nebraska, of being met by my mother and driven out to Wahoo, I remember only my fog of exhaustion, but I have a clear recollection of awakening that first morning in her house, a week before Christmas.

My mother helps me walk to her kitchen table and sit down. The smell of her body, her sensible soap and lotion and slightly intoxicating hairspray, floods me with memories of childhood, but I cannot remember ever feeling this tenderness from her before. Except for a few things she has brought from her first marriage, such as the Danish blue plates lining the walls, the house and everything in it are her new husband's, which is strangely reassuring. I do not miss our old kitchen or wish ever to return to the house where I grew up. For the first time, she does not criticize me or talk about my father. It seems that she wants to care for me, wants me there with her.

It is a pleasure to be out of bed, a greater pleasure to watch Ben's bath. He is nine months old, which means he is dancing rather than standing in the sink; he is laughing, pulling at the washcloth, teasing my mother, trying to entice her into teasing him. Which she readily does. How does a baby learn how to make a joke? He is a canny, blond charmer of a baby, and I love him more than I have ever loved anyone. I feel a pang because I long to be bathing him myself, but the hands that are holding and washing him belong to my mother, and they are next to my own.

We are back in the body, and I am firmly on earth. The time I spend in my mother's house, more dependent on her than I have been since I was a very young child, entrusting her, too, with my baby, is like finding myself in the belly of the whale— trapped in the body in the body—undergoing something like another gestation. I find that she deeply loves me, something I didn't know for years.

Now she brings Ben to the table, which she has covered with layers of towels. I can't manage the diaper pins—we agree paper diapers are too expensive and wasteful—but I can smooth his skin with lotion. My fingers are bent and clawlike, but eventually they will straighten, although they'll never be absent of pain. For the moment nothing matters but being able to stroke my baby's skin.

I think of the story of Jonah and the whale, a story I'd remembered from childhood as one of many that emphasized the certainty of terrible punishment. Now the story seems to be about my mother and myself. Not about obeying her, but about being returned to her body, to the body itself, returning again and again until we cannot escape ourselves.

Tom Sleigh

THE INCURABLES

Fifteen years ago, in a place that now seems less likely than anything I could make up, I find myself sitting in a room in a Mexican clinic that treats patients on whom conventional medicine has given up. In other rooms there are other patients, some of them within days or weeks of their deaths. Perhaps to call this place a "clinic" is too grand. The fact is, we have retreated to a converted motel, in better days served as a retreat for Hollywood stars like Gloria Swanson and Dorothy Lamour. At least that's the myth we patients trade among ourselves, compensating for the cracked ceilings and walls in our rooms, the chipped and dirty swimming pool, the haphazard palm trees and overgrown bougainvillea that clings to the faded whitewashed wall that surrounds the clinic grounds.

Removed from the world, we drink specially prepared juices each hour for fourteen hours, we eat vegetarian meals, we try to detoxify our bodies with frequent enemas. At the end of our first weeks, if the treatment is working, our immune systems will react with astonishing ferocity: Our organs and tissues will begin dumping toxins into our bloodstreams, the cancer patients' tumors will start to dissolve. The result of all this purifying activity, in which the body supposedly gears up to heal itself, is high fever, nausea, acute pain in joints as calcium deposits break down, foul odors, the sweats, sudden intense chills, even mild forms of mental disturbance and psychosis. The challenge is to stay ahead of the flood of poisons.

Only the fear of imminent death could make anyone stick to this regimen. Six, seven, or more enemas a day—the treatment seems lunatic fringe at best. But what can we do? Fasting, visualization, macrobiotics, laetrile, wheat grass juice—we've read the literature, we've given these other alternatives a try. And still we're sick, our doctors still tell us there's nothing they can do. As our chances for getting well diminish, as pain or weakness turns us more and more inward, the only force turning us back toward the world is hope.

Having lived with a chronic blood disease for close to twenty years, I've become acquainted with the mercurial shiftings of hope. Hope is my ally when my health starts to decline, convincing me that I can raise myself up; but hope is equally my tormentor: In a good stretch of health, hope can lull me into thinking that my life is more or less normal—until the inevitable downswing, when hope seems merely self-delusion.

My illness is as rare as it is unpronounceable: paroxysmal nocturnal hemoglobinuria—which in simple English means "blood in your urine at night." The first time I noticed it was on a dank, hot Baltimore spring morning a few months after I'd turned twenty-two. To keep my fear in check, I walked the floor of my apartment a few times, halting now and then at the window to look down at a plane tree that was just beginning to leaf out above the Dumpster in the alley. I managed to convince myself that the blood lazily diffusing in the toilet water was only a fluke of biochemistry—a verdict which the various doctors I consulted over the next three years tended to agree with. None of them came remotely close to making the right diagnosis—a fact which

I don't hold against them. There are so few cases that most doctors, including blood specialists like hematologists, have never actually seen a walking, talking PNH patient.

The disease (my disease, I should say) has no known precipitating cause—but somehow a gene that should make a protective protein on the membrane wall of a red blood cell has gotten switched off. So when I get an infection or if I'm overtired, my oxygen-carrying red blood cells break down abnormally fast. In fact, if I contract a particularly fierce fever, my red cells begin to explode so quickly in my bloodstream that unless I get to a hospital, I can die—from loss of blood, from blood clots, from heart attack. And those are only the acute dangers: In the long term my disease can develop into leukemia, or my bone marrow can give out altogether—what the Merck Manual calls "aplastic anemia." But when my blood count is stable, I take an almost macho pride in my body's ability to adjust: A normal person reading this essay would probably faint in his chair and be in serious need of a transfusion if his red cell count were to plummet to the level that I now consider "healthy."

In these good periods, as if my illness were a demon lover, my muscles flex and bend: I try to appease my illness with feats of strength and endurance, to blind and nullify it by swimming and hiking and taking long walks.

But then, as always, comes the crash—I get a fever, my blood count starts to dive, hope neutralizes fear by fueling what I know is the excessive intensity of my fantasy life: As if to counter my lack of physical vitality, my daydreams grow wildly involuted. While the skeptic in me scoffs, I dream up obscure and mystical compensations for the knowledge that sooner, rather than later, my body will fail me.

The hope that my death means something, means something not just to my intimates but to the world at large, drives me in the most shameless and childish way to concoct extravagant, even grandiose, fantasies. The more elaborate the fantasy, the graver the circumstance: Snowed in beneath hospital sheets, as I wave good-bye to my construction worker roommate (whose blood count had inexplicably plunged to the level *up* to which I'm waiting to be transfused), the orderly slides me out of bed onto the green, plastic-pillowed trolley and wheels me off to X ray. I'm to undergo a scan for blood clots in my lungs. While I breathe in the radioactive gas that will illuminate my lung tissue, I fight back my fear of death with a fantasy in which I embrace death: The plastic mask erasing my features, suddenly I'm hectoring and stoical, casually unconcerned by the approach of my impending execution. I spend my final hours convincing my closest friends that the soul is imperishable . . . then, without a tremor, drink off the fatal hemlock that my weeping jailer prepares for me. Unlikely or laughable as it seems, I'm reenacting Socrates' state-ordered suicide, my so-called crime to incite free thinking in the young. The fact that I'm terminally ill, and my death is less a sacrifice on the altar of free thought than it appears, is my closely guarded secret.

In the *Phaedo*, the dialogue of Socrates' death and his attempt to prove the immortality of the soul, I sense beneath his manner of disinterested, logical argument wild swings of hope and fear: hope that death will reveal ultimate truth, fear that all death means is that one's heart stops beating. How confident the philosopher seems in his talk of mind disencumbered of body, pure immortal mind! Yet beneath the deliberate cool with which he elucidates the doctrine of the divine, eternal forms, showing how "Beauty and Goodness possess a most real and absolute existence," I sense in his willingness to take the poison something murkily self-destructive, almost suicidal. At the same time, his conviction that the soul is immortal is more than a little self-interested: As his proofs elaborately unravel into counterproofs, he demonstrates not only the immortality of the Soul, but of his soul in particular. But these spookily contradictory motives aren't simply the product of an unacknowledged death wish or a manically hopeful need to reassure himself of his own indestructibility—the philosopher seems equally intent on comforting his followers. Tenderly stroking the head of Phaedo, Socrates asks his young friend if he intends to cut his hair tomorrow as a sign of mourning. When the heartbroken Phaedo laconically replies, "Yes, Socrates, I suppose I will," the philosopher jokes that if his arguments fail, both of them will have to shave their heads today.

What I find most moving and troubling about this dialogue is the moment of Socrates' death, when he pits his own hopes for immortality against the implicitly skeptical method of his argument. Each time he establishes the soul's indestructibility, he encourages his followers to contradict him, to poke holes in his conclusions until they are completely satisfied that the case has been proven. At last all doubts are vanquished, his followers accept his reasons, his approaching death and his eerily hopeful embrace of it are in precarious balance.

But now my fantasy takes over, the soul of Socrates inhabits my lungs, lips, teeth, tongue that have been arguing against the body as frail, corrupt—while the hemlock numbs my flesh, my friends feel my feet, ankles, knees, thighs to keep track of how far up my body the chill of the hemlock has progressed. My philosophic abstractions, my denigration of my own flesh are entirely forgotten before the mystery of my dying body. The elaborate dance of my intellect can't distract me or my friends from the sorrow and fascination of flesh passing away, flesh that means me, my hand stroking my friend's hair. My vision is blurring . . . to spare my friends the sight of my face, I've drawn a cloth over my head. But now a sacrifice that I've overlooked to Asclepius, the divine healer, keeps nagging at me: I uncover my face and, fixing my eyes on Crito, the friend I trust most, I tell him, "Crito, we owe a cock to Asclepius. Make sure the debt is paid." When he assures me it will be done, I—

But here the fantasy comes full stop. I'm no longer Socrates; his soul has passed out of my flesh . . . my fantasy gives way to the fact that for almost twenty years, I've anticipated daily, whether consciously or not, the moment of my death. . . . The fact of my death, my *real* death, is a scalpel that cuts through tissues of ego and daydream: In another, starker vision of the end, I see my body shiver a little while my lungs stop breathing. But my mind can't rest there, death is too reductive, it can't keep hope from spurring on my imagination: Now Hermes appears and leads my soul flittering like a bat to the underworld. The soul of my dead father comes winging up to me, shrilling in a frequency I don't yet understand—except for the strange vibration of *hope*, the lone syllable in the language of the dead that is anything like the language of the lives of earth.

My father comes to me in a dream. His fur is white, his antlers branch above him, his muzzle is elongated, his nostrils quiveringly suspicious. His eyes see me but don't see me as he lowers his head to drink. The water drips from his jaws when he raises his head again, and now his eyes, which before were liquid, uncomprehending, wholly animal, stare back at me with human recognition. He seems to know me, but he himself—I can't tell what he's feeling or thinking. He takes a step toward me and as I put my hand out to touch his fur, his head jerks back, he looks at me warily—but then allows me to put my arm around his neck, blood-warm, his fur more bristly than it looks. I feel joy to have him next to me, his fur, his muscled legs, the ridge of his long backbone—but the next moment he flattens into two dimensions, I realize that I'm looking at a mosaic. A voice that I can't locate says, "Stop, just stop it!" When I wake next moment, I can tell that my health, which has been poor for the last few days, is better, magically better, and that the renewed strength I feel in my arms, and especially in my legs, has something to do with my dream.

In A.D. 174 Pausanias, the Greek travel writer, visited Epidaurus in southern Greece, the center of the cult of

Asclepius. He tells us that Asclepius's father is Apollo, god of medicine, music, light, and prophecy, while his mother, Coronis, is mortal. The polarity of an immortal father and mortal mother underscores the ups and downs of the god's fortunes. In one story of his birth, his mother leaves him to die on a mountain (ironically named Mount Nipple), while in another he is snatched by Hermes from his dead mother's womb just as the flames of her funeral pyre engulf her. Entrusted by Apollo to Chiron, the wise centaur for his education, Asclepius brings the healing arts to such perfection that the gods of the underworld complain that they are being cheated of their dead—and so Zeus incinerates Asclepius with a thunderbolt. But the cult of Asclepius springs up all over Greece: Pausanias describes the god's many statues as being made of ivory and gold. The god is seated and a dog lies next to him. One hand grasps a staff, the other is held above the head of a serpent. As the god's birthplace, Epidaurus becomes one of the healing centers of the ancient world.

In Asclepius's wild oscillations of fortune—his exposure on the mountain, his rescue from his mother's funeral pyre, his ability to raise the dead for which he himself is put to death—I perceive the force of human ingenuity struggling against the brute fact of death: Asclepius's brushes with death and his miraculous escapes seem an emblem of the human mind faced with its own mortality as it ricochets between hope and despair.

What in Epidaurus was called the Hieron, or sacred precinct, of Asclepius, finds its counterpart in the clinic dining room. This is the sacred space of our hope to get well. To an outsider, in our short-sleeved shirts and sandals we look as casual as tourists on a Mexican holiday. But the pallid woman who sits across from me, who seems to labor to bring her spoon up to her lips, the hoarsely breathing man next to me whose skin is more jaundiced than tan, concentrate on their food with fanatical intensity. In our sect of the sick, in which we secretly speculate on the ones among us who are too far gone to make it, our cardinal rule is to convince each other and ourselves that health can't be far away. As we sit eating at the battered wooden table, novitiates like myself glean knowledge from the old hands:

"Had your first fever?"

"No, it hasn't hit me yet."

"Mine lasted about four days—a hundred and four degrees, nausea, the works. The docs here are right about the peppermint tea. It washes out your stomach real good. And you should do double duty with the enemas. It really helps to knock the fever down."

I stare into an unseasoned soup of potatoes, onions, and leeks. My ears fill with the hum of an industrial juicer reducing crates and crates of kale, celery, beet tops, apples, carrots to messy pulp squeezed by a hydraulic press into the elixirs we drink. All of us smell subtly of the Vaseline we grease our enema tubes with.

"Are you doing full-strength coffee enemas?"

"No, they told me to try tea for a while—just to go easy, at first."

To traditional practitioners of medicine, all this sounds crackpot—a hypermoralized quackery that stresses "cleansing," an almost ritualized regulation of eating habits and bodily evacuations that seems reminiscent of certain practices of ancient mystery religions that stress the need for purification and rebirth: Initiates into Mithraism were placed into a pit where the blood of a sacrificed bull streamed down on them from above, washing them clean of their sinful past lives; like Socrates' devotees, Pythagoras's followers believed in transmigration of souls, soul passing from body to body until it became so pure that it was released from the cycle of death and rebirth; Orphic cults prescribed ascetic practices to believers—no beans, no flesh, the wearing of certain kinds of clothes. Such ancient rites and disciplines may seem oddball at best, akin in certain respects to the healing cult of the Virgin Mary at Lourdes. Mystical mummery, faith healing, it all sounds pretty dubious . . . but I wasn't going to discount the miracle that could cure me!

In the sacred groves of Asclepius stretched a long covered

colonnade where patients consulting the god would sleep, see certain visions in dreams, and come forth cured the next morning. Did my dream of my father as a stag have a clinically measurable effect on the sudden improvement in my health? The temptation to link my dream with the therapeutic power of mental suggestion is hard to resist—especially when doctors can accurately describe the biochemical chain reactions that make me feel sick, but offer nothing concrete in the way of a cure . . . except for a potentially risky bone marrow transplant. High doses of radiation and chemotherapy to wipe out my bone marrow mean that I would have to live in hygienic isolation from infection. Temporarily without an immune system until the new marrow infused into me can take hold, I would be defenseless against the most innocuous of microbes.

When I contemplate undergoing a marrow transplant, I begin to allegorize the stages of marrow transplantation into a quasi-mystical passage from disease to health. First, the ritual ablution, in which my sinful marrow is destroyed: Through an intravenous needle, Cytoxin swirls into my bloodstream, or I lie on the X-ray table absorbing megadoses of radiation. Then, in a germ-free plastic tent, I'm kept in isolation from the world's manifold pollution: Utterly nauseous and wiped out in my high-tech chrysalis, I pass through the stages of my rebirth. My clean new marrow is IV'd into my veins and sucked up by the hollows of my bones; gradually, over a week or two of obsessive monitoring and blood tests, my new marrow cells proliferate and take hold . . . and if all goes well . . . if the graft is successful and my defective red blood cells don't return . . . if, during the month or so of my sojourn in this germicidal void, I've successfully avoided pneumonia and other life-threatening infections . . . then—at last!—my day of deliverance arrives: I take off my surgical mask, I leave my tent; through the hospital's automatic doors I step out into the microbe-infested air, I reenter the world of temptation and risk.

Of course, a bone marrow transplant ought not to be mystified; it isn't an allegory of sin and salvation, of spiritual death and rebirth. But the relatively neutral phrase *bone marrow transplant*—nothing in the term hints at how extreme the treatment is. Of course, that neutrality buffers me from the knowledge that my doctors must deliberately bring me close to death as part of my cure: not quite as theatrical as being washed in bull's blood, but a whole lot riskier! Who can blame me for indulging in a little mythmaking? Even if I don't succumb to infection while my new marrow is grafting, I'm still subject to the irony that to make me well is to make me ill. Released from the hospital, in full possession of my new health, I'm haunted by my treatment's future consequences: Just what are the long-term effects of high doses of radiation and chemotherapy?

In one case recorded at Epidaurus, a sleeping patient woke to find the spearhead embedded in his jaw miraculously extracted and placed into his hand. And there are other accounts where hysterical or similar afflictions were cured by the influence of imagination or sudden emotion. True or not, these stories were much like the stories we told each other over meals at the clinic. To an outsider, there isn't much spiritual uplift in these tales. In fact, in our relish to recount the history of our own bodily functions, we sound a little like the sinners in Dante's hell as they eagerly recount the history of their sins:

"My hands and feet began to sweat this afternoon in the weirdest way. But when they stopped, the headache I'd had all afternoon was gone."

"I was nauseous for a while this morning until I vomited up a lot of bile."

"My skin feels so greasy I have to keep taking showers. The doctors say I'm throwing off a lot of ketones."

"I did three extra enemas last night, and the pain in my kidneys isn't nearly so bad today."

"Every time I breathe, I smell this really strong whiff of motor oil. They say they have to paint the walls sometimes just to get the smell out of the rooms."

A bluff, relentlessly positive-thinking shoe salesman with lung cancer; a young English woman with cancer of the uterus, soft-spoken, determined to live for the sake of her new baby; a terribly frail, once beautiful middle-aged schoolteacher, attended by her infinitely patient husband, her stomach cancer arrested, the tumor apparently neither shrinking nor spreading; the middle-stage multiple sclerosis patient, her legs tingling, numb, so that walking was becoming a struggle—we all listened with rapt, intense hope to each other's stories of toxins released and evacuated, of former patients restored to health resuming their lives, free of the ominous, chaotic fears that had driven us here: us, "the incurables"—or so we'd been labeled by conventional medicine that, for all its ingenuity, had reached its limit to help us. In an ironic swipe at the medical establishment that was naturally hostile to the clinic's methods, and with not so subtle hucksterism, the clinic used that label of "incurable" in its promotional literature, attempting a little mythmaking of its own: "Incurable" could be changed into its opposite; from cranks and outcasts obsessed with our own bodily excretions, we now became the elect, the superheroes of death and disease!

We had our stars of recovery, stars more luminous in our quietly desperate eyes than Gloria Swanson or Dorothy Lamour: the Alabama housewife with a brain tumor who was given a few weeks but now, completely recovered, had written a book about her cure; or the truck farmer with an almost certainly fatal, wildfire variety of melanoma, who was now so healthy that he allowed himself a drink and a cigar from time to time. An entire book chronicling the miraculous cures of the incurables was always ready to hand—we looked to it for encouragement, we convinced ourselves that our cases weren't nearly so dire, that all we need do was follow the regimen to be saved. And undoubtedly many were saved—the treatment did work, we met the survivors, talked with them, relived their medical histories, from their abandonment by their regular doctors to their resurrection at the clinic. And of course many died—their condition was too advanced, for some physiological reason they couldn't tolerate the treatment, their immune systems were far too impaired by radiation, by chemotherapy, by sheer exhaustion.

After a few days at the clinic, as the doctors had promised, I began to have a "healing reaction." The day was hot, in the fields surrounding the clinic the weeds burned gold. Across the road from the clinic I was taking a walk in the tiny village where most of the nursing staff lived: a slab of concrete for a basketball court, small cinder-block houses painted pastel blues and with corrugated roofs, roosters and hens, dirt roads wandering up the hillside the village was built on. The eerie sense of normal life going on beyond the confines of the clinic made me realize just how extreme my state of mind was—hope that I would get well, that I could be as stolid in my health as the roosters and hens obliviously pecking at the dirt had narrowed my attention to an obsessive concentration on my body's functioning. The sporadic drifting noise of conversation, of the sound of sweeping, of clothes being washed outdoors by hand on washboards and in tubs, of the backfire and drone of cars and small tractors, all these signs of daily domestic chores and routine labor argued against my own quiet monomania.

That my hope (and fear) could so limit my responses to the world showed me how sealed off I and my fellow sufferers were in our infinitely self-regarding battle with disease. The appalling self-involvement and secret egotism of the dying! Our tyrannical self-awareness tracked moment to moment the subtlest fluctuations in our breathing, body temperatures, and heart rates, while the day-to-day world we wanted so desperately to get back to, the world of easy sleep, of unregulated food and drink, of routine contact with one another—we automatically blocked out. Oblivious to life outside the clinic, all we could think of were the mortal chances of our own sorry, aching flesh. To break ourselves of the fear of death, to face it with the apparent confidence of a Socrates!

At Epidaurus, the temple of Asclepius was filled with votive offerings—marble eyes, ears, legs, hands, feet, all the parts of the body that the god had healed left behind in simulacra as a remembrance of the god's grace: the wounded arm exchanged for the well arm, the blind eye left behind for the sighted one. Long lists of cases inscribed in stone slabs record the method of consulting the god as well as the manner of his cures. The god's way of treating wounds (dressings and cautery) and broken bones (various kinds of splints) must have seemed to the patients more common sense than miracle. But the cures that depended on supernatural intervention—the miraculous mending overnight of a broken vase, for example—tease my imagination most. Why shouldn't I wake up some morning with all my cracks seamlessly mended? But my skepticism returns; I shrug off such hopes. My oscillations between belief and doubt mirror exactly what the god's patients must have felt: It seems that in later times the efficacy of the old faith healing fell into disrepute, and the priests substituted for it elaborate prescriptions as to diet, baths, and regimen—in many particulars quite similar to the treatment I was following in Mexico.

But here in the village, removed from the clinic, in the hot sunshine, I was outside of my obsession, my body seemed for a moment like any other body. Someone looking at me wouldn't have known from my appearance that I was sick. Why didn't I behave like Socrates in the face of my own death? To buy a rooster from a villager, slit its throat, and offer it up to Asclepius was no more eccentric than enemas, "healing reactions," and the company of the other incurables. Hope? Was this alien state of mind part of the punishing operations of hope? Malignant hope that kept me frantically pursuing health? Would it be a form of suicide to refuse to compromise with mortality? To abandon hope, to inure myself to physical suffering and eventual death . . . if only I could keep my head clear of my body's special pleading, "Do this and this, you'll recover, you'll get well."

Perhaps I was addled by the heat, and certainly I was in the first throes of the "healing" fever that the doctors at the clinic had predicted. But at that moment, in a village whose name I can't even remember, I felt free of the clinic! The houses' pitted cinder blocks and mortar scalloped between the courses; the wooden fences around dirt yards; the scrounged camper shells ingeniously propped on cement foundation walls and used as tool sheds and bedrooms—these imparted a sense of almost supernatural order and normalcy, of unimpeachable certainty of well-being.

This state of well-being was impersonal: It had nothing to do with me or the relative state of my health; a diamond absolute, it held sway no matter what kind of doctor or medicine I put my trust in, no matter who got well or who died, no matter what hope promised or failed to deliver. If the clinic in its extremity mirrored the sacred groves of Asclepius—last refuge of the sick and dying—then the village that afternoon was like workaday Epidaurus, seat of unselfconscious well-being, normalcy, and order. Yet how foreign those words sound in the ears of "the incurable," inspiring both awe and despair. Though I could sense that power as operative in others' lives, I myself had never felt so far from health, even at the very moment when the sunshine and heat seemed most resplendent with health-giving qualities.

Now, when I think of Asclepius's power, I see kings as well as peasants, each praying to be healed, lying down for the night on the cold marble. I see the god in his benevolence appearing to the sleepers, filling this head and that with its own special, miraculous dream. Even Alexander the Great's father, Philip of Macedon, visited Asclepius's sacred groves and left his breastplate and spear on the god's altar. But then I imagine the sick and dying whose dreams weren't colored by the god—wouldn't the god's decision to heal some but not others also make him a figure of dread? But small matter if the god favored Philip or chose instead to cure the poorest bondsman in his kingdom: Both visits would be punctiliously added to the other inscriptions, more evidence of the god's influence and power.

Shortly after my fever spikes, my stay at the clinic comes to an abrupt end. My nausea and chills, my red blood cells breaking down so quickly that my urine turns black—it's quite clear to everyone that unless I get to a hospital immediately, a real hospital, I might die.

While my mother drives us toward the border and a hospital in California, I focus on the emergency as if it's someone else's body, someone else's life at stake. My mind is weirdly cool and distant, my body aches, aches and shivers, fever blurs my vision: I feel afloat in a plunging elevator, only the elevator is my body descending farther and farther from that untroubled, expanding light that is my own awareness watching, detached, invulnerably serene, unmoved by the tense voices talking far below . . . my voice, my mother's voice discussing what to say to the doctors, deciding *No*, we can't tell them about the clinic; that *Yes*, the body in trouble may need a blood transfusion.

The farther my body falls, the more attuned grows my perception of how weak my arms and legs feel, how light my pulse—my breathing, too, is beginning to plunge, my body and breath separating so completely that body seems infinitely heavy, stone-stupid, elemental. . . . Now we've reached the emergency room, the neon keeps twisting and writhing, wrenching itself away from the fixture, then starkly dissolving into the shadows. In the bed next to mine someone is moaning about his headache, a headache so terrible that his moans create a disturbance like a heat wave or a mirage, only it's an undulating plaque, a force field of blank pain.

From far outside my body I feel my heart speed up, beating so quickly that the darkness the neon dissolves into rises into my eyes and flows over and around me, reaching even to the place where now I'm nothing but hovering Being above my own voice crying, "I can't breathe, I don't believe I can breathe." A hand grips mine, the headache, the moans, they belong to this hand— tears come to my eyes when I realize that no matter how fierce the pain the headache and moans spring from, the hand that belongs to this pain has come to comfort me, to calm me so that I can breathe until the nurse gets there with oxygen.

My body is still free-falling, my heart flutters so quickly and faintly it seems about to stop. I sense panic trying to pierce the spreading blackness that holds me until I hear inside my head a voice so authoritative, so utterly self-convinced and godlike that it might as well be Socrates arguing over the soul, or Asclepius come to me in a dream: "Wonder Bread builds strong bodies twelve ways, Wonder Bread builds strong bodies twelve ways, Wonder Bread . . ." The oxygen mask fits over my face, through my strengthening breath my brain and body begin to fuse back together; now my heart starts to slow, the slogan from the old TV commercial that has surfaced from my childhood, and which I used to chant to myself whenever I was worried or afraid, inscribes itself on pure untextured mind—which again feels the impress of my identity . . . and with that comes fear, naked, raw fear. . . .

That I knew this could happen, that fever almost always results in my red blood cells' obliteration, drives home that I am ill, chronically ill, that my disease can kill me, has almost killed me. My desire to get well, my hope to return to the unconscious ease of assumed health, now seems wildly absurd. I can't stifle the voice needling in on every side, _How can you lead your life if life means that you must be ill?_

More than a decade later, I'm sitting at my mother's dining room table, still one of the incurables. I'm about to play a role that I've played many times—the survivor, "the old-timer" of death, the _philosophe_ of disease. I always feel a little fraudulent— but my feelings aren't the point: My mother has invited over her neighbor's seventeen-year-old son who has lymphoma. He's tall, with an athlete's torso and legs—but his muscle tone is beginning to slacken in his chest and abs, the result of his illness's onslaught, of radiation and chemotherapy.

"I'm out of school for a while," he says, "but hey, that's okay—" and gives an ironic smile. I recognize the style of humor: slightly deadpan, rueful, making much of negatives, already he's realized that the world can't easily tolerate more direct displays of emotion.

"I'll bet it really hurts to have to miss school, huh?"

"Oh yeah, I wake up weeping every morning!"

We trade jokes back and forth, each of us instinctively understanding the fear that drives our joking, but also enjoying our shared sense of being different from other people; of being members of a club that in theory everyone belongs to, but that only some of us, and only at certain moments of our lives, are truly enrolled in.

"It's not going so bad—my hair fell out in patches so I just shaved my head. I like wearing a cap anyway, so what's the difference?"

"Hey, my hair just falls out on its own!"

Around and around we go, slipping in bits of our medical histories. The more I learn about his condition, the more despairing I feel about his chances; one reason why he's asked to meet me is to let me know, a stranger uninvested in his life, what no one else near him can bear to hear: that the odds aren't good, that in a year or two he may well be dead. But it's not only despair we feel underneath the joking—our laughter is genuine. I sense in him an intense pride in carrying himself bravely, in his refusal to say too much, in his stoical restraint.

I've played this scene before in more fraught circumstances. I'll meet with the friend of a friend of a friend scared, vulnerable, valiantly keeping in check anxiety and dread. We talk about alternative treatments, both of us knowing that if the doctors pronounce you terminal, a miracle is required . . . and miracles, our glances agree, are in short supply. . . . After our conversation I always feel drained, I wonder why I put myself in these situations: Am I a kind of death junkie, getting off on intense emotion? Does it reassure me to see someone sicker than myself?

This kind of self-accusation becomes its own dodge; how much easier for me to cocoon myself away from such people, to keep myself insulated from their pain and dread. My motives for meeting them may be less than altruistic, but wouldn't it be worse to refuse to meet this young man, so dignified in his fear, so intently matter-of-fact about the prospect of his own death? Yet in my role as elder statesman how dislocated I feel, the incurable still secretly lusting after a cure, my acceptance of my fate a not so subtle ruse to trick myself into thinking that my condition is as routine as the sunrise. The constant threat of mortality has shaped me the way wind shapes a tree, bending the trunk in the direction that it habitually blows. Or I sometimes think of myself as moving in a different gravitational field, the heaviness and clumsiness of my movements contrived to look almost normal. It's only when I meet up with someone like this young man that I understand the extent of my own psychic accommodation to this field's warping force. Akilter from the sudden, strange intimacy we share, I realize I'm a little afraid of him—no, not him, but of everything he's suffered and may still suffer. Does he feel the same about me, as if fear and despair were infectious? Yet what greater consolation can we offer than the physical reassurance of our failing but still bravely persisting bodies?

I suppose the point is to overcome what is negative in these feelings, to recognize in our jokes our shared sense of a common fate, even in our veiled, perhaps mutual fear, a genuine bond. But aren't these things also sources of estrangement—from ourselves, from other people, from the world?

Now we finish talking, we say good-bye. The tension I've felt the whole time we've been together tightens inside me, I feel helpless to protect him or myself, inadequate in the face of the enormity of the trial that each of us one day will face. I consider what may be his fate—and realize, almost with a kind of envy, that he could soon know more than I about what it means to be "incurable." . . . As I watch him walk away, unexpectedly he turns and calls out to me, "Good luck!" For a moment I'm a little ashamed: Shouldn't I be the one wishing him luck, I, the old-timer, "the incurable"? What have I given him, after all? Is it simply the fact that I'm still alive, striving to lead a relatively normal life, that makes me seem special in his eyes and so spurred him to seek me out? As if, by pretending to be healthy in the eyes of the sick, I might slip out from under the watchful gaze of my own fate and actually cross back over the border between disease and health? Yet I, too, wanted to meet him, to share this intimacy of our estrangement from the world of free and easy flesh. How young he is, how vital his body seems despite the alien pallor beneath his tan—my hand moments ago held his, and I can still feel his skin's warmth fading from my skin.

The voice you dream is mine—bend down to me, come listen: I'm one of Asclepius's yellow snakes, the one his hand reaches out to; or else I'm his dog stretched dozing under his chair. In snake language, in dog language, he whispers why you people suffer, why you, among all these others, are fated to get well, and why you, with the same illness, already belong to the gods of the underworld. His voice in my head inhabits the marble of his statue, the stone so cool against me reassuring in its chill. You patients who leave me offerings, I barely notice you I'm so intent on the delicious cool that rises and flows through me. . . . As I lie here, my belly listens to the marble, I hear it whispering to me in the voice of the god. At night when you're asleep and my tongue licks into your ear, you, too, may learn what the god knows. Bend down to me, come listen, in the god's own words, to the reason for your life and death, the reason for your suffering and pain, the reason why the god will or will not heal you.

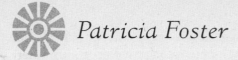

Patricia Foster

LITTLE SHELTERS
OF REPAIR

Christmas night. Mother lies alone in the dark while my father has gone to a party. Cautiously, I open the door, tiptoe into the room, and stare curiously at her as she sleeps flat on her back, a wet cloth over her forehead, the room a blue fog of stillness. The drapes are drawn, my father's pajamas left strewn on the floor. At noon Mother rushed around the table, serving roast turkey and dressing, green peas, scalloped potatoes, and the special biscuits she made at midnight. The table, set with the best china, the best crystal, the embroidered tablecloth topped with gleaming silverware and goblets, was meant to remind us of the loveliness of our lives. But when Mother lifted her fork (she told us later), a migraine exploded like a bomb behind her eyes, heat flashing in waves so intense she could barely move.

What startles me now is her stillness, a stillness more extreme than the stillness of sleep. I keep expecting her to shift positions, a knee to poke through the sheets, her arm to move away from the wet cloth she holds like a clamp to her head. But she never moves.

As a child I'm terrified by the sight of my mother lying alone, in defeat. I learn early that illness represents weakness, and behind this weakness, despair at the body's sudden anguished halt. And yet as I grow older, the picture I carry inside my head is always this: *a woman lying alone in bed, the room dark, the man gone*. When I think about it this way, it's the man gone, the absent partner I focus on. More than anything else, illness comes to represent for me the interruption of that sexual duet.

My own story begins in 1981, the year David and I live in the Ugly Apartment. Three streets from the Pacific Ocean, Santa Monica has designated certain buildings as rent-controlled apartments: brick-breeder units with concrete lawns and palm trees rioting in the wind. Ours is owned by a real estate tyrant who refuses to improve the premises in this three-story building with its peeling paint, its rusty drains. The stairwells are dark, the elevator stinks of pee, and yet the day we see the apartment, we're stunned by the rooftop patio of tar, felt paper, and gravel that opens from our apartment, giving us a 180-degree view of the ocean.

"We can live here," I say, excited, squeezing David's arm. "We can afford it and it's not too horrible."

As if to bless us, the first night's sunset is vibrant, orange-purple explosions of smog-filled air. A breeze sweeps in from the water, clean and fresh, and we lean against the railing, eyes closed, hands held, breathing the soft ocean air. I can imagine lying on this roof, the late night fog sweeping across my face, the mild tropical air wiping away the day's disasters. David and I wander like newlyweds into our apartment to make love, curling around each other in sleep, then wake to the smell of gas fumes flooding the room, spreading with the rubbery stink of bad perfume. I sit up, sniffing, coughing. "What's going on?" I shake David, then hear the cars shifting into gear, the mufflers exploding. I realize our bedroom is over an open garage, the exhaust fanned right through our windows.

It never occurs to me that this might endanger my health, the fumes entering my sinuses, clogging my lungs, interrupting the synapses of my brain. I consider this simply the inconvenience of being poor. I want to be an artist and every artist I know lives in compromised circumstances, in grungy studios in downtown L.A. where winos and prostitutes roam the streets, hustling, tricking, loud and obnoxious, their talk frantic and slippery, or in ramshackle rooms near the beach where roaches and silverfish crawl up the drains. Besides, I've worked with chemicals for years, dyes and paints, and the thick, suffocating stink of photographic fix. I've learned to mask the smells, to turn away, breathing shallowly until the noxious fumes are absorbed into the air. Today I get up quickly and plunge into the shower, then put on the blue silk dress Mother sent from Mobile, a dress I wear at least twice a week to one of the many temp jobs that pays my bills, jobs that allow me time to make art, to write stories. As I rush out into the sunny morning, I think only about time: how to gauge the freeway so I'll arrive at the parking lot in downtown L.A. before all the slots are filled, how to make it home before our neighbor Lenny lies naked on the roof, a green washcloth covering his genitals, his long, hairy limbs exposed to the sun.

I *never* think about health. I think instead about the peculiar weirdness that swirls all around me, how Lenny and Jill rush into our apartment to say hello, Jill wearing no top, her breasts swinging freely as she turns and turns, looking at everything in the room. *Is this your book? Is that your computer? Do you want to know how to fix the cable company so that they won't ever cut you off again?* While Jill talks, Lenny stares through lenses so thick I expect to see fish swimming behind the frames. I think of him lying pale and blind on the roof, the green washcloth picked up by the wind and sailing out to sea. He always looks mad, fuming quietly as if all those years in North Dakota have left him afflicted with a claustrophobic fury.

When they leave, David and I collapse into hysterics, drawing the drapes, covering our mouths. We wait until dark, then creep out onto the roof and dance, alone under the stars.

It's several months, in fact, before I become aware of some malaise, a weariness I can't seem to name. I drag in the mornings, take longer, hotter showers. I drink more coffee, suck on Coffee Nips throughout the day.

"What, you want to be Dopey or Sleepy?" David teases because I'm frequently tired, exhausted, caught somewhere between lethargy and sleep. What puzzles me is that I've lost appetite of even the most elemental sort, the kind that sends you to the kitchen for buttered popcorn or Häagen-Dazs, to the library for a book, or even outside to the deck to watch the red-gold sun sink into the Pacific Ocean. Instead of curiosity, I have great bouts of inertia in which I lie on the couch, caught in the grip of a strange new fatigue. But surely this is the result of my numerous jobs, the uncertainty of my future, even the dinginess of our apartment. I stare for a moment at my favorite couch, a postmodern affair with a chrome frame and a pin-striped futon. In this new apartment it looks deserted, barren, the astringent light uncovering all its flaws: the coffee stains and jelly smudges more obvious in the stark, treeless light of L.A. than they were in Seattle, where the light filtered through fig trees and maples. Yet David feels no ill effects from this change; he seems inspired by our move to the ocean, working longer hours at his design studio in Culver City, reading late into the night when he's home. It must be me. *All in my head. Lighten up*, I tell myself. *Focus on what you love.*

But I can't focus. It's Friday afternoon and I've come home from work to lie on the couch, staring at the ceiling, unable to concentrate. When David wanders out to the roof, watching the surfers glide toward shore as graceful as ballerinas, I listen to the traffic heating up, the horns blaring, the cars surging like waves of thought.

"Wanna go see the new Fassbinder film?" he asks, coming

back in. He leans over me, his hand stroking my arm. "I hear it's pretty good."

I shake my head. I don't want to move. "You go," I say, snuggling deeper into the couch.

But he scrunches up his face, withdraws his hand. "Jesus, it's Friday night, Patricia. What's wrong with you?"

"I don't know," I whisper, feeling guilty for a life thrown suddenly into shadow.

The next morning I step into the shower, sneeze, and as the hot water pummels me, I feel the deep ache in my arms, those limp spaghetti strings I used to grab on to the monkey bars with as a child, lifting myself up in order to hang upside down. Now I want only to stay in the shower until my skin starts to shrivel, my brain drawn down to its tiniest nub. Here no one expects anything of me. I expect nothing of myself.

"I can't seem to do anything," I tell David days later as we walk to the ocean, past the body builders and bums, toward the crashing surf. At first his face shows alarm, then a slight irritation.

"Maybe you're just tired," he says, glancing quickly at me before he turns to the ocean.

Maybe you can't handle it that I'm sick. And yet for a brief moment I feel whole, content, staring at the surfers paddling out to catch the next monster wave. Maybe he's right, I think, my face lifted to the breeze. Maybe I simply need to rest.

A fierce wind blows dust through the door. It's the Santa Ana winds, hot, dry, and dusty, bringing smog from the mountains, spreading it in thick gray clouds of pollution. I want to get up and close the glass door, but I feel too tired to move. I cough, then sneeze. I don't want the air to touch me, the sofa to touch me, human hands to touch me. My body's turned a corner, lost feeling for what once made it thrive. I no longer touch myself, no longer make love to David in the middle of the night. Instead, I sleep all the time, turned over on my side, arms pressed in, folded under me like wings. I remember the first time I felt like a woman, not a child-woman desperate for any touch, not a sex-starved teenager, but a woman in love.

It's a warm sun-drenched day and we drive through deserted early morning towns, window open, the smell of the sea just over the last hill. Last night we slept on the beach near Cresent City, California, but today we've turned inland to the silence of fields. Hot green plants sprout out of crumbly dirt. "Let's stop," I say. "Let's stop right now. I've never been to Oregon before."

David stops the car beside a field. There's no one for miles, only the hum of insects, the flick of leaves in the wind. We walk through the dirt. Then run, laughing, until we're in the middle of alfalfa. We stop, breathless, lying down, arms and legs in the dirt. David closes his eyes. I see the freckles splattered across his lids, his breathing short and jerky as we roll and roll, mashing leaves, weeds, plants, moving, I think, to the center of the earth.

Now as I lie on the couch, listening to the Santa Anas ruffle the palms, I worry about my womanliness, worry that my husband may lose his desire for me. Only this thought can make me drag myself up, first to close the door, then to the bathroom to brush my hair, my teeth, to put on lipstick and blush.

It seems inevitable that I'm not only afraid of what the illness will do to my body, but the ways it will stretch and tear at the fabric of marriage. Illness, I know, degrades your sexual presence, and it's my sexual presence I've believed to be the key to my survival in the world.

Before I moved to California, before I met David, there were days, weeks, even months when I thought something would break inside me if I couldn't find someone to hold me, someone whose voice started that sweet humming inside. It was all I lived for, just to feel that sound, like a low-pitched *aaaaa* right beneath my rib cage. Without it I didn't know what to do, who to be. I tried to work, to distract myself, but all I could think about was being held, being loved, as if the two were synonymous. It was a time in my life when sex seemed like a sponge, something I couldn't get enough of, a reckless abandon, a substitute for the love I might never have. Surely everything would be okay if only I could be held, my body stroked and kissed, my lover like a cat purring above me. But of course, I wasn't really held. Instead, I went from boyfriend to boyfriend with long periods of celibacy in between until at age twenty-nine I thought I was toughening up, getting it together. I was finishing an MFA in art, working furiously, learning to be alone in my bed.

I've thought often about my need to be touched, this insistent desire to be held, and though I have nothing but my own speculations, feelings that emerge from the depth of insecurity, I see how that need is entwined with my mother. When I was very young I thought of my mother as my exclusive property, my private and amorous indulgence. Because I was the baby of the family, the one who almost died at birth from Rh factor complications, my mother took me everywhere she went: to my father's clinic to deliver his lunch, my hand on her leg as she squeezed the lemon into his tea and opened the little packets of sugar so he could quickly dump them in, then off to Mrs. Bruce's backyard with its sharp rows of beans and corn to pick up the caladium bulbs and the big fat heads of cabbage tilted from a bag. Mrs. Bruce had three wobbly chins and black hairs growing defiantly from the mole on her cheek. She tried to pinch my face, but I bent my head into my mother's hip, making her carry me along with the sack of cabbage and the caladium bulbs bulging from her purse. Sometimes we went to the dry cleaners or to Mr. Gosse's apple cannery to make applesauce, or to Stella Fry's house to return the plastic permanent roller rods. In pictures I look like an appendage: a towheaded kid strapped to one side of a woman's body, hanging on for dear life.

I don't remember when my mother stopped touching me,

when she let go of my hand. It may have been, in fact, that I dropped hers, that in a moment of rebellion I flung myself away from her in a dramatic rage. What I do remember is sitting curled up beside her on the sunporch of our house, my body nestled next to hers as she turns pages of lessons on magnets she'll teach that day. I hear the whispery flutter of paper, smell the cloying pungency of gardenias floating in a bowl of water as I snuggle closer, inevitably drifting back to sleep. But after second grade, this kind of intimacy disappears. I begin to touch other things, an anxious, nervous touching, my hands picking, rubbing, stroking, grabbing. The hem of my skirt, the strap of my purse, a leaf, a rubber band, even other little girls' hair, obsessed as I am with the way their ponytails dip and sway as they walk ahead of me toward the cafeteria. I love the way their hair feels, straight and bushy like a horse's tail or a long thin rivulet of silk, my own a Brillo pad of corkscrew curls. "Stop that," the girl in front of me in line says, yanking herself free from my hands. But I don't want to stop. Touching means I exist. I'm not a shadow, a dream, a fraud.

Recently, I watched a TV special about one of the new treatments in Canada for anorexic girls (I suffered from anorexia when I was twenty-two), a treatment focused on touch, the bestowal of overt affection and physical acceptance (the girls hugged and cuddled, even carried and fed by a counselor, "Com'on, love, just another bite") as a way of reaching that furious need for relationship. As I watched a counselor pick up a starving girl and carry her to her bed, I felt something lift inside me, a longing so old it felt like mourning.

By the time I met David in 1979, I'd made a rather tepid decision to be alone for the rest of my life, to buck up and keep my body to myself. And yet within six months of our meeting, I moved into his studio in Culver City, a forty-by-forty-foot room with a loft fifteen feet off the floor, a small office, and a bathroom shared with a real estate company that owned the front rooms.

David and I divided the territory, set up space for my work, built a darkroom, hung a trapeze, and daily climbed the ladder up to the loft, where we kept books, a desk, and a futon. But as we lay down together each night, what a shock to discover that my earlier sexual presence had been a sham. I'd never had an orgasm before, had never masturbated, and had no idea what pleasure I might want. I was still longing to be a little girl, wanting someone to hold me, his arms cradling my body, while I dressed in tight jeans and tank tops, waving a red flag for attention. How stultifying that seems! And yet I know the truth lies in this very attenuation, this great need to be wanted, not to be abandoned. I'm sure that much of this tension involved my own lack of confidence, my confusion about what it meant to be a woman, and from that confusion came an inability to relax, to be truly generous, both to myself and to others. And yet once David and I had decided to be together, some of that psychic tightness—and thus the physical strain—seemed magically to dissolve. For me, it was the beginning of a consciousness, a self growing up, no longer timid or silent, as full of demands and reprisals as I was of conciliation.

There is the afternoon we're driving home from the Boy's Market after our weekly grocery shopping. It's a typical southern California day, full of blue skies and a pulsing sun, a sameness I've begun to be weary of. By this time what I see in southern California is contrived weirdness, a posturing that reminds me of my younger self. While I stare out the window, David's talking about the studio, about what we need to do to keep it straight.

"You've got to start cleaning up better," he says, looking quickly at me, drawing my attention back to the two of us, to the dust and rags and scraps of fabric that have littered the studio floor.

"Better than whom?" I turn from the window to stare at him. Recently I found several apple cores on his side of the futon, shriveled skeletons that look ancient, anthropological.

"Your stuff's all over the place downstairs. You leave dye out in those little plastic containers and you never clean your brushes. It's making the studio a mess."

I turn away from him to watch a skater swiveling in and out of the crowds. She has on a bikini with fringe splashed across her breasts. The fringe sways with her movements, back and forth, back and forth, a mesmerizing frenzy. "You never do the dishes," I say, seeing the cluster of my dye pots heaped on a chair, stacked up near the sink. "And you never hang up your clothes. They're in little piles all over the place."

"Oh, c'mon. That's not the same."

"Why not?" Of course I know the division he's making: Work space must be clean; personal space can be compromised. Not that it matters; we're fighting the fight about who gets to scold whom, who makes the rules.

"Jesus, you have no sense of reason," David says as he turns into the studio driveway and parks the car. "You're just arguing to be arguing. Why don't you admit you're being a pig? Admit you're wrong, that you need to clean up. That's all you have to do." Having said this, he gets out of the car, hefts sacks of groceries in his arms while hot flashes of fury race through my body. Without thinking, I reach into a bag and grab, making a wild throw. I watch fascinated as the broccoli arcs through the air, then splatters against the garage, florets scattering into tiny pieces.

And suddenly I laugh, feeling happy, released from being a good girl. What pleases me is this new anger, this little storm of feeling I've shut deep inside myself for so long.

David doesn't move, the sacks balanced neatly in his arms. His eyes move from the scattered broccoli to me. "Not a very good answer," he says. Then he walks away from me into the studio.

Looking back, I can see that our fights were often childish, our demands foolish, and yet what was important was that we fought fully, hauling out the dark, dirty secrets of our lives, untangling the petty contrivances, the easy honesties. We yelled and glared, willing to be wrong; in essence, to feel. It was during this first year that we set the pattern for our marriage, fighting openly about what we wanted from one another. Of course, this was so hard on our nerves, we also spent time alone, exhausted, uncertain, both attracted and repelled by our life together. And yet in many ways these fights smoothed the way for the conflicts of illness. When illness came, it wasn't a secret weakness, a hidden wedge. Though I would often be the woman lying alone in her bed, the room was not dark, the man never totally absent.

The doctor is tall and gaunt, too young to look so tired. He says I have environmental allergies and this strange, new diagnosis called candidiasis (candida-related complex), illnesses resulting, in part, from heavy use of antibiotics in my teens and twenties and the constant inhalation of fumes. At home I try to describe it to David. "Imagine that the most aggressive fungus inhabits my digestive tract, sprouting hydralike chains that penetrate the gut wall, releasing antigens into my bloodstream, toxins swimming merrily toward my brain." I can visualize these bacteria mutating, sprouting long athletic arms. It's the major waste product of yeast cell activity, acetaldyhyde, that's tricky. The liver can convert it into alcohol, making me feel drunk, or more specifically, hungover, wiped out. One afternoon when the city's trapped by heat, the smog settled over us in a drape of brown haze, I read about a Japanese man who's been on a twenty-five-year binge due to candida in his gut. When I read this I laugh and twirl around the apartment. I'm not alone. I'm not crazy. I don't have Alzheimer's.

Of course, the great irony of becoming ill is that it forced me to look at the distortions I'd created. I'd spent so much of my twenties needing physical intimacy that this obscured the larger story, the mental attention I craved, my brain a kind of secret exploding volcano, vain and hungry and hot. Once I settled down with David, my ambition became focused, directed. I believed I was "finished" with the business of self-deprecation: all that sloppy uncertainty, the reproachful gazes in the mirror, the panicky fissures of hope. Now I wanted to read all the time, to study literature and writing, to withdraw from the hustle of L.A. life into the solitude of my room. I knew what sacrifices I'd have to make to paint and write, and so it seemed only a cruel joke that one of the main symptoms of candidiasis is called *brain fog*.

"Why can't I *think* today?" I'd mutter, looking at my books, my desk, the work I'd planned to do. I would put my head in my hands and a few minutes later surprise myself by moaning. Had I emerged from the neediness of my twenties only to be saddled with mental fatigue, to have words dropped from my vocabulary as easily as dead cells sloughing off skin? So it seemed. On a bad day I sat in my room and tried to remember the names of foods: tomato, broccoli, squash, apple, raisins, peanut butter, and what was that food we ate in front of the TV with the white puffed-up kernels? I felt a dizzying fear until in a few minutes I remembered. *Popcorn*.

And then there was the afternoon my friend from college called. "Listen," she said, "Sarah's just been selected to Mortar Board."

"That's wonderful." I thought of Sarah, lovely Sarah with her inquisitive brown eyes, her hooting laugh. I wanted to ask about the ceremony, to find out when Sarah would be inducted, thinking how nice it would be if I could attend, if we could celebrate together her daughter's success. But I couldn't think of the word *induct*, couldn't think of any word like *induct*.

"When is she going to be indoctrinated?" I whispered, as if she were joining a subversive group. I said it softly, barely uttering it, allowing just enough sound to give her the gist of meaning. I was relieved that she didn't correct me. Each correction brought with it a fresh wave of despair.

*   *   *

"You're still you," David says when I complain about the cognitive problems, how I feel like a blanket's been draped over my brain. We've moved from Los Angeles to Iowa and then to Florida, where I've entered a Ph.D. program. "And you're going to have to work with this," he continues, "and not lapse into depression. You're going to have to do research, and temporarily, at least, accept the limitations."

I screw up my face. "Fine for you to say. You get up every morning and dance around the kitchen waiting for the coffee to perk." But I don't speak the underlying question: How can I accept my limitations when I still have to make a living? I'm teaching now and I know that in order to teach well the next day I have to be rested. That night as I get under the covers, I hear David clanking and banging, working on an art piece, the sounds resonating through the walls, the clink of a chisel as he shapes a bas-relief sculpture. I sit up in bed, suddenly furious, jealous that he feels well enough to make art while I have to conserve all my energy for other people. I shove my face deep into the pillow, my heart beating rapidly, my mind caught in such a torment of envy, all my weariness evaporates. Is this the only way I can come alive, through the madness of jealousy? I hate my jealousy of other people's energy as much as anything else about myself; it seems so small-minded, so petty, the very things I've been taught to fight. But tonight I let the jealousy explode. I bounce my body against the mattress, kicking and beating the covers as if I'm beating up all that training to be a nice girl. I make an especially vicious kick, one that drowns out the noise of David's drill. That's it. *I'm not nice.*

David and I sit across from one another, eating salad and soup. Tomorrow we're having a yard sale, and I don't want to think about it. I'm in one of those gray-weather moods, irritated at the thought of tagging clothes, then starting a paper about Leopold

Bloom. I don't have time for such foolish things as yard sales. But we need the money.

David's talking about the new Oranda fish he's named Edo, how this remarkable fish has eaten an entire lettuce leaf during the day, swiping little bites when David's back is turned. David tells the story dramatically, enacting the subversive eating habits of the Oranda, the secret nibbles, the floating, drifting lettuce, an entire island of food. As he talks I see the fish swimming and eating while my own energy's ebbing away, water swirling fast down a drain. Now David's telling me something about himself, and though I pretend to be listening, I've moved off on a side road, fretting about the brain fog I've had lately, wondering if I'll ever finish this Ph.D. when I'm so tired and spacey much of the time.

"Well," he says, and I look up only because there's a pause in his voice.

"What?" I ask, as if I've simply missed the last comment.

"I said, *I think I'm getting the flu*, but there's no use even saying that to you because you'll always be sicker. Your illness eats up all other illness."

I blanch at his words, want to argue that I'm not competitive about illness. But there it is. The devil in our lives.

"Okay, you be the sick person tonight," I say with a little flash of anger.

But he only stabs a slice of green pepper and lifts it solemnly to his mouth.

It's now that the doorbell rings. A sound that shatters the house. I jump up to answer it, wondering who could possibly be bothering us tonight in the middle of an argument. When I open the door, two large black women stand on our porch, dressed as if for church in nice clothes and heels, jewelry shimmering around their necks. They peer through the screen.

"We've come about that yard sale," one of the women says. "Your ad said you've got clothes and we're looking for clothes."

Of course I should tell them to come back tomorrow when the

yard sale begins, but suddenly I don't have the energy to refuse. "Just take what you want," I say, and let them rummage through the pile, paying me whatever they like.

By the time they leave, David's gone off to bed, the dishes are in the sink, the table cleared. I stand for a moment in the silence of the house, then walk outside as if I can walk out of this life. Darkness surrounds the house like a glove, a thick humid darkness, the moist air moving in from the Gulf. I stare into this darkness, suddenly frightened of what I've become. I feel pathetic, shamed, that hairshirt of illness: Sorry for being so much trouble, for being inadequate, inappropriate, for making so many demands. There it is. Guilt! The old stumbling block. *I can't do, can't make . . .* But I haven't come this far only to capitulate, to slink back inside my hole.

I begin researching a new doctor, a new cure, making all the awkward phone calls, telling the same story to bored receptionists who put me on hold, to doctors who have little time or inclination to speak to a potential patient. I call medical practices in New York, Denver, Dallas, but the closest doctor who practices environmental medicine is in Atlanta, so I gear up for the five-hour drive each way.

Every two weeks I make this journey to a doctor who is laconic but meticulous; his thoroughness, his innovative strategies make me think he'll help me get well. But the trips are marathons, expensive in both time and money. After the third trip, I'm especially tired when I get home, my head throbbing, my eyes red. "Just let me lie here," I say to David when he comes into the bedroom, where I lie sprawled across our double bed. He has three aquariums now and wants to tell me about the parrot fish who's pregnant. "She's becoming a spook," he says. "She won't have anything to do with the other fish. She's isolating herself completely." While he talks, I look toward the window, where a black ant crawls methodically through the tiny crack in the screen. A green fly buzzes above a decaying moth. When David leans over to touch my shoulder, I flinch, then say apologetically, "I can't stand to live with all these bugs."

But what frightens me most is my pervasive weakness. I can barely move. My legs and arms ache with a new kind of heaviness, and I think of all the diseases I don't want to have. Multiple sclerosis, rheumatoid arthritis, lupus, fibromyalgia. I'm terrified in a way that surpasses my imagination, as if I've been split open, exposed to the void. Overwhelmed, I begin to think of paring down my life, making the complex simple, getting rid of all the unnecessary demands. Where to start? Should I drop out of the Ph.D. program and devote myself entirely to getting well? Or should I simply quit teaching, take out yet another loan, reducing the stress in one area even though I'll be increasing it for the future? Or perhaps I should chuck it all and move to Atlanta, close to my doctor so I can be right under his wing, a baby bird needing so much care and attention. I think that the delicate, careful structure that is me is collapsing into so many pieces, all I can do is keep them from blowing away. I hug myself, cradling my ribs, my stomach, as if I can hold myself together. And in the midst of my panic-stricken thoughts I see the one thing I can do: regulate my sleep. It seems so simple it crashes around me with the brilliance of relief. Most nights I stay up late, then wake several times during the night, discomforted, worried, unable to go back to sleep because of David's heavy snoring. And it's here that I make a decision.

"I need to sleep alone."

David's sitting at his desk, looking at me with an expression of perplexity and reproach. "Why?" he asks. He's never had a sleepless night in his life.

Again, I feel guilty, making what I imagine is another selfish demand. *It's not just the food, the environment, but now you've got to move out!* The second bedroom isn't as comfortable, the mattress older, the window uncurtained, boxes piled in corners, stuffed full of an unexplainable mess of David's papers. I can't sleep in this room for the very reason that it's an allergic nightmare. But more important, it's the first time we've slept apart, the first time illness has so clearly disrupted a night's intimacy. And yet I believe we can survive anything, that we're rock, stone, boulder, our lives threaded together with the silvery strength of loyalty. Now we go to bed at different times, wake up separately, no limbs touching, no sleepy caresses, no recounted dreams in the early morning light of day. We don't meet at the breakfast table or laugh as we slide by each other in the bathroom. Still, sleeping alone seems a tiny crack, barely a fissure in the lives of two busy people.

By the third week, David's schedule has become more chaotic than mine; he's been staying up late nights, trying to finish a project for a demanding client, and I've agreed to take up the slack, to do the more onerous domestic chores.

We're eating dinner one night, sitting at the kitchen table. I've been grading papers all day and I'm preoccupied, not really noticing David's mood until he says in an irritable tone, "These peas are cold."

I eat some. They are cold. "Well, warm them up," I say, holding out my plate.

He scowls as he jerks the plate from my hands.

"It's not a crime," I say, trying to make a joke. "I wouldn't blame the peas." But then I see how tired he looks, his body slumped as he stands at the counter. "I'm sorry," I say, and get up to stand beside him, taking the plate of peas and putting them in the microwave. He pours some coffee and looks intently at me. "I really am. I'm sorry it's not a good supper."

David takes a deliberate sip of his coffee and looks away from me toward the window where the dogwood blooms look like confetti in the late evening light. It's that moment just before darkness when the light flutters above the trees, illuminating their tops with a silvery halo. The room around us seems to soften, to gather us together. I feel our busy lives come to a halt. All my sickness and studying, all of David's deadlines and worry drop out of sight. I look at David, wanting to rub his neck, to be close, and yet it's now that he seems to take possession of himself, to become separate, no longer acting the part of a fussy man, but a person who's lost something of great value.

"Patricia," he says, his voice soft, barely above a whisper. "I have to go away for a while."

And I feel the fine mesh of lines scattering in all directions, the cracks coalesced, forming a seam that's widened and split. But for the moment I don't say a word.

When he's ready to leave, I'm anxious, unhappy. I ask where he's going and how long he'll be gone.

"I don't know," he says. "I just want to wander around for a while and find whatever I find."

I know this is true. I also know it's much more than that. I walk back inside the house. From my study window I can look into the shadow of the oak tree. The kids who lived here before us hung a rope swing from the tree, though the wooden seat has long since fallen out. Now it's just a dangling rope with frayed ends. It looks lonely and purposeless. Staring at it, for the first time I feel like a woman who's come full circle: ill, alone, the man gone.

"Why did you leave that time in Tallahassee?" I ask David this summer while we're sitting outside in our backyard, the squirrels running over rocks near the fence, the light fading to dimness. I ask this question every few years, trying to understand whether it was the restrictions and distress of illness that divided us or something more elemental: the realization that our dreams might not be achieved. Or was it simply sleeping apart?

"I don't know," David says, and his eyes stare not at me, but out past the fence where weeds and summer ferns grow beneath the maples and pines. "I think I'd just had enough."

I feel a familiar shiver inside, a noise in my brain like a zipper being unzipped. Though I've asked the question, I'm not sure I want to hear any more.

"You were often sick, you know, and when you weren't convalescing, you were studying or grading papers or talking to your friends in the Ph.D. program. I just felt like I came in last."

I nod, remembering nights of suddenly feeling good, my mind cleared, the achiness released from my body. I'd pull out the Victorians, become absorbed in Charlotte Brontë, George Eliot, reading with the hunger of a captive, ravenous and undeterred. If David stepped into my study I'd give him a quick hug, then return to my book. I had to focus, sabotaged by days of recuperation.

"Besides, I was lonely and tired from working so hard that year."

And this, too, I remember, how he got up at five, went to bed at midnight, saw clients even on Sunday. There were fewer days of the laziness of love, of languorous play, of time out from ambition. In Los Angeles, we'd discussed each other's art, printed photographs in the darkroom, worked side by side on collages with fabric and paint. We'd made love on the beach, in the car, in the middle of the day. But in Tallahassee, debts settled around us, locking us inside their hungry jaws.

David stares at me. "I also felt tricked."

At the sound of that word, I stiffen. *Tricked* is a word with an attitude. "What do you mean?"

In the dark I can't see his face, can't read his expression, but I hear the uncertainty of his voice when he says, "Our lives seemed so impulsive, so free when we were first together, then after you got sick, it reminded me of when I was a kid." He sounds sad, embarrassed. He tells me a story I've heard once before, how as a child he had to take care of his severely depressed mother. "She stayed in bed all day and left me to supervise my brothers. I'd open the door and tell her it was four. She'd be snuggled under the covers, only her face showing. A pale, bloated face. And she'd mumble, 'Wake me at five.' Then at five it'd be another hour, and on and on." His voice picks up emotion. "While she was in bed my little brothers and I were hungry. We were tired of staying in. Sometimes she didn't get up at all, and I . . . I just wanted to run away."

This time I hear the story differently. What plays inside my head are these old stories from childhood, the ones that terrorize us, that we dare not repeat. I don't want to be the woman ill and alone, and David doesn't want to be the caretaker, the one left responsible because of someone else's illness. How terrifying to know that the past never lets go, but transmutes itself, coming back into our lives, breathing its raspy breath down our necks.

We are quiet for a while, the smell of the grass seeping up from beneath our feet. Night darkens around us, and we hold hands, still quiet, still together.

What seems miraculous to me is that I'm getting better, an incremental process, one step at a time. I feel particularly good one December evening after we've moved across the country to Iowa. We walk through the woods on our way to a coffeehouse in town. It's a snowy night, the air powdery with tiny flakes that glisten beneath the pale light of a quarter moon. The earth looks newborn, no movement beyond the trees, nothing except for the fast-moving ripple of river which eddies when the wind comes from the northwest. Snow coats everything, every inch of sidewalk, yards, clotting in thick clumps in the split trunks of trees. Even the wires overhead are painted with snow. We walk slowly, bundled in our winter clothing, coats, hats, gloves, and even hoods that cover most of our faces so that our shadows look like monsters. Tonight we have new names, Shadow and Hedge, silly names we've given each other over supper, though I can no longer remember why. Throughout our marriage we've given each other various names, anything with an ironic twist will do, anything to extend a moment, make us laugh. Tonight I think about the resonance of the word *Shadow*—my husband's playful name for me—the way my chronic illness has fixed me in the shade, a phantom wife, *now you see her, now you don't*. I think of this because tonight I feel the weight of illness lifting.

"I'm back!" I want to yell, aware that I'm hungry in every possible way. Only lately have I been dreaming of sex again, feeling a nostalgia for those days before I was ill when we used to spend days in bed. "Let's have a date tonight," I whisper at the coffee shop, leaning close, my breath still laced with frost. I'm suddenly horny.

David sighs. "Do you have to plan everything? Even our romantic moments?"

I'm crestfallen. I think of stabbing him with my knife. But then I nod yes, I guess I do. I realize that illness has made me choreograph my life. And this both annoys and frightens me, this need to arrange intimacy instead of letting it happen naturally. Whatever that now means.

"Oh, just forget it," I say, not one to suffer rejection well. "I have too much to do anyway."

The next day as I nurse my hurt feelings, I have the small revelation that there's a keen symmetry between wanting a cure for illness and wanting the cure for the fragmentation in one's psychic life. Most of the time I've lived my life as if on hold, waiting for the magical moment of perception, the instant when the pattern will be exposed and I can understand who I am in the complexity of things. Each morning when I get up, I feel this same sense of defensive wanting, hoping that today will be a good health day, that today something unsuspecting but healing will occur. I know that the healing will be a wonderful power, that I'll feel it throughout my body and spirit, and this is the same wanting I have for my psychic life, this desire to be blessed. I know that the wanting doesn't stop, that part of healing is accepting the frustration of desire, then peeling back that frustration to know some deeper sense of peace. I also know that this is hard, if not impossible. Marriage, it occurs to me, is not so different.

But a good marriage has its intimacies, its little shelters of repair. It's Sunday morning and I'm sitting at the kitchen table in a kind of stupor, a glass of pureed spinach, a baked potato before me, an unusual breakfast by any standards, but rather normal for me. (I've had to eliminate wheat, yeast, sugar, dairy, caffeine, and all processed foods from my diet.) I'm frowning over the paper, grumbling to myself because I don't yet feel awake, don't feel like a person, my limbs still aching, my mind wrapped in cotton. I'm like my mother before her first cup of coffee, "not quite there." Across the table, David is happy, reading aloud something from an editorial, some snide comment he wants me to hear. Jealousy rises above my head like smoke. Even he can see it, the envy—fat, white, and dirty—that gathers in my glance. He can tell in my scowl that I'm not "with" it yet. He stops reading.

"Come on," he says, getting up, motioning me into the kitchen for some kind of play. Reluctantly I comply, move toward him, a complaint already forming on my lips. He stands before me, his arms out, his feet planted solidly on the floor. "Get on," he says.

"I don't want to," I say, already defensive. "I'm not in the mood."

"Just climb aboard," he demands. And I'm too passive to argue.

I step up on top of his shoes so that he holds me like a dancer, my feet on his feet, my head now the same height as his. Then the two of us glide around our kitchen, my arms around his neck, his breath warm against my ear. We are dancing, swirling and swooping around the room, the clock on the stove blinking, the crumbs from the toaster scattered across the counter. I feel the hard bone of his neck, the soft rush of his hair. And this is the moment David tells me he loves me, loves me even though I feel ill and afraid, even though I can't wipe that ugly scowl off my face, even though I'll probably be more myself by noon. I know that we'll make love soon, bodies naked, tongues like darting fish.

"You might as well smile," he says now. "It really can't hurt."

And inevitably I do.

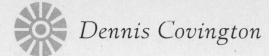 *Dennis Covington*

THE GOOD PART

My sister Jeanie has lupus, and occasionally, when her brain swells to the point that she gets confused and starts having seizures, she has to go to the hospital to have her blood cleansed. It's a painful process that Jeanie endures by telling stories. The last time my wife, Vicki, and I visited her in the hospital, Jeanie was telling us about a pair of shoes her husband, Bunky Wolaver, had found at a discount shoe mart in Birmingham. The shoes were Florsheim Imperial wingtips, an expensive line of men's dress shoes, but this pair was on sale for $5.88. "You know Bunky," Jeanie said. "He couldn't pass up a bargain like that."

The only problem was that the shoes were a size six, and Bunky wears a size nine and a half. So he had been trying for days to find some man who could wear a size six dress shoe. That morning, for instance, he had phoned Jeanie just as one of her doctors, Dr. Birdley, was making his rounds.

"I'm so glad Dr. Birdley is there," Bunky told her. "What about leaning over the bed and seeing if you can tell what size feet he has?"

A few hours later, another lupus patient, a member of Jeanie's support group at the hospital, stopped by to give her encouragement. For the most part, this was a somber visit, as both women are in advanced stages of the disease. But when Jeanie told her friend about Bunky's Florsheim Imperial wingtips, the other lupus patient started laughing so hard, the chair she was sitting on collapsed.

Jeanie's stories have always seemed particularly Southern to me, and on the way home from the hospital that night, Vicki and I entered a serious discussion about the nature of Southern storytelling. The good part of Jeanie's story, I thought, was Bunky asking her to check out the size of her doctor's feet to see if the shoes he had bought on sale might fit. Vicki thought the good part of the story was the moment when the other lupus patient's chair collapsed.

We didn't resolve the issue, but we did conclude that every story, Southern or not, has to have a good part. "Have you gotten to the good part yet?" we often ask each other when one of us is reading a novel the other has recommended.

But what exactly constitutes the good part of a story? And since our lives themselves are stories, where in this sea of misery, this vale of tears, does the good part lie?

The answer itself is a story, I think.

When I was a boy, my friend Bert Butts and I decided to sell armadillos. We'd seen an ad in a magazine called *Fur, Fish, and Game*. The ad said that Wild Animal Enterprises of Port Arthur, Texas, was offering a dozen armadillos for thirty-six dollars. Bert Butts and I had never seen an armadillo, but they were only three dollars apiece. If we sold them in Birmingham for, say, twelve dollars each, we'd quadruple our money.

So we sent a money order to Wild Animal Enterprises in the amount of $36 for a dozen armadillos. Then we placed our own ad in our local paper, the *Birmingham News*: "Armadillos, twelve dollars," followed by my phone number. The response was overwhelming. "What kind of dog is this ar*mah*-dillo?" one caller asked. Another caller, an apartment dweller, ordered two after we told him they didn't bark. We promised another armadillo to a young married couple, just starting out. Within a day or two, we had sold all twelve armadillos.

The only problem was that the armadillos never arrived from Port Arthur, Texas. We tried to call Wild Animal Enterprises, but the place wasn't even listed in directory assistance.

About that time, and quite coincidentally, my father's oldest brother, Uncle Brother, had a heart attack. Uncle Brother was my favorite uncle. He had fought in World War I, and he happened to live in Galveston, Texas. He even had a wife named Texas. Uncle Brother and Aunt Texas.

"Don't you think you ought to go visit Uncle Brother?" I asked my father. Dad had recently lost his job at the steel mill, and he was reading the help wanted ads.

"Why? Brother's doing fine," Dad said. "He should be out of the hospital in a day or two."

"But he had a heart attack," I said.

"Uh-huh."

"And he lives in Texas."

"Oh," Dad said. He put away his newspaper. "I think I see what you mean. You'd probably like to go to Texas with me, wouldn't you? Maybe we could stop on the way in Port Arthur."

Are you at the good part yet?

The very next day, Dad and Bert Butts and I left for Galveston to visit Uncle Brother. It was a fourteen-hour drive. On the way, we stopped in Port Arthur to look up Wild Animal Enterprises. The company proved to be nothing more than a ramshackle frame house with a couple of caged skunks and a barn owl on the front porch. The man who lived at the address, a Mr. Kenneth Foote, said he'd been trying for weeks to fill our order for armadillos, but the weather had been too dry. The armadillos were all holed up in their burrows somewhere.

"Y'all try again after we get a good rain," he said. Then he returned our money order for thirty-six dollars.

When we arrived in Galveston, Uncle Brother was doing fine. He and Aunt Texas were also very surprised to see us.

Are you at the good part yet?

After the trip west, Bert and I had to do something, so we ordered our armadillos from another outfit, this time in Florida. The animals were more expensive, though, and we hadn't factored in the shipping costs. In short, it looked like we were going to lose money on our armadillo venture, but the worst part was that I had not yet gotten to see an armadillo.

When the crates from Florida finally arrived, I was at summer camp. Bert distributed all but two of the armadillos to our customers. He wanted me to be in on delivering the last two. But on the night before I returned from camp, my father, who was keeping the armadillos in a cage in our garage, forgot to secure the latch to the cage. The next morning, when I got home and ran to the garage to see the armadillos, I found the cage empty. The armadillos had escaped.

It was a blow to both me and my father. In retrospect, though, I can see that I was merely disappointed; my father seemed injured in a permanent way. He knew how much I had wanted to see those armadillos, and he felt entirely responsible for their escape. What he didn't understand was that this had been no ordinary summer. I was almost thirteen. When I looked into the empty cage that morning, I had quickly moved past my own disappointment to his. I think this was the first time I had ever allowed someone else's pain to supersede my own. I see this only in retrospect, having been married now for nearly twenty years and with children of my own. I hurt for my father because I knew that, in ways, he had invested more in those armadillos than I had. And because he was so much older, time would repay him less generously.

Are you at the good part yet?

*   *   *

My father and I remained close until his death in 1988, although our lives diverged in certain ways. My father never drank, for instance, but I grew up to be the kind of drunk you wish you'd never met. Fortunately, Vicki and I both sobered up in August 1983. There's no use going into details. We had "bottomed out," as they say in AA: the usual blackouts and brawls, the lying, the thieving, the whoring around.

When we stopped drinking, our two girls, Ashley and Laura, came along, and our writing careers started to jell. There have been tragedies along the way, including my father's death, and the deaths of my oldest brother and his son. But the last thirteen years have been good ones. We have come to our senses and watched our girls grow up: spend-the-night parties and softball games and pets too numerable to mention by species, let alone name.

But then last spring, things took a bad turn. In July, Vicki and I had a fight, an all-day, frantic shoot-'em-up. It was fueled by jealousy, and it was low and vicious, like something straight out of our drinking days. In the months prior to the fight, we had both been having affairs, something that hadn't happened to us since we sobered up. And on opening night of a play Vicki had written, her boyfriend and his wife had shown up. They sat in the seats next to our daughters. I thought I was going to throw chairs. Instead, during intermission I went across the street for coffee with one of my former students. She and I didn't make it back in time for the beginning of Act II. We had to wait in the wings until the lights went down.

"Where have you been?" Vicki whispered through clenched teeth.

That was the source of the argument the next day. I was furious that her boyfriend had come to the play on opening night, and that he and his wife had sat next to our daughters. Vicki was furious that I had missed the opening scene of her second act.

"Is that why you came in late after intermission?" she said. "To get back at me because he was there?"

"You should have told him not to come," I said.

"He's an admirer of my work."

I thought the veins in my temple would burst. "Your whole family was there."

"Well, he's not the one who embarrassed my family," she said.

"And I suppose you're saying I am?"

She nodded.

And then we said unspeakable things that don't make sense outside the pathology of our particular marriage. Vicki clawed my arm until she drew blood, and I made the confession that I knew would be the last word.

After the play, I told her, at the cast party at a friend's house, I had found myself alone in the kitchen. An abandoned glass of white wine sat on the kitchen counter next to a half-empty bottle. I told her I had glanced around to make sure no one was in the room. Then I grabbed the glass and took two sips. I put the glass back and stepped away from it, looked over my shoulder again, and then returned to the counter, grasped the wine bottle, and took two more sips. I had been one month shy of thirteen years without drinking a drop. And then July came along.

"Why are you telling me this?" Vicki said.

"I don't know." But of course I did. I had drunk the wine because I wanted to, but I had told Vicki about it because I knew it would hurt her in ways that nothing else could ever do. Marriage between alcoholics can result in an odd set of unspoken vows. For Vicki and me, the most hurtful infidelity will always be the one we are on the brink of having with alcohol.

Are you at the good part yet?

Two days later, my younger daughter, Laura, and I flew to central Florida for a long-anticipated camping trip, just the two of us, something my father and I had never done, unless you count that trip to Texas with my friend Bert Butts to visit Uncle Brother in Galveston.

Laura and I pitched our tent at a state park a few miles away from a patch of palmetto scrubland my father had bought in a massive real estate scam more than thirty years before. These two and a half acres were the only investment Dad had ever made, and he deeded the land to me before he died. In the intervening years, though, a group of hunters had tried to steal our parcel of land, along with thousands of adjoining acres. The hunters had fenced the property, posted armed guards at the only gate, and denied access to individual owners like me.

I was determined to reclaim my inheritance, no matter how insignificant it might appear to be. As Laura and I drove past a fire tower on the road to Frostproof, Florida, I pointed out the window and said, "Straight through those trees lies the property your granddaddy left us."

At precisely that moment, we saw an armadillo on the shoulder of the road. I pulled onto the shoulder, and we walked back to the spot where the armadillo was rooting around in the grass. A few feet away lay another armadillo, crushed by a passing car.

I picked up the surviving armadillo. He was young, a juvenile. He didn't appear to be injured. He waved his sturdy legs at me and blinked his eyes.

"Can we keep him?" Laura asked.

I took the armadillo as a sign. "You'd better believe we're going to keep him," I told her.

Are you at the good part yet?

We put the armadillo in an empty Styrofoam ice chest until we could get to a hardware store in Frostproof and buy a wire rabbit hutch. We assembled the hutch right there in the store; the salesman helped. And then we took the armadillo to the local café for breakfast. Nobody there had ever seen a live one that close up before.

Next, we took the armadillo to the front gate of the hunt club. The animal was a conversation piece, and the wife of the gatekeeper let us in to look around the place. The land was a wilderness of palmetto and pine, lily pads and frog song, Laura's idea of paradise. I was glad she'd been able to see it, and I resolved anew to get our part of it back.

But there were complications in this armadillo story of ours. When we left Dad's property, the state park where we'd camped wouldn't let us bring the armadillo in, so we had to find a vet who would board him for the night. It took a little persuasion. But that night we slept soundly for the first time during our camping trip.

The next morning, we stopped by the vet's office and picked up the armadillo. We bought a pet carrier designed to fit under an airplane seat, and the vet gave us documents so we could take the armadillo with us on the flight from Tampa to Birmingham.

"Does this mean we can really keep him?" Laura asked.

I nodded.

"Then I think we should call him Joey," she said.

But in Tampa we discovered our airline didn't allow animals on board, even in the cargo bins. Another airline did allow animals, at an exorbitant price, but there was one stipulation. "They have to be warm-blooded," the clerk said.

"But he is warm-blooded," Laura said. "He's a mammal."

"Well, all I know is he's not a dog or cat," the clerk replied. "We can't fly an armadillo to Birmingham."

So Laura and I didn't fly to Birmingham, either. We rented a car instead. It took us two days, but we had our armadillo.

Are you at the good part yet?

That Sunday afternoon, tired and proud, we brought Joey into the kitchen of our house in Birmingham and set him on the table for Vicki and Ashley to admire. Joey was asleep, so we didn't take him out of the cage.

"Is he all right?" Laura asked.

"Sure," I said. "He's fine."

But later, Joey started breathing through his mouth and wheezing, exactly as my father had done toward the end of his own life. I tried not to panic. I left a humorous message on our vet's answering machine. "I know you don't usually treat armadillos," I said, "but we have one here that appears to have a cold."

By the time our vet returned the call, Joey was dead.

Wait a minute. What happened to the good part?

I don't think the good part of a story is the same as the turning point, or critical moment, or *denouement*, whatever that is. I think the good part comes much earlier than that. I think the good part is the moment when things really get interesting, where a story that is meandering aimlessly along suddenly seems to know in which direction it's going to head. I don't mean the point where complications arise, because I think the good part of a story has more to do with character than with incident. The good part demands a surrender from the reader. You give up a little piece of your own life and fall heedlessly into the lives of your characters. If they head for Texas, by golly you're going, too. If they get armadillos on the brain, well so do you. The good part is the indispensable part of the story. It is the part where you know you won't be able to put the story down.

But what about our lives? The good part, for me, has been elusive. That night in July, it was just a few sips of wine. I didn't get a buzz. But I have never been more aware of how precarious my sobriety is. I am hanging by a slender thread. And when a July like the last one comes along, I wish I could check into the hospital, like my sister Jeanie has to do, and have my blood completely cleansed.

Like her, I think I could bear the pain by telling stories—stories with good parts in them. I know there must have been a good part to our story this past July. On its precise beginning, though, Vicki and I will disagree. I think the good part of the story may have begun the moment Laura and I passed the piece of property my father had left us, and we saw the armadillo rooting in the grass along the shoulder of the road. Or maybe it was the moment I picked him up, and Laura said, "Can we keep him?" and I knew in a flash that we would try.

But Vicki thinks the good part of the story came later, on the day after Joey died, when she came into the kitchen and found Laura crying.

"Are you crying about Joey?" Vicki asked.

Laura shook her head. "I'm crying for Dad."

We buried Joey in our side yard, where we had buried our favorite golden retriever and innumerable frogs, chipmunks, and mice. Then we tried to replace him with a green iguana the girls named Javy, after Javy Lopez, the catcher for the Atlanta Braves. Ashley lets Javy climb up the front of her shirt, but Laura has had a hard time warming up to him. Tonight, though, as I write this, she is feeding him a strawberry by hand.

And I am thinking about armadillos past and present. Who could have foreseen that an armadillo would come again into the life of my family, that it would leave us as suddenly as the others had, and that Laura would bear my pain in the same way I had borne my father's? And who could have foreseen that after thirteen years of sobriety, Vicki and I would fall into simultaneous affairs and hurt each other like the true drunks we are? Who could have foreseen the little deaths that lay in wait for us last July?

I still haven't made sense of it yet. The question is not why I relapsed that night, but why I stopped after only four sips of wine. Perhaps I was anticipating and bearing Vicki's pain. Maybe that's what our marriage, every marriage, is about. All I know for certain is that a year has passed, and it's almost July again. Vicki and I are still sober and together, despite our crooked hearts. And I am beginning to think we have finally gotten to the good part of our story, the place where we have become so interested in the lives of our characters, neither of us will be able to put the story down.

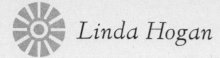 *Linda Hogan*

PLANT STORIES

"I felt her deep exhaustion and her sorrow, wakened and warmed . . . like soil stirred, the sorrow of its ruin reflected in her, the human and the land interlocked like doomed lovers."   —Meridel LeSueur

"It's about a pine tree, great big pine tree. . . . You could see it from here, you could see it from Fort Washakie."
—Emily Hill, Shoshone

"Our earth is turning over and turning green."
—Emily Hill, Shoshone (from Judith Vander)

In the darkened bathroom, my daughter sits in a bathtub filled with hot water. I kneel on the floor beside her, pouring hot water over her back as she cries from the pain of a migraine. I can offer only compassion and small comfort. While I think I understand pain, I do not know hers. Skin, between humans, divides and separates us, and pain is a distinct companion that visits each person differently, carrying her to its underworld, a country ruled by an invisible and unjust dictator.

I am thinking of mythology, the story that tells of Demeter and her daughter, who was stolen by the lord of the underworld, where seeds and roots dwell under the skin of earth. I tell myself that there are twin energies in the world, hope and hopelessness, that breaking is followed by healing. In the story of Persephone and Demeter, after life is withheld from the vegetable world, after the hunger of mortals on the skin surface of earth, a compromise is reached; the other side of this descent, as the story goes, tells us that the daughter Persephone ascended, after all, like a new plant back into the light. The girl returned, if only part of the time, to her mother on the surface of the world, and Demeter, who in her anger had withheld the plants, allowed them to return to their upward-rising fullness, both bearing and borne by spring.

My own daughter will be well again. As for me, I am not only the mother who loves a daughter, a mother hoping for the return of life and spring and healing to the world, I am also one of the stolen ones; part of my life is lived beneath the skin of ground, in the dark world, the interior landscape of pain, invisible to the eyes of those uninitiated into the world of sickness, separated from them only by virtue of skin.

Maybe this story of illness and pain is something of a plant story, a story that grows from a darkness deeper than the one in which I bathe this beloved daughter. It is a story of the dank world where ants, shrews, and earthworms carry on beneath the vision of humans. It's a story of the loss of light and the place of ultimate death where living bodies decay. It's a story like that of Persephone which says a girl has been stolen and taken away. But it is also a tale of life and movement toward light, one that addresses itself to a kind of wholeness, imperfect perhaps but certain as the trees and grasses that are determined enough to push away stones. Like in the mythic world, it is a story that contains creation, swelling seeds and shoots, the place where plant roots spread their first reaches of tendril and thread in the dark interior in a journey of upward rising.

For over ten years, I have hidden pain and illness from others, descending now and then into a darkness indescribable to those who have not been there. There are days I can barely get out of bed, days I don't answer the phone because there is no energy even for speaking. On these days, these nights, I am living in an underworld, unseen, unseeing.

Physical pain isn't just an event; it is a country—one whose citizens recognize each other on daily streets just by the expression on their faces. And it has such presence that it is impossible to ignore. A day of it warps time and is a lost day, although for short-term pain, like that of my daughter, we can bear it because pain also has the shortest of memories. But a month of it can change a life, changing even the body's chemistry. Years of it seem powerful enough to twist all eternity, to obliterate a human being and her history.

On those days when I dwell in the territory of pain, it is this human history I try to recall, what it was like before the darkness of pain, the mighty physicality of this body as a child, hanging upside down by my knees from a tree branch in a forest of trees, believing, as all children do, in my own strength, that this body would not fail me or grow old or break. There are fields and meadows in my remembering, the sharp hay and animal odor in barns that, years ago, carried me to the heart and muscle of my own body. I recall the joy of the physical playing in red and yellow rich-smelling autumn leaves I'd just raked into a pile, the smell of the dark, moist clods of earth, and the welcoming feeling of coming in for a home-cooked dinner after horseback riding with a boyfriend through fields, my hands dirty and alive with the smell of horseflesh. I remember, too, the trees we rode beneath, the shading willows that grew by creeks and were a language telling that water was there. Even rooted in earth, they were divining rods, as if nature were telling its own story of water, attraction, and elements beneath the ground. And I see that there are stories of plants and trees in the human body. The first world around me, the first world around us all, is the world of plants rising from soil, their breathings, their turnings toward the sun.

When I was first sick, told that my diagnosis would probably be multiple sclerosis, I came home from the hospital determined to heal myself. I went to bed in daylight, an unusual thing for me "before" illness because I hated to waste my days, days when I would roam the countryside and nearby creek, looking at the insects, animals, and plants that shared my world, plants like mullein with its velvet leaves and tender dew-filled centers. There were mariposa lilies and wild snapdragons, yucca with stalks I called candelabras because of how they seem to light up in the night. In Celtic traditions, the forest was considered to be a place of power and depth. For the Yaqui, the enchanted plant world shows up in Deer Dance Songs, in which even the drum is considered a flower, and in which a pathway into sacred time and space is considered to be something of a flowering, a beautiful growing. The flower world is the entryway into the spiritual world of the ceremony.

Now I tried to think of the lost days as lying fallow. Now I didn't walk through the world of plants around me. Now it seemed I was wasting away with the kind of exhaustion that would later immobilize me for long periods of time when I was too fatigued even to sleep. But I believed in healing. I believed I could visualize wholeness, could find a healing dream or vision.

One afternoon in bed, barely able to move, I dreamed that my spine was the stalk of a dry plant. In this dream the stalk turned green and alive, pushing upward with leaves preparing their first budding out.

At the time I believed that this dream was a language of my body, grown out of it, and that it meant a physical change was taking place, that it signified healing, that I was walking the fields with another part of myself than my feet. And this would become my pattern, always believing a cure was working, that this illness would go away if I found the right things. Hope is a food for sick people. My search for a vision, for "right thinking," soon gave way to a realization that this was not the path to healing, or at least not a complete path. But later I would see this dream as that which originated inside the first fall of my body through time—chronos, for chronic—and earth, as a fore-shadowing of my later interest in, and search for, medicinal plants.

I suppose it was because of this dream, its unbidden presence in my psyche, that I turned toward the healing tools of my ancestors, of all our ancestors if you go back far enough.

Recovery for me has been in the return, the renewed look again to the life of plants and the traditional uses and knowledge of plants in various tribes and peoples. Now I call plants "the vertical gods," and like illness, like the stolen lives of women and girls, they grow in the darkness underground and rise up alive, seeking health, from deep places of the interior and with a strength unrealized by most humans.

And so I went to traditional healers who used herbs and ceremonies and prayer. I was cared for by an indigenous Pueblo woman who'd served an eighteen-year internship with a Hopi healer. Smoking me with cedar and sage, she offered me her remedies and told me the stories of gathering plants, the weeks it took to harvest them, the relationships developed with land and plant and tree. I visited others, finding even a woman who sang new songs into my body. These were healers for the spirit as well as the body, and their medicines have worked for many, but this illness that cohabits my body is one that is new. This is an illness that originated, as I believe, in our newly poisonous American soil; it's a modern disease. Like bindweed, it grows from disturbances in the land.

Within a year of one another, my sister and I were both diagnosed with an unusual form of multiple sclerosis, thought by some physicians to be genetic, even though it is an illness that occurs only in industrialized countries, with two clusters appearing only after the presence of military or the use of chemicals. The diagnoses for both of us are even now, over a decade later, sometimes still in question. For her, there is the loss of eyesight and other neurological difficulties. For me, while there were neurological problems that interrupted the direction my life might have traveled, what has endured as the most difficult aspect of illness has been the secondary illness of fibromyalgia, an almost-constant deep fatigue that is not restored by sleep or rest, and its partner, chronic pain. It was an illness beginning with eye pain, gradual muscle tightening, even of the optic muscles. Stress, I believed at first, as we are inclined to blame our lifestyles, and rightly so, for the damages to our bodies. It is this painful nerve and muscle disease that is the hardest to bear because chronic pain, unlike that which is acute, is too seldom understood, treated, or even relieved by medical professionals. Its presence wears a person down. This is an illness, as René Dubos said, that doesn't take life, just ruins it. Disabled for a year and a half, I was unable at first to button a shirt or pull on a pair of slacks without lying down to rest afterward from pain in the muscles used, and from fatigue. I was in constant pain and kept the phone beside me in case I needed to call a neighbor to help me get up. It was a terrible helplessness, and at times I was reduced from walking to crawling. It seemed my life had ended. As writer Susan Griffin states about her own illness, it felt to me, also, "that the world is dying within one's own skin."

In indigenous systems of knowledge, the human body and the body of earth are the same shared being, the same matter, the selfsame creation. It is known, it is a given, that the life of the human body is in all ways rooted in the deeper, older world; we are alive with the lives of fish, plant, animal, air, and water. We humans are a brief, small measure of the same processes of life and evolution and health that are at work in all species, animal and plant. Because of this we are subject to the same vulnerabilities. What happens to the world happens also to the people:

Trees and grass same thing
They grow with your body
If you feel sore . . . that mean somebody killing tree or grass
You feel because your body is that tree or earth.
Tree might be sick . . . You feel it.
What you do to tree is in your own body.

—Big Bill Niedje, aboriginal elder

Now, in recent Western science, the heart of what is being learned reveals that this ancient, indigenous knowledge about the body of earth holds true. The old intelligence of tribal peoples is coming to new, Western terms. Humans are no longer considered as individual, unrelated organisms. We are this landscape, the same physical matter, the same unseen atoms, the same energy or life force. There is common ground between matter and matter, matter and spirit. As physicist David Bohm said, "The body enfolds not only the mind but also in some sense the entire material universe."

In the same way indigenous knowledge asserts there are such relationships, this new science of unity states there are genetic affinities between all living things. We are finding that skin is truly permeable; the doors of ourselves are always open. We have wrongly thought that there is skin, a separation, between us and the rest of the world. But our recent invasions by virus, radiation, and pesticides show us how vulnerable are our bodies. Because of this commonality of all matter, it is in our bodies where the brokenness of the earth is witnessed. In our cells, skin, muscles, in illnesses, in genetic changes. We are the repositories where many things come to rest, and within us they begin their work at consuming or changing us. Neither toxins nor viruses are kept at bay by our seeming containment.

My friend Mary O'Brien, a botanist who researches endocrine disrupters in the environment, writes about how easily toxins enter the human body, how intricately connected are our children and ourselves with the world beyond our seeming skin. And vulnerable. "We all know and feel the story of life as exchange. The land gives its soil to the rivers, the rivers give their sediments to the ocean, and the sediments are borrowed for a while by bottom-feeders. The bottom-feeders are given into fish and the fish are taken into seals. The seals give their fat to the Inuit and both the seals and the Inuit give themselves and their milk to their young. We are an earth of exchanges. Exchanges of air and moisture and protoplasm. We have to take care with these exchanges because what we give, we give to exquisitely balanced systems." And, she says, "Much of what we humans give in exchange to what we have received from the earth is disorder." She writes that in a world of such balanced systems, "we have to be careful, religious, really, with what we exchange with the Earth." We've witnessed the consequences: "Tumors forming in children's brains; farmworkers going into convulsions; birds born with beaks that won't work because they're crossed; babies born with their spinal cord outside their back."

Even if we forget or fail to acknowledge the physical, worldly context of our lives, we participate in and with this planet and its atmosphere in an endless, skinless dance of give and take.

What I remember most from high school is the day I dropped acetone on an elm leaf and looked through glass at the green slide of life within it, the fluids moving inside that delicate cathedral light of leaf. And the cells, so named because they looked like rooms green and clear as jewels. Up until then, there was little about school that interested me. I had seen nothing alive in it, but suddenly, here was a world before me. Even so, I believe it was my first step at trying to learn the wide spread of a world by peering at the small and minute, by looking through things instead of at them, although the rest of my education would focus on this. In the seventeenth century, Leeuwenhoek noted that the world was made up of small, nearly invisible particles. Galen set forth the theory that germs were the cause of disease. Until recent years, we'd inherited and been taught a tradition, it seems, of seeing the small and rote, a world broken down to individual particles, minute and unrelated.

Because of this "method," as the exploration and process of science is called, we have failed to see, and never understood, the large and communal, the mysterious elixir that pushes the life into motion within a plant, the magic of the ancient transformations of our bodies into plants, their lives into our lives, the filaments that connect us with the rest of the world, from soil to cloud to river and back again to soil.

Nor were we told, in those days, that plants spoke a language of their own, a tongue of nitrogen, carbon, air, and light, or that for many plants, most of their root systems can distinguish, in an intelligence we don't possess, between toxins and nutrients, or that Linnaeus said time could be told by observing the movements of plants. Or that tribal elders say you can tell when rain is coming because of the way leaves turn and curl in order to hold the precious water inside themselves. The past knowledge of native peoples didn't develop in such isolation as that of Western science; and by ignoring native knowledge our schools and books never taught us many of the real properties of plants.

Some of the healing potencies in the world are so simple we wouldn't think of them. In her book *Sastun*, Rosita Arvigo speaks of learning from indigenous women how rose petals stop bleeding during a hemorrhage after a child delivery. An elderly Nahuatl midwife sent Arvigo out to gather rose petals: "Dumbfounded, I did as I was told. She boiled the petals and leaves, and when the mixture was cooled she spooned it gently into Margarita's mouth and gave her the baby to suckle at the same time. In eight minutes the hemorrhaging had stopped."

And the Comanche medicine woman, Sanapia, looked out at her world, prairie, field of grassland, and said, "I can just sit here and look at them bald prairies and see four kinds of medicines growing. I bet you can't even see them."

In Rupert Sheldrake's book *The Rebirth of Nature*, he writes that near the home of his youth, "I saw a row of willow trees with rusty wire hanging from them. I wanted to know why it was there, and asked my uncle, who was nearby. He explained that this had once been a fence made with willow stakes, but the stakes had come to life and turned into trees." Willow, the painkiller, the first source of aspirin. Sheldrake later writes that "If hundreds of cuttings are made from a willow tree, each can grow into a new tree. Pieces of wound tissue from plant stems can regenerate roots and shoots; and even single cells from such wound tissue, grown in test tubes, can form entire plants."

It is magic, how a tree forms, how redwoods grow out of their fallen elders, how banyan trees create others from themselves, how bark forms a layer over wounds. The nearby cottonwood, accidentally cut by a neighbor last year, sent out numerous new shoots this year in its move to survive, and the young aspens chewed by the deer have become smaller, bushier plants, but they, too, have increased their numbers. The bulldozed elms at the corner are trying to sprout new leaves from their amputations.

But the human body is another story.

I remember not only the leaf from biology class, but further back, younger, to times when, with my sister or friends, we would go to the nearest Sears Roebuck store and visit the shoe section and stand at the X-ray machine to view the bones of our feet. We spent many hours looking down through that machine at the inner landscape of our bones, looking through ourselves, making what was unseen visible. As with Madame Curie, who died of the invisible, we didn't see the danger; one day the machines were removed from all the stores because of their threats to human health.

We thought so many unseen things were safe. We thought so many things wrongly. And one day we woke out of the fifties to find ourselves in an endangered world and endangered bodies. And years later, many of us found ourselves ill from sources we couldn't identify.

There were many possible sources in addition to radiation. Before the publication of Rachel Carson's groundbreaking book *Silent Spring,* about the hazards of DDT, many of us in my generation had been exposed, almost daily, to DDT, even sprayed with it as children to keep chiggers, ticks, and horseflies from our bodies. We had been subject to crop dusting in Oklahoma and chemical exposures, radium buried beneath the ground in east Denver. In the sixties in Colorado there were numerous small earthquakes that resulted from the pumping of toxic chemicals into the earth. There were nearby drums of chemical weapons and nerve gas eroding only a few miles away. We later lived in Leadville, Colorado, a place now visited by chemistry classes to measure and observe the lead that runs down streets in the rain and snowmelt. Lead, which was once used in European medicine as a healing agent and preferred by chemists and physicians over herbs, is now known to be poisonous. The town where I currently reside only recently had uranium tailings removed, tailings we didn't know were there. And just two summers ago, at my aunt's house in Martha, Oklahoma, in the heat of summer, a yellow crop-dusting plane flew low above us. We ran inside, closed the house, and sat indoors at the kitchen table as the plane passed over, thinking and hoping that the walls would protect us. Yet we could smell the pesticide and it rekindled my memories of the planes coming over the houses and acreages of my kin.

This life of mine is a common life. I am exposed to no more toxins than any other American is, or will be, in a close future. As Mary O'Brien says in her essay "Where Do Things Go?" there is no "away." Even the water beneath the ground moves north, passes beneath the continent in watershed to Baffin Island, where it carries high concentrations of dioxins to the breast milk of native mothers. Now our water runs down the mountains into Denver, where it is picked up and used.

And yet, even with what we do know, a war is being waged on land, forest, on topsoil and plant, and because of the relationship between us, on humans. Not only are we being poisoned, not only are ancient ecosystems, ones that held the world intact, being destroyed, but along with them the remedies are also disappearing. In Richard Preston's *New Yorker* article "Crisis in the Hot Zone" (October 26, 1992), researchers say that viruses are emerging from areas being deforested and as those areas are being destroyed, so are the medicinal plants that are used for the illnesses caused by the viruses. The viruses themselves are coming out from the destruction, emerging out of darkness and depth of verdant rainforests and jungles into human bodies and then disappearing back again.

This is the inheritance of a way of living greatly different from the older forms of indigenous knowledge and ways of being that sustained and protected the world, the ceremonies and stories that contained directives for how to live and maintain life of the world.

It is hard to speak or write about physical pain because it is a state of being that, by its own existence, brings on a sense of sadness and defeat. Accompanying it are many losses, including the loss of selfhood. To speak about it is to address the worst state of our human being. It can't be measured, and because of this it is too often left untreated, as was the case in a recent suicide assisted by controversial Dr. Jack Kevorkian. His patient was a woman who shared with me this same painful illness. I not only had compassion for her suffering, but also an understanding of how she came to the decision to die. I was in Japan reading the newspaper, traveling with a friend. I said, I know how she feels, and I wept. Like her, I felt that this illness was a terrible and lingering death. It's an illness ignored by many in the medical community, not even considered an illness until recently. A medical doctor at the University Hospital, speaking to a full auditorium of people who suffer from fibromyalgia, said he did not see it as a disability, only a syndrome. With this, many in the audience stood and walked out. Who could believe in anything else he said? He was so young and vibrant, not an inhabitant of this country, not even a visitor, yet talking about the residents and terrain, as if he understood them, to make it fit his beliefs.

It is an illness so overwhelming to all aspects of daily life that in the beginning it was hard to imagine months or years of it. Unable to work, I, too, went untreated until, with all my resources and after years of suffering, I found a knowledgeable doctor who was willing to offer to me the medications I needed, medications other doctors withheld, afraid I might become dependent. What they didn't know was that their hesitance and the laws that created it doomed me, and many others, to a life without life. And, although the newer knowledge on pain is that for those who suffer it allows for normalcy without addiction, as if the body needs it and uses it up in different ways, legislation and practice have not kept up.

Because of the herbs I have experimented with for so many years and a compassionate doctor who allows medications for pain, I am one of the few people able to work and travel and write, to live a life that is nearly, but not quite, normal.

It would be easy to blame the physicians—this was stated in the case of Kevorkian's patient—for they of all people should have compassion. And she did not receive it. The presence of Kevorkian must have been a great comfort for a person in chronic pain. But in defense of medical doctors, I know the truth is that those who don't have pain can't imagine what it is to endure it. For those who haven't visited this terrain, it is unimaginable what a body can endure; it is territory as unmapped as that of the underworld from which Demeter could not rescue her daughter because there was no path in, no path out, except to wait, to let the world around her become dormant, bare of life, and begin its return.

In the new M. Scott Peck book *Denial of the Soul,* he writes about pain, about the mistakes, crimes, and sadism, he calls it, of modern medicine in its unwillingness to offer relief from pain. "Forget about overconcern with addictions. Forget about formulas and schedules. The most common reason that medical professionals inadequately treat severe or excruciating pain is simple lack of empathy. They are dealing with something foreign." And ironically, we live in a time, unlike in previous generations, where there is compassion for emotional pain, but not for human physical suffering, and perhaps, as so many have stated, it is because in the Western way of thought there is such hatred of the body. And the human body, instead of seen with the wider view, in its context as an extension of the earth, part of community, is seen from a Christian-influenced point of view as the apart-from place where punishment takes place, as the curse we have to bear in this life. In fact, the word *pain* even shares the same linguistic and moral root as the words *punishment* and *penitent.*

But whatever the reasons, a woman who is depressed or anxious is more likely to be taken seriously and medicated than a woman suffering from physical pain, particularly if it's chronic. With these values, a person is more likely to be given a prescription for emotional difficulties, or for obesity, than for physical pain.

I find it so interesting that in indigenous communities the body is sometimes seen as more real and significant than the spirit, and yet at the same time, the traditional people honor and respect the life in each thing on earth. How different from the Western way, in which the soul is more important than the body, and yet the world is seen as having no life. This is part of a painful American history, too. In the early days, at first contact, the Europeans, believing they were saving souls, read charters to tribes in Latin. If the tribal people did not answer in Latin, they were killed, considered to be in need of salvation.

The judgment of the ill is so prevalent a reaction that for years I said little, except to my closest friends, about my illness. In our times, it is as if being sick means that I am less. In truth, it does mean this; I am less than what I was, unable to live my life the way others do. And I am seen by others as less, weak not only in body but in character, and vulnerable in ways humans pretend and desire not to be. In our time we are people who want to believe in individual cause and effect, and so, as we students did in that biology class years ago, we look at the world through glass, and it is a small and isolated view.

But my reluctance to talk about illness has been overcome as I've learned that this is not a private tragedy, not just an illness of my sister and myself; our personal loss and suffering is only a small part of a larger pattern of illness affecting large numbers of Indian people. Immune system disorders are proliferating among native people. In addition, both fibromyalgia and chronic fatigue syndrome bear enough similarity to the Gulf War syndrome as to increasingly be medically categorized with it, and the Gulf War syndrome is now known to originate with chemical poisoning and nerve gas exposure, bearing witness to the fact that what is in the earth and air and water comes to rest inside our bodies, creating change.

According to journalist Terry Hanson, ninety-five percent of the members of the northwest Shoalwater Bay tribe, enough to warrant the building of a new clinic, suffer immune system disorders such as the one that affects me. Pesticides used in local cranberry bogs are one probable cause of the Shoalwater Bay illness in Oregon. On that reservation, in addition, there have been no live births to native mothers in over six years. A Choctaw physician in Seattle says that at least fifty percent of the urban Indian community show the same illness and symptoms.

There have been other clusters of illness in Native America, many of them related to pesticide, nuclear, and other chemical hazards. In one village in Alaska that has high cancer rates, even in the children, it was found that the nuclear waste of the Manhattan Project was buried beneath their village, a move that can only be seen as an act of ongoing genocide.

There may be a particular genetic susceptibility or sensitivity in native people, but as Indian people, we are especially vulnerable for a variety of other reasons; not only are a large number of us still mostly in poverty, with inadequate, nontraditional diets, but our remaining lands are polluted and irradiated, and even now are being targeted for nuclear waste and chemical storage. As surely as when smallpox was purposefully introduced to the tribes, we are dying of the diseases caused by the aggressive technology, medicine, and lifeways of a society now failing even those who uphold and believe in them. And our illnesses alone tell us we are of a piece with the world, extensions of it, and skinless.

Father Berard Haile was a priest who kept voluminous notes on the Navajo ceremonial called Upward Moving, sometimes also called The Emergence Way. This ceremony, or Chantway, details the significance of plants to healing in Navajo medicine. Plants that come upward from the dark earth play a key role in the Upward Moving ceremony. The patient wears a dress made of spruce branches. Herbal mixtures are taken. Pollen is dusted on the people. The patient's hair is bathed with yucca and medicine bundles are made, containing sage, grasses, and watercress. In the last nights of the ceremony Haile says of the healer, "He raised the entire bundle of plants and permitted them to rain over the patient."

These ceremonies, as with other tribes, contain not only the plants, but mythic accounts of creation and the first people, and the knowledge of how a regional ecology works. In the Navajo Chantways, these narratives and accountings are far more complex than those in the Western biblical near-equivalent. Even as a Catholic priest, Haile felt the Navajo ceremonies and their supporting literatures to be "magnificently structured narratives," as he wrote, containing arithmetic, geology, and geometry. Their complexity and structure, as he maintained, are proof of their validity. The Emergence Way, in particular, recounts the upward-moving direction of healing and rebirth. The ceremony itself is something of a living plant, he says, growing from roots in a deeper world.

Perhaps in my own body I have always known this process of upward rising. I know spring is a healing time, a time of recovery and regeneration. There is a planetary and vegetable movement, life from the mineral underground, a calling of the sun, and movement is the ally of life. The plants have stamina and persistence and will push aside stones in order to emerge. So it is with me; I am in a constant search for healing, on a journey upward like a plant in darkness, moving upward even from the inherited trauma of history. And I believe in this movement of spring now rising outside.

But while there is movement upward, there are two directions of energy in this world, there is also its companion. There is also the down-dwelling reach of roots. The vertical gods, in their season, like Persephone, descend.

This is what plants know, that downward, too, is essential. It is part of the same life that contains rising. The life force begins in darkness, like the plants in my shed moving toward sun that must, at the same time, send an anchoring root toward the place that is mineral, gravity, and underground water. In the plant world, descending energy is necessary. And for everyone and everything, eventually, as the earthly cycles go, illness, decay, and age claims us. Gravity is a powerful force. The whole planet is held to its rules. Our deaths may be in us at birth, may be in the land around us, and even as we rise to adulthood, we are falling toward those ends. And my body claims this understanding, too. Illness has taught me that, like roots, growing down, not up, is sometimes the direction life takes.

*   *   *

For now, it is spring. Yesterday was the first warm day I had my hands in earth, cleaning out the flower beds, the dead leaves, looking for new shoots of delphinium, columbine, lupine, the first signs of a fern I try to keep alive in this mountain earth where they do not usually prosper and need a human hand.

It is a good feeling to be working in the rich-smelling earth, a world renewed after the dark, cold season of winter, and to have my hands dirty with life in this spare, dry mountain soil. It is work to eke out a plant or two in this place; this is not the black, lusty earth of richer, wetter places. Here, a garden is not a natural thing; nature itself tries to overcome it. And as a gardener, I don't want to wage a war on the land to grow and produce what I desire, so I try to live with it, the way I try to live with my own body, tending and nurturing what will grow and giving up what won't—except for that one beloved fern—in this terrain.

I am not restored to health, but am restored to love, comfort, to a vision of the world that is moving into a wholeness. I have learned a small portion of the plants, a beginner's knowledge, really, even in so many years, but it's enough to teach me to respect their company, their movement in wind, their enchanted blooming and dying, their grace and dignity. I have also learned that if we lose one piece of the world, one species of plant, the entire foundation crumbles.

Perhaps people came into this world, after all, by way of a reed as it says in so many emergence stories. It's not so much more fanciful than the creation story of evolution, to think that matter could be so transformed and shaped from some brilliant heart of creation from fish into bird, from a rib of clay into a woman. They say it was, after all, a garden that was the center from which human life sprang, formed of clay by a God who set forth a tree that contained knowledge.

*   *   *

Out in the dark shed with its cracks between boards where light falls across the ground, white-leafed plants are sending themselves upward in a search for light; they stretch from the bare earth floor beside rake and shovel, trying to find a single crack of light. Tenderly thin and pale, they seek what is remembered from before their first growth, from the spindly darkness of their lives beginning inside earth. Even in darkness a plant will grow toward the light. Demeter, who saw a dark god steal her beautiful daughter, would understand both this darkness and this persistence in a plant growing, bending, grasping for light. They want to live. So do I. I embody the world. Think of me as plant. Pollen. Leaf. Stamen. Root. Seed. Upward Rising.

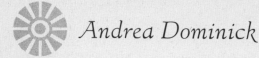

Andrea Dominick

PAMPHLETS

The doctor is telling me she will insert a needle into the lower part of my eye socket and immobilize the muscles in the eye. I stare at the white walls while she explains the procedure and hands me a pastel pamphlet giving me the statistics on diabetic retinopathy. It tells me I'm not alone, but also makes me realize I'm not one of the fortunate ones who detected their condition early.

My eyes dilated, I turn the pamphlet over in my hands, barely seeing the print. I almost laugh at the irony. I wonder if there is a closet in the back of the office somewhere used only for the storage of pamphlets. In the waiting room, I looked around and noticed that every patient seemed to be holding a green, pink, or light blue pamphlet. Different colors for different conditions. And I guess there is some comfort in having one to take home. It's as if they know you will remember nothing they have said. They send you away with a reminder, something tangible. This pamphlet has a picture of the inner eye. An eye that's not functioning properly.

And I guess I feel better in knowing someone went to the

trouble to write it all down. I think if there's a pamphlet about it, it can't be that rare. I calculate in my head that there are approximately ten million diabetics in the United States and eighty percent who have had the disease fifteen years or longer develop retinopathy. I should not be surprised to find myself in this office, because I developed diabetes when I was nine years old and have gone fifteen years without complications.

I squint to see the framed diplomas on the wall, but I can't make out any of the writing. There is a huge diagram of a retina next to a degree from the University of Iowa. A healthy eye. None of the blood vessels are leaking. The room is all white and a large piece of equipment stands between the doctor and me. Just minutes before, she used it on my eyes, allowing her to see the blood vessels which have weakened and exploded. She gazed at them a long time and it was during those minutes I knew there was a more serious problem than I had first anticipated.

I came into this office with my father, thinking I had a retinal tear. A common condition. Blood behind my pupil was clouding my vision and causing blind spots. I know there's even a pamphlet on retinal tears. My friend Joel had one last year, but this pamphlet in my hand says *Diabetic Retinopathy* in large, white letters. Something I already know a little bit about. I've read some of the books on diabetes and I know that lack of oxygen has caused the vessels in the back of my eye to weaken. Fifteen years of Type I diabetes can have this effect. A few vessels have already broken and caused some vision loss in my right eye. The debris from the hemorrhage is floating around back there, preventing light from hitting my retina. I will have to undergo laser surgeries to cauterize the other vessels and prevent those from bursting as well. During this surgery, a powerful beam of light will be focused on the damaged areas, forcing the leaking vessels to regress.

The doctor gets my attention by tapping on the pamphlet in my hand with her pencil. She knows I have not been listening because she sees ten of my kind every day. She gives me that knowing look, as if I am going to be one of the difficult ones. The young woman who leaves today and then returns with a list of written questions next week, so she continues to talk about what she knows. Procedures.

"And about that injection into your cheek . . ." she begins again.

She says this nonchalantly, as if another needle shouldn't be a problem for a diabetic. Doctors frequently do this. They believe I have no fear of needles. It's as if they are about to tell me it will pinch for a second before remembering who I am. Then they say nothing. They do this with booster shots, Novocain, and even when they're drawing blood from a vein. I know this woman will probably do the same thing when I go in for surgery next week. She will remember that this is diabetic retinopathy. That I am a diabetic. And she will give me no reassuring words before insertion, but will be frighteningly silent, even though she has a lot to say right now.

"You'll need to notify your primary physician. Do you have a physician?" she asks.

I simply stare at her and nod my head, knowing I will not report this to Dr. Manning. He will be too concerned. He will make a big deal out of it and insist on blood tests and kidney checks. He'll want to search for other diabetic complications. He's very thorough.

During my initial hospitalization for diabetes when I was nine, Dr. Manning came to see me in the hospital every day. He made sure my blood sugars were normal and told me I didn't have to wear the hospital gown if I didn't want to. He brought me little peppermint candies to keep by my bed in case I woke up with an insulin reaction in the middle of the night. He made me realize that I had some control, but those nurses who took my blood when I was first hospitalized refused to believe that I was already an expert with the syringes. They kept me in the pediatrics ward for thirteen days, teaching me how to count calories, test my blood and urine, informing me of the complications associated with diabetes, showing me the proper way to administer an injection. But I knew how to give a shot. I had watched my sister hundreds of times, but the hospital's idea of standard procedure deviated from my sister's. Denise would simply pop the needle in and out of her leg before she threw on her jeans and headed off to high school in the morning. The nurses in the hospital insisted that I clean the area with alcohol, carefully draw the insulin, tap the syringe for bubbles, insert it into the subcutaneous layer of fat at an eighty-five-degree angle, pull back the plunger to check for blood, and then insert the insulin. That was my first real experience with the medical profession. I was in fourth grade and learned quickly how to behave in their presence.

They made me practice giving shots on oranges in the hospital during those two weeks. Every day around three o'clock a nurse would come into my room with an orange, two syringes, and a vial of water on a silver platter. She would tell me to set the orange on my leg and give the piece of fruit ten shots with each needle. Swab the rough skin with alcohol and run through the entire procedure, because she claimed practice made perfect.

Sometimes, if she left me alone with the orange, I would peel and eat it instead. She would get angry with me and call down to the kitchen for another orange. Then she would sit there and make me stick the needle into the fruit in front of her. But after I returned home, I gave my shots just like my sister did, without alcohol and holding the needle at a ninety-degree angle.

And Dr. Manning was there every day checking on me, watching me grow up in the following years. Now I don't want to tell him about this eye problem. I don't want him to think I haven't taken care of myself. He has always been too concerned about my health. The first year after the initial hospitalization to regulate me, he made me visit his office every month for blood work. I was too young to understand why they had to take blood from my arm the first week of every month. The veins in my arm are narrow. Doctors aren't sure why, but diabetics have small vessels and trying to find a vein that would "cooperate" was always difficult. His nurse would poke around with that needle, sometimes missing two or three times before she could get any blood. I would offer up all ten fingers instead, but she said she needed more blood. I asked her to take it from my fingertips. They were tough from multiple finger sticks.

"It has to be from a major vein," the nurse would sigh.

I would cry and open my arm.

I didn't understand the tests, but I understood what having diabetes meant. I had grown up with needles in my house. My sister had already had the disease ten years when I was born. I used to dig her needles out of the trash can and fill them up with water, transforming them into water guns and shooting my brother.

Then the needles belonged to me. And Dr. Manning had made that a positive experience by teaching a nine-year-old how to control her life. But this eye doctor before me seems to be the authority now.

"Who is your doctor?" she asks.

When I tell her, she raises her eyebrows and suggests I find another doctor, one who specializes in diabetes. I need to monitor my blood sugars more closely. High blood sugars are probably what leads to the weakening and breaking of these vessels in the first place, she says. She is telling me things I know. She writes down the names of some doctors and hands me the paper. I stare at her immaculate fingernails and tuck the little list of faceless names inside the pamphlet. It's as if she believes these people will save my life. She assumes I have faith in doctors.

And to a certain degree I do. I have to. I need to trust this woman before me, because she called my case severe. I wonder what she sees when she looks through that lens into my eyes. I have no choice but to trust her. This isn't a lesion on my skin or a pain in my gut she is talking about. This isn't something I can look in the mirror and see. The breaks are behind the lens of my eye and no one can see them but me and her. I glance at the diplomas on the wall again, looking for something tangible to place my trust in.

"We do several of these surgeries every week," she reassures me. "You are a bit young to have developed this condition, but we've seen younger."

And I was, by far, the youngest person in the waiting room here. Most of my friends just go to optometrists. They read the eye chart and get their new glasses, but the people in the waiting room of this office had eyes sixty or seventy years old. I think one can reasonably expect some problems by then. But there was one small child who came out of the back room while I was sitting in the waiting room. A nurse was leading her by the hand through the door. With a white patch covering her left eye, the child stretched her other hand in front of her, feeling her way through the air toward her parents. The little girl's mother was holding a pamphlet and brushing away tears as she rose to put her arms around her daughter. When the girl finally focused on her mom and saw the tears, she started crying herself. I watched them together, stared at the child's tanned legs and scraped-up knees, wondered how long it would be before she played outside again. Wondered if she was going blind, because she couldn't have been more than four or five years old.

". . . and then you'll have to wear a patch for a while," the doctor continues.

She tells me about the gauze patch required after surgery. It keeps the light out of the eye and I can take it off after eight hours. There will be a little bruise under my eye where the needle was inserted. After I take the patch off, I will have to put drops in my eye for three days to keep the pupil dilated and the muscles relaxed. My vision blurred, it will feel like someone punched me. The trauma to the eye from the laser surgery will also cause me to see spots for several days and I will lose some peripheral vision in the dark.

She is going to cauterize the outermost blood vessels my eye uses to see when the pupil is dilated. And then I will have the vision of the old. I've heard their complaints about the way they can't see the lines on the road at night and how the headlights of other drivers make visibility hard. I will learn how to drive again.

Seeing in a dimmed room will also be difficult after the surgeries. I will buy another lamp for my living room and use brighter light bulbs after the surgery. I will learn to use my hands to find objects in the dark and my sense of touch will become more keen. I will rely on my fingertips to find the keys in the bottom of my purse or open my car door at night. Vision loss is a result of this treatment. This doctor tells me it's inevitable.

Inevitability will become interchangeable with my destiny. I will try to learn to accept the fact that my fate is in the hands of the doctors. Never having asked for help before, I will be forced to rely on them to stabilize the condition. I will learn to ask. Lowering my eyes, I will tell my friend Ann that I can't drive again tonight. She will maneuver her car across the busy streets of Des Moines and come ten miles out of her way to pick me up. Some evenings my mother will cook for me because I can't tell which can is which in my cupboards. I will learn to swallow my pride, pick up the telephone, and dial the telephone numbers of my friends. Running my fingers over the buttons and hesitating as I press what I think is a two or a seven, I will hear a familiar voice and then the sound of my own voice. Asking.

"You shouldn't lift anything over ten pounds, either. No running. Don't do anything rigorous," she continues.

"For how long?" I ask.

"We're not sure. We only know that sudden increases in blood pressure or simple physical strain can cause vessels to unexpectedly break."

I wonder who the "we" is she is referring to. Doctors always talk like this. As if when one speaks, they all speak. I think of the

Borg character on a *Star Trek* episode I saw last night. The collective. Every brain is connected to one big database and no independent thought is permitted.

But this doctor is human and I struggle to remember that. She probably has children and a dog at home. Maybe even has medical problems of her own. I don't know about her life, though I find myself longing to know something about her. Something other than what I see before me. White coat. Brown hair pulled away from her round face. Manicured nails wrapped around a clipboard. Moving easily around my chair, she feels at home within this starch, white room. I want to know what she does when she leaves her office at night, but she continues to talk about what the surgery will be like. And when she notices that I am not listening, she sighs. The sigh a parent gives to a small child. A sigh that she gives to my kind every day. And like the pamphlet, I find some comfort in that as well.

So I let that woman with perfect nails perform four surgeries, two on each eye, over the course of the next two months. Just before the fourth surgery, I was sitting on the hospital bed, waiting for her to arrive, and I picked up my medical chart. She had written the words "severe, high-risk, proliferative diabetic retinopathy" on the top of one of the pages. The words scared me. She walked in while I was reading and took the folder from my hand, as if I hadn't the right or the knowledge to understand its contents. So I never returned to her after that day. I decided I wasn't going to go anywhere else, either, because I had been reading a medical book on diabetic retinopathy and had discovered that two surgeries were usually sufficient. But a week later another vessel broke.

I was leaning over to turn on my television when I saw the familiar blood and debris behind my left eye. I watched the vessel break and bleed and block my vision as I listened to the weather report. I could see the tiny nerves scattering behind my retina, so I closed my eyes. I sat on my living room floor and listened to the broadcast about the killings in the Middle East. The reporter was referring to pictures on the screen, but I kept my eyes closed. And I thought about having to go back to that woman. So I dialed information and got the number for the University of Iowa Hospital. Their Ophthalmology Department ranks in the top five in the nation. And I hoped for a more compassionate doctor. One who would tell me that the insertion of that needle was going to pinch for a minute.

This doctor tells me to stare at a spot on the ceiling. I have to keep my eyes open as he inserts the needle into my eye socket. I shift my gaze from the ceiling to his eyes as he pushes down the plunger and I feel the numbing solution enter my muscle. I stare at him standing above me, trying to cling to the image of his sympathetic hazel eyes as everything goes dark. The left side of my face goes numb. Reaching up to touch my own cheek, it's as though I am no longer a physical presence in this room; I'm unable to feel my own fingertips resting on my face, unable to see my own hand. The doctor leads me through a door marked DANGER—RADIATION and I sit down behind the familiar machine and rest my chin on the towel. Laser lights fill my eyes. I count the blasts to keep my mind occupied. Tears stream down my face. I'm not in pain, just tired.

The drive to get to the University of Iowa Hospital was long. My father and I left Des Moines last night, but the interstate was closed about thirty miles east of the city due to the weather. Blinding snow enveloped our car, and my father couldn't see. He leaned toward the windshield and opened his eyes wide, trying to catch a glimpse of other cars we knew were somewhere ahead of us. I stared through the windows into pure white. My heart racing, I kept glancing at my father as he strained to see.

Luckily we found a hotel room along the road, but we got no sleep. I could sense my father's nervousness the entire night. As if he should have had control over the snowstorm or was failing to get his daughter help. I told him not to worry, that the blood was already beginning to settle out of my eye. I sat on the double bed next to him and pretended to read a magazine even though I could barely make out the photographs of the models in the advertisements.

All night my father kept reaching over and taking my hand, asking me if I needed anything. Stuck in this hotel full of college kids who had been trying to get home for the weekend and businessmen missing their wives. Finally, my father leaned against the headboard and pushed buttons on the remote control, staring at the wall above the television. He was worried, but we made it here this morning after they opened the interstate.

And today the doctor is doing what he referred to as "heavy laser" on my left eye. He explained that after this surgery I could notice the most significant loss of vision yet. There are still hundreds of weak vessels back there, vessels that if left untreated will explode. And if more and more break, the fluid might accumulate behind my retina and cause it to detach. He said then we'd have an even bigger problem on our hands. So he's using laser on those weak vessels to make them shrivel up and die. And then it takes several weeks to know whether or not the eye has responded to the surgery. He said it can take up to two years for this condition to stabilize in someone my age. They don't understand why, but a person over sixty might only need two surgeries, whereas someone in her twenties could require more than eight.

"You're not going to go blind," he says, as if reading my mind. I've counted to five hundred. "You've lost some peripheral vision, night vision, and things will be dimmer, but you're not going blind right now."

I say nothing. There is comfort in those words. My sister had always said she would kill herself before she would go blind, but Denise never had any problems with her eyes. Most of her friends through high school and college didn't even know she was diabetic. My mother always said it was because Denise had developed the disease when she was so young. In the early sixties, no one knew much about diabetes and people were scared of it. Kids on the playground used to tease my sister in grade school, pretending to make syringes with their fingers and poking my sister in the arm. Even the mother of one of her classmates didn't want to invite Denise to a birthday party because of the illness. The woman had been scared my sister would ask for a slice of birthday cake. My mom says Denise never wanted anyone to know after that, because she thought people would treat her differently. Everyone would think she was so fragile.

But she wasn't. She was tough. And when she died two years ago, everyone was shocked. Shocked that they had never known about the disease. She was thirty-three years old and never talked about it with anyone but me. She had been the one who sat on the edge of the hospital bed when I was nine and told me not to worry. She said people didn't have to know and having diabetes wouldn't change my life.

But now it has. My life is different. Not just because I can barely see to drive at night or because my father is reading entire novels to me. My life has changed because I am finally facing who I am. Who I have become. I was always in complete control of my life, and now I have to accept sacrificing this control to other people. I need their help and I'm learning to face this reality. I have to try to believe the doctor's words and have faith in them as I would a religious scripture. And in three months, this is the first time anyone has told me that I wasn't going completely blind right now. I had been afraid to ask. Scared to say the word *blind* out loud and afraid of what they would tell me. But this doctor said the words. You're not going blind right now.

It could happen in the upcoming years from glaucoma or macular degeneration or retinal detachment, but not right now. Not from this condition. And I will remember this doctor's words in the upcoming months. When my eyes don't respond to these laser treatments, while I wait for those little vessels to shrivel up and die, I will accept my condition. My vision will get worse, but I'll adjust to it. And eventually it won't seem like I'm waiting to go blind or waiting to die as much as I'm learning how to see the world more clearly. I will simultaneously lose and gain my vision.

The next time I'm in this hospital, the doctors will tell me that the vessels aren't responding to the surgeries like they'd hoped they would. They'll say that some people go through twelve to sixteen laser treatments and there still isn't any improvement. The doctors will stand in the examining room with me, holding photographs of my retina, and contemplate a course of action. But my heart won't race anymore in their presence. When the vessels in my eye refuse to shrivel up and die from their treatments, refuse to be burned and shrink up and continue to grow and break, I'll embrace their will to survive. Their desire to grow in response to the doctors' attempts to kill them. And next month, when the doctors line the pictures of my retina up before me, side by side, and talk about risks and options, I won't tense up. I'll sit back in the chair and close my eyes and breathe. Because I'll believe in my life, the life my body is fighting for.

But right now, my back tight and neck cramped, I hold my breath and count the laser bursts, feeling the rays of light like little fires inside my head, thinking for a moment about radiation and cancer. When my count reaches 735, the doctor pulls me away from the machine. He pats my shoulder and talks about the advancements that have been made in treating diabetics. I feel safe with this man.

I saw the diplomas on his office wall. His wife is expecting their second child. They've been married for six years and the wedding band on his finger is too tight for his chubby hand. His hair is thinning and his glasses are scratched and he knows about diabetes. He had talked to me for a long time before he inserted that needle into my cheek. He even let me see my medical file when I asked and explained to me what the jargon meant. He showed me pictures of my retina. He never handed me a pamphlet.

"How is it, then, that diabetics so often go blind?" I ask.

He sighs. But it is a thoughtful sigh. And he tells me that it is mainly people who do not seek care.

"They ignore the blood they see in their eyes," he says. "They assume it will go away and things will just heal up if they leave it alone. Sometimes by the time they get here they can't see anything through all the debris behind the lens. And we have to wait to do surgeries because we can't see anything, either. Other people don't even know they have diabetes, but there are some diabetic eye conditions we can't do anything for at this time. However, you're so young . . ."

I can barely see him, but I nod because I know there is compassion in his eyes.

". . . and we're seeing more and more young people like yourself with this condition," he continues. "Individuals who developed diabetes as children and ran high blood sugars through their adolescent years. They tend to think themselves invincible. They don't listen to medical advice."

I understand what he is telling me. My sister hated doctors. She said they could kill you if you weren't careful. My sister and I had been living together almost two years in an apartment outside of Des Moines when I found her body. I was on summer break from college and had gone to visit my brother in Minneapolis when I came home and discovered her. She had been dead three days and the July heat sped up the decomposition process. The fan in her bedroom window was blowing on her hair, producing the only movement in the room. But I sat with her for the longest time before I called anyone. The coroner did an autopsy because the cause of death couldn't be determined. She had always refused to go to the doctor for physicals and had no primary physician or medical records. The death was ruled a heart attack. And I wonder if she would have let a doctor save her life anyway.

This doctor pats my shoulder, smoothes back my hair, and tapes a gauze patch over my eye.

"Do you have any other questions?" he asks.

I shake my head. The questions I have are not ones he can answer.

He breathes deeply and settles back into his chair. "You have to be sure you're testing your blood sugars every day, Andie," he says.

"I am," I reply.

And I'm not lying when I say that. I have been giving myself four shots of insulin a day for the last three months and doing my blood work at least twice a day. I have read every book I could find on diabetic complications, prevention of them, treatments. I am taking megadoses of vitamins C and E, and flaxseed oil. One of the books in the library recommended those for diabetic eye conditions. I had even been doing yoga because I heard it could heal the body. But the headstand position had resulted in more broken vessels. The first night I tried that pose, the blood rushed to my head and I saw that familiar red behind my eyes again.

I had even gone to Dr. Manning and asked him about new diabetic medications to help control blood sugars. He had narrowed his eyes and asked me if I was having some kind of problem. I told him no, but that I had decided it was time for me to really start being more careful. He prescribed a new drug called Metformin. It was supposed to aid in the utilization of insulin, but it made me sick. I stayed on it for three weeks, throwing up every morning. And my blood sugars weren't any lower. It only worked if your pancreas was still secreting some insulin and mine had been completely dead for many years. So I stopped taking it, but I just read yesterday about a new medication that should be approved by the FDA this month. It's supposed to slow the absorption of carbohydrates and keep the blood sugar from elevating so quickly. I'm going to go back to Dr. Manning and ask him about that one next week.

"I am being careful," I repeat to this doctor sitting before me.

"Good," he replies. "You have to think about your kidneys. Your eye problems are a sign that the disease has harmed the blood vessels in your body. That means the nerves in your feet, legs, and some internal organs might not be getting the oxygen they need, either."

I know this, too. The books talked about these things. My father knew this, because diabetes runs in our family. The books said that diabetes usually skips a generation and my grandfather had the disease, too. Then my cousin and my sister and myself all developed it. One medical theory is that certain individuals have the predisposition to develop diabetes from birth. They say it's totally genetic. The insulin-producing cells in the pancreas called islets will eventually die, but it's a matter of time. In some people it takes two years and in others it might take up to seventy. It has taken my body nine.

"And you've had the disease for several years," he continues. "You've got to think more than you probably want to about where you're going to be in five or ten years."

My head is starting to ache and I don't feel like talking about the future right now. I start to stand up and he takes my arm, leading me back to the waiting room, where my father is reading a magazine. With the Valium weighing on me, I will sleep while my father drives a hundred miles back to Des Moines through this December blizzard. I will not respond when my father tries to talk to me about an article he read in the waiting room. I will be lost in my own thoughts of fear. Trying to get a mental picture of myself a year from now, five years from now, I will hope I am still reading books and able to see the screen in a movie theater. As the snow beats against the windshield, images of my future will flash through my mind.

In eight hours, I will pull slowly and carefully at the tape on my cheek as I stand before my bathroom mirror, removing the gauze patch and expecting to be engulfed in blackness. But I never am. I will see light through the lens of my eye, but won't be able to read for several days and then only large print for a few weeks. My father will come to my apartment and read my class assignments to me.

My dad walks me down the hall to the elevator. I can see out of my right eye, but that, too, is blurry from broken vessels and repeat surgeries over the past few months. I'm not paying attention and I run into a medical cart. Something falls, but my father says nothing, grasps my arm more firmly, and maneuvers me around it.

When we get outside, the sun is blinding. My dad eases me onto a marble bench and I wait in the cold while he goes to get the car. I keep my eyes closed, but I can feel people walk by. I assume they are staring. Wondering to themselves what could be wrong with the eyes of such a young woman. A man hesitates in front of me. I can smell his cologne and he asks in a sympathetic voice if I need help getting somewhere. Holding my chin to my chest, fumbling for my sunglasses in my purse, I tell him thanks anyway. I can hear him hesitating as he walks away. And others continue to pass by. But I am sure I only hold their attention for a moment. They are carrying pamphlets in their pockets. Detached retinas, macular degeneration, cornea transplants, AIDS-related eye complications. I am not alone as I feel the familiar grasp of my father's hand.

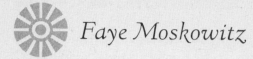

Faye Moskowitz

BECAUSE I COULD NOT STOP FOR DEATH

My mother was a shy woman, modest about her body as women often were in her day, and I scarcely recall ever seeing her fully unclothed. But as she grew more ill, she must have found that modesty a luxury, for she began to ask me to help lace up the corset she felt obliged to wear as long as she was able to get dressed in anything but a gown and robe. . . .

I was fourteen or fifteen at the time, crazy with concern about what I considered the limits of my own body: the floppy breasts with their inverted nipples, the insistent belly, the outspoken thighs, all of which I hid under long baggy sweaters or oversized army surplus shirts. And there she was, her naked body nearing forty, a softer version of my own except for the one searing difference: in the place where her left breast should have been was a thin pillow of flesh; satin scar tissue, still an angry red, forked around it and into her armpit.

Over the next few years, for good or ill, I would slowly come to usurp my mother's place in her home. How she felt about that, I can only speculate; for my part, I took some satisfaction in my growing status as mother to my two younger brothers and as surrogate "wife" to the father I adored. Among my many relatives, I became known approvingly as "the girl with the golden hands," the one whose mother allowed no one else to touch her.

An army of well-meaning women marched through my house in those days, my aunts Bessie, Bernice, Frieda, and my Bobbe Brocha—clucking, sighing, exchanging meaningful looks, rearranging cupboards and closets so nothing was ever where we thought it might be, filling our refrigerator with covered dishes of food that didn't quite taste like my mother's cooking, food that got shoved to a back shelf by more dishes, food that eventually bloomed with exotic flowers—pink and red and green—and was thrown out to more clucking.

No matter what we called them—maid, cleaning lady, or housekeeper—no one would work for long in a house with so many mistresses. I came to recognize with dread the ever more sullen face, the tray set down on the porcelain sink with too deliberate a clatter, the damp mop wielded like a weapon over the kitchen linoleum: all signs that we would soon be poring over the situations-wanted ads one more time.

As I had for several previous years, I kept a diary for 1947, my sixteenth year and the final twelve months of my mother's life. When I first opened that red-bound book again after more than thirty years, I was stunned to find only a scant handful of references to her sickness. Instead, I meticulously record almost daily trips to the butcher shop, the grocer's, the bakery. The many mornings I couldn't bring myself to get up for school are documented; I write about my hopes for an acting career and my growing interest in Zionism. The days go by. I cook corn soup for my brothers' lunch: a can of Premier Cream-style Corn, a can of milk, a lump of butter. My brothers are twelve and six. We eat salami sandwiches, washed down with Vernor's Ginger-ale. I attempt to prepare a brisket for my father, "the way he likes it," roasted forever, then sliced and roasted some more so it will fall

apart in a gravy of carrots and onions. I take my little brother to
the J.L. Hudson Company and stand in line with him for hours
waiting to see western star Bill Boyd, and when we finally reach
the white-haired actor in cowboy boots and ten-gallon hat, my
brother says, "Was that really Hopalong Cassidy or was it only a
dream?" I wash clothes when the latest cleaning lady fails "to
show" yet again, check the oil level daily during winter so our
house will stay warm. And endlessly, in purple ink and even
more purple prose, I examine my relationship to various
boyfriends with an obsessive scrutiny that breaks my heart today.

For much as I basked in the approbation of my relatives, I
hungered for life as a normal teenager. When everyone who
counted spent Friday nights at meetings and parties, what was I
to do with a mother who might be lying alone, hurting, needing
me to take her to the bathroom or just to talk to? Often, my
father would stay out until after midnight. How could I blame
him for fleeing the sadness of our house? I couldn't face it even
in my diary. Toward the end of her life when my mother was
heavily sedated, her doctor told me that she was actually "quite
comfortable," that she continued to cry out from the memory of
pain and nothing else. I took that to be another of the well-
intentioned lies with which we sought to protect one another.

My dilemmas seemed global. How could I keep my mother's
condition a secret from the world outside my house, when it was
friendship I was seeking, not pity? I was convinced that having a
sick mother made me different from other girls at a time in my
life when I would have killed for conformity. Nothing was too
insignificant for my envy. I even coveted the little wooden nail
brush with which my friend Malcah scrubbed the bathroom sink
after we washed our hands at her house. She mustn't forget or her
mother would scream, she told me. I saw that tiny brush as an
emblem of the distance of my life from hers. My mother had long
before given up sovereignty over such small concerns.

And there was something else: Like most girls my age, I

wouldn't have deigned to ask my mother's advice about much, but I bitterly resented the illness whose gravity not only diminished the importance of my problems, but closed off the possibility of answers had I *wanted* to ask. One afternoon after days of endless consultations with Malcah and any number of unsatisfying shopping expeditions to Hudson's, I snuck into my mother's closet and took a black rayon dress embroidered in sequins to wear to a formal party. As if my mother would have denied me the use of that dress. As if she would ever be able to wear it again anyway. Better to simply take it, I figured, than bother a dying woman with anything as frivolous as a decision about a party dress.

Day after day, while my mother was still capable of moving about, she waited in her bedroom for me to come home from school so I could help her undress. In the fashion of the time, a large doll in a black velvet gown sat with skirts spread over a chartreuse taffeta bedcover, a sweet smile fixed forever on her porcelain face. My mother's cedar chest stood nearby. Among the embroidered linens from the Old Country, a long brown braid of my mother's hair, glistening with naphthalene, lay coiled like a small animal. In that long-ago room, surrounded by her possessions, I turned my head from the disconcerting image of her mutilated body, her dark sex, and the salmon-colored harness with its unyielding bones and twisted laces . . . held my breath so the scents of her in the hollows under her arms, the folds of her skin, the woman smell between her thighs would not invade my dreams. . . .

I managed to bury the memory for years, but perhaps it was back then that I first came to believe I, too, would have breast cancer one day. If my mother's body and my own so resembled each other, I reasoned, why was the sickness not inevitable? Superstition, a stowaway from the Old Country, had caught a ride in steerage with brass *shabbas* candlesticks and featherbeds and lurked at every corner to feed my fatalism. I ingested old wives' tales along with my Cream of Wheat, and not solely from my Jewish relatives in Detroit's ghetto. As a child, in small town Jackson, Michigan, I watched a gentile neighbor pick heavy clusters of Concord blues one fall from an arched trellis that stood between our houses. Suddenly she shivered in the balmy September wind. "Someone is walking on my grave," she mumbled, staring past me in the wine-drenched air as if I weren't there at all.

Such a strange thing for that woman to say, I thought, and forgot about it until, years after my mother died, I first read W. Somerset Maugham's retelling of a folk tale named "The Appointment in Samarra." As the story goes, a serving man menaced by the figure of Death in the Baghdad marketplace begs a horse from his master that he might ride the sixty miles to Samarra, hide from his pursuer, and thereby avoid his fate. Later that day, the master goes down to the market and asks Death why he threatened the servant.

I can still remember how the story's closing lines caught me unawares with the shocking pain of a trap sprung. "That was not a threatening gesture," Death said, "it was only a start of surprise. I was astonished to see him in Baghdad, for I had an appointment with him tonight in Samarra." "Oh," I said, putting down the book, shuddering as the neighbor woman's words of long before came back to me. "Someone is walking on my grave," I told myself and of their own accord, my fingers leapt to my left breast. I took the tale as a reminder of how futile it was to try to escape my destiny.

Though I am an educated woman who reads whatever she can get her hands on, I never read about cancer if I could help it. I began going for yearly physical checkups only late in life and, despite my worries, or perhaps because of them (what I don't know won't hurt me), I never practiced self-examination. Occasionally, I would run my hands down my breasts in the shower and mutter a prayer of thanks when I found no lumps or bumps. I smoked like the proverbial chimney long after my friends all quit, and it wasn't until I turned sixty that I conceded to an annual mammogram, and then because I was bullied into it by my family doctor.

In short, while I fully expected I would get breast cancer one day, I tamped down my fears and simply ignored the prospect as much as I was able. This is not a prescription I would recommend even to my enemies. Some nights, when my chronic insomnia provided me no hiding place, I would lie next to my sleeping husband, alone as it is possible to be, weeping as the drumbeat of my anxieties matched my heart's terrified rhythms.

That wasn't the end of it, of course; in the dark, stripped of my defenses, I assumed every mole, every headache, every digestive disturbance was also an indicator of an incurable disease already too far gone for anything but sympathy. All this is not to say I took my self-imposed prospects completely lying down. Like the serving man in the myth, I had a plan to outwit Death, and it was devilishly uncomplicated: I would simply keep myself too busy to get sick.

And so, semester after semester, as students fell around me, like flies in the days of Flit—from flu and mono and strep and stress—I maintained my snowy attendance record. "Ah, the youth of today . . ." I would say to anyone who would listen, but, just as my mother had, I always muttered, *"Kayn aynhoreh!"* to placate the Evil Eye in case it was hanging around waiting to punish my chutzpah. I was everywhere: the consummate wife, mother, grandmother, and friend; teacher, writer, lecturer, doer of good, with a life so slick and seamless, no illness could find purchase on it. After the surgeon announced the malignancy to us, my husband and I left the doctor's office and walked to our car in silence. What is there to say? I thought, my bowels loosening in fear, but then the words came out of my mouth anyway. "I don't have *time* for this," I told him.

I still find it hard to think of myself as having been "sick." Thanks to mammography and the early detection it provides, to sharp-eyed technicians, wise and able doctors, good fortune, and perhaps, even, yes, my dead mother looking out for me somewhere, my cancer was contained and needed only a lumpectomy with follow-up radiation. I never felt unwell for a moment; once or twice I've considered the entire episode akin to a particularly unsettling nightmare with no more aftershock than the usual vague unease that fades with morning. But of course, that's fantasy, wishful thinking. Six months after my last radiation treatment—checkup time—I'm just beginning to grab hold of what has happened to my life.

Still, it's not my nature to think too closely about illness; denial is more my style; I find writing about it even more difficult. As if they were soles on a newly waxed floor, the words stick, come away with a reluctant thwack. Perhaps it's my belief in the magic of language. Even now, I can hardly bring myself to type the word *cancer*. When my mother was dying, the name of her illness, for all I knew, might have been, "Don't ask," for that was the response whenever anyone inquired.

One day not long before my mother's death, I heard the rap of her cane through the kitchen ceiling, the signal that she needed my help. By then she could no longer even walk to the bathroom, and I had pretty much relinquished her care to two shifts of visiting nurses. Perhaps they were between shifts because for the first time in weeks my mother and I were alone together. Now the green taffeta spread hung folded on a quilt rack at the foot of a metal hospital bed; the doll, banished from my mother's bed, sat on the cedar chest with her velvet skirts fanned out, smiling her sweet painted smile. I thought of that braid of dead hair underneath her, bits of moth flakes shining in the strands like melting drops of snow. Anything to avoid looking at what lay in the bed. "Faygeleh," my mother said, plucking at a fold in the blankets, smoothing them, trying to make the words casual by the homely gestures. "Tell me something," she said at last. "Do you think I'm ever going to get better?" How could I answer her truthfully, when I was bound as inextricably as she was by the complicated deception we were playing out? I think by then I had guessed she was doomed, but my family's rules allowed no such admission. Uttering the word might affirm it. I could only say, "Of course, of course you'll get better," and in doing so, help conspire to keep her wrapped more tightly alone inside her fear. She never asked me that question again.

So I grew up considering *cancer* a word so powerful that like the name for the Almighty it was best uttered in euphemism. After my surgery, I would drive around with my car windows rolled up, forcing myself to practice saying out loud, "I have cancer, I have cancer," fully expecting, at first, to spontaneously combust like Krook, that character out of Dickens's *Bleak House*. The first time I spoke about "the cancer" to my friends, I felt as if the word fluttered in the air above my head for a moment, a banner in the wake of an advertising plane.

I've read and heard so many accounts of lives turned around by bouts with serious illness or perilous situations; no such dramatic changes have occurred for me. So far, I've found no sudden metamorphosis from my old passive there's-not-much-I-can-do-about-sickness (except ignore it) self into a proactive, assertive patient. Which isn't to say that I'm not working on it.

My OB once gave me an approving fatherly pat on the shoulder moments before he ordered the scopolamine that would obliterate all memory of my impending delivery. "She's a good girl," I heard him say. "She never makes waves." I drifted off to La La Land on the tides of what I, then, took to be the ultimate compliment.

Decades later, true to form, I relied on my internist's referrals and got no second opinions until long after my radiation was completed. I haven't read *Dr. Susan Love's Breast Book* yet, and I'm not sure I will. Though I call myself a feminist, I realize I didn't seek out women doctors for a disease that afflicts mainly women; my internist, my surgeon, my radiologist, and my oncologist are all white males, and I hardly gave that fact a thought until well after the fact. So, in a time of need, I fell right back into the familiar patriarchy of my Orthodox Jewish upbringing. "The apple doesn't fall far from the tree," as my mother used to say.

And because my diagnosis and the start of a new semester at the university coincided, I also responded to that situation in my own typical fashion: I set about ensuring that my normal life would be disrupted as little as possible. Five mornings a week for thirty-three days I went to the hospital for radiation treatments. There, I undressed, wrapped myself in a green hospital gown, and lay down on a table under a space age machine that to my mind had the aura and physical dimensions of *Challenger*. Some days I imagined it malfunctioning, refusing to stop on its downward trajectory toward my breast, saw myself flattened under it like a cardboard cat out of a Tom and Jerry cartoon. I learned to pull my gown off one shoulder to expose my breast, reach back with my left arm, and grasp the bar provided, thereby contorting my upper body into a parody of a provocative pose: Marilyn Monroe in *Some Like It Hot*. But I hadn't time for ironies; by 8:30, I was at my desk at school, another treatment reduced to one more tick on my calendar. To my shame, I'm still driven to boast that I didn't miss a single day's work.

No one but my husband knew of my problems at first. I saw no reason to worry my children during the preliminary tests, but as the days went on, the silence itself became an issue, something else to ultimately explain and justify. I said nothing to my morning walking partners, my two dearest friends, and as we headed for the National Cathedral, chatting about our grandchildren or our busy lives or the latest headlines, my secret fell between us like a scrim. I knew my husband was as frightened as I was, and so, intending to shield him, I foolishly pretended to business as usual, thereby isolating each of us from the comfort of the other. I will tell everyone when I find out this was all a mistake, I promised myself, but by the time the date for surgery was set, I determined that my silence was really self-serving. I wasn't sparing the people who loved me from pain. Rather, I was shutting them out of my life, denying them any opportunity they might have to show their concern for me. I was condemning myself to the isolation once imposed on my mother.

One night, a couple of weeks into the radiation, and on the wings of two glasses of white wine, I burst into tears and told my friend Sue that the most awful part about the situation was just having to admit that I was not the strong one, after all. I couldn't deal with how ashamed I was of being sick. "Dey got Chahlie," I said, doing my best Marlon Brando impression, laughing, crying, mopping my eyes with a paper napkin. It was just so hard to finally admit to a vulnerability that had been my ugly secret for so long.

Today I can look back and find much good in what has happened. I've had my memento mori, but I see no reason to keep it constantly in view like those skulls sitting around on tables in the paintings of saints. There's a strange kind of relief in having finally faced what has threatened me for so many years. Like Mersault's father in Camus's *The Stranger*, who went to witness every public execution he heard of, I have caught a glimpse of death and this time, at least, I have walked away. For that, I am profoundly grateful.

In some ways, my identification with my mother is deeper than it ever was, for now I can more clearly imagine how alone she must have felt with no permission to speak of her illness, and no one in whom she could confide her fears. To speak of it would have been to confirm the worst, and that she was never allowed to do. Most important, I've finally learned to stop being angry at her for getting sick, and that lesson has stretched to include forgiveness for myself. I know I'm not to blame for my breast cancer, any more than she was, and if, God forbid, I have a recurrence, it won't be because I brought it on myself. How simple and obvious this all seems, and yet I have had to come so far to reach this understanding. And there's more. . . .

"*Mir zol zein far dir*," my mother would say when one of us children was sick or hurt, "it should happen to me instead of you." Years ago, when my own son Frank was about five, he became gravely ill with spinal meningitis. For days his small body, limp and feverish, lay curled up on a cot in a closet-sized hospital isolation room. Whatever was happening in our lives then, our ambitions and our daily concerns—house, work, even the welfare of our other two children—fell away in the face of our terrible grief. Outwardly, we were on a kind of automatic pilot, my husband and I, asking what we thought were intelligent questions of the doctors, giving out bulletins to anxious relatives, advising each other to eat, get some sleep. Had we been able to step back and look at ourselves, we might have said we were proud of how well we were "holding up." But one day our pediatrician pulled us out into the hospital corridor and told us that Frank would have to undergo yet another diagnostic procedure, this time a painful spinal tap.

We both fell apart then; I remember we leaned against opposite walls of that narrow hallway and cried, so devastated we couldn't even touch each other. To see our child suffer: Nothing in our lives had prepared us for such agony. I knew then as I know now that I could have said, "*Mir zol zein*," until the end of time, and I would not have been able to absorb one moment of my child's pain. So we both did the one thing we could do; we took turns holding our son in our arms and let him feel the blaze of our love leap like silver lightning from our bodies to his.

That scalding memory has taken its place in my recovery, too. I have seen how moved and sustained I've been by the embrace of family, friends, colleagues, and the professionals involved in my getting well. Susan and Ruth set their alarms for an insane hour each weekday so I didn't have to give up my morning walk; my husband took it on himself to drive me to every radiation session, though I certainly could have gotten there myself; my friend Dan appeared in the hospital anteroom many mornings after my treatments as if he had just happened by at 8:30 A.M., waiting to walk me over to the university; my four children called every day, just to "check in." I felt them all, and so many others, too, gathering me up in a bountiful harvest of compassion. Once or twice I've given a cheer for the girl with the golden hands. I was a good girl, wasn't I? It's easier to say that now.

My cancer was discovered at the close of what had been one of the happiest years of my life. Some months before, almost sixty-five with an unconventional academic career, I had been granted tenure at George Washington University. With tenure came a sabbatical spent reading long delicious books and writing when I was moved to do it. We wintered in Florida with the retirees, feeling absurdly young in their midst, exchanging congratulations like the rest of the "snowbirds" whenever we heard a weather report of blizzards back home. I sat in the sun, learned to swim, found a saucy new hair color, lost twenty pounds. In short: heaven. Still, my mother would have said that somewhere in those glorious months, I let my guard down, got too careless, forgot to whisper, "*Kayn aynhoreh,*" knock on wood. I know better, of course. I know that my calm and joyful year provided sustenance on which to feed during the sadder one that followed.

In the context of illness, the primary meaning of recovery involves returning to a former state of good health, but I see now that my road to wellness has allowed me or forced me to recover so much else. In the wake of the cancer, memories long lost, connections never made continue to flood my consciousness. Somewhere in my adolescence, for example, in the years my mother was ill, I formed a friendship with Emily Dickinson that remains to this day. Her enigmatic little poems with their breathtaking first lines enchanted me.

Ours was a three-bedroom house on Burlingame; over time,

we all moved from room to room to accommodate the various stages of my mother's illness. After the night nurses came to stay and my father needed my bed, I would sit in the basement room to which I had been exiled and read Dickinson's words out loud, commit them to memory. Though I shut doors and curtained off my space with heavy damask draperies salvaged from the attic, I couldn't drown out the terrible sounds of my mother's crying. Sometimes I sat cross-legged on my chenille spread, rocking back and forth, fingers in my ears, feeling the oil furnace vibrating nearby, while I stubbornly recited Emily's words. Death, an uninvited boarder, a guest at our dinner table, became a familiar part of my lexicon, too, and thanks to Dickinson, a less daunting one.

Not surprisingly, I found myself drawn to other poems about dying. How I squared lying down with kings and my budding socialism, I can't recall, but I even deigned to take comfort from "Thanatopsis," William Cullen Bryant's poem we were assigned in school. I mourned for A. E. Housman's rose-lipt maidens and lightfoot lads, seeing in their untimely deaths a shadow of my own mortality. Days when I was feeling particularly sorry for myself, Walter de la Mare's "An Epitaph" could teach me a lesson about mutability, could tear me apart in a peculiarly consoling way: "And when I crumble, who will remember / This Lady of the West Country?"

But it was Dickinson I came back to again and again, and for some reason, to the poem that begins, "Because I could not stop for Death, / He kindly stopped for me." Perhaps the notion of death as a courtly suitor appealed to my teenage romanticism; perhaps the personification helped domesticate a state that seemed, at the time, so wild and foreign to me; who knows? I hardly considered the individual words, just let the images wash over me. But lately, those opening lines have returned with a strange insistence. One night, sitting in my darkened study, unable to sleep, I suddenly realized that I had been missing the irony in them all along. "Because I could not stop . . ." And I thought of the task of perpetual motion I had set myself once, as if sickness and death wait for the caesuras in our lives, as if we can name the time of our assignation. I understand now that sickness makes no appointment and is not impressed with busy lives or concerned about interrupting them. Sometimes the old clichés hit the nail on the head: You can run, but you can't hide.

So, yes, I have my old life back, and a sweet one it is, but there is a difference now. I am caring for myself (in both senses of the word), and that means experiencing the time left me—and I pray it's many years—in a slightly different way. My days are as crowded as ever, one stepping on the hem of the next, but I'm trying to spend my hours more deliberately now as if each were a golden coin, luminous and precious as the full moon. I am learning to say another new word besides *cancer*, and that word is *no*. No to people I don't want to see, no to things I don't want to do. And I'm rediscovering the beauty of *yes*. Yes to what pleases me; yes to what will make me feel good.

We learned during the Depression never to throw away anything that was still useful. Perhaps the economy was a holdover from frugal days in the Old Country. In any event, there was no disposable society for us. Shopkeepers wrapped bundles in twine that unreeled from a great ball hanging over the counter, and I remember that my mother never cut the string when she unwrapped the packages at home. She slipped the string off whole and tossed it into a drawer, where the bits and pieces of twine over time formed themselves into a coil as dense as my mother's shorn brown braid. One morning I would come rummaging for kite string or a length of twine for a cat's cradle, and then would begin the tedious process of searching for a beginning in all that tangle. But then, we don't call that loose thread a beginning, do we? Rather, it's an "end," we look for. And so it is with my story. What is beginning? What is end? Aren't they, perhaps, both finally the same?

Tracy Thompson

THE GIFT OF A NORMAL LIFE

It is deep in the night; morning is a mirage. And the thing I have dreaded has happened: The beast is outside my window. It is a mechanical beast, and it screams—steel against steel, a heavy thundering of weight. There is the oppressive sense of something huge and black. It is confined for now, but it threatens to bolt loose, breaking all natural laws; if I move, it might notice me. I lie motionless, trying not to breathe. The beast slows, grumbling, then shudders, slides and finally comes to a raucous, banging stop outside my window. Somehow the silence is worse than the cacophony that preceded it. It is a silence of something about to happen, broken at intervals by another metallic groan as the beast moves, muttering in its sleep. The fear is a bubble that rises from the pit of my stomach to my lips. Then there is a shadow in the doorway: my mother.

"It's a freight train, Tace," she says tiredly. "Go back to sleep." In a minute, I hear her voice across the hallway, in my parents' bedroom, "I swear, I think she can hear those trains the minute they leave the station in Chattanooga."

*   *   *

It is summer, and I am in the backyard, a shelter under a close, cool canopy of oak trees. My mother's chaise lounge rests on bare dirt, next to the duck pen. She is sitting with the mother of one of my playmates, and they are sipping iced tea from tall frosted metal glasses, and I should be comfortable. But I'm not. I feel a familiar, gnawing fear. What's wrong? Something's wrong. I keep waiting for it to happen. "It's so nice to sit back here when it's raining, the trees are so close you don't get wet at all," my mother is saying. Somehow that casual remark is branded in my brain as if she had said, "The Russians are bombing us" or "I am dying." Those were the things I expected to hear.

It is years later. I am in fourth grade. One day I leave my seat in the classroom and go down the hall to the girls' room. I walk close to the wall, trying not to take up space I feel I have no right to. Inside the restroom, I crouch behind a toilet, my arms wrapped around my knees. I do not cry; I am just wordlessly sad. I have been wordlessly sad for quite a while. People seem to take this for granted. "My hill and dale girl," my mother calls me, and I have no way of knowing that the way I feel is at all unusual. I only know it feels unbearable. And so for relief I sit behind the toilet, where at least it's cool and quiet, away from the boisterous classroom and the noise that seems to hurt my skin. Unable to figure out why I am sad, equipped with only a child's logic, I eventually decide that it is because President Kennedy is still dead.

Even then, this rationale did not seem satisfactory.

And so over time, the typical anxieties of childhood became something else—merged into a different and altogether darker pattern, the way drops form rivulets that wear paths in stone. Something a bit like that was going on in my brain. But it would be years before I knew the word for what was happening, and decades before I truly understood what that word meant.

The word was depression—a milquetoast word, really, one

that does no justice to the ancient shadow on the brain it supposedly describes. How can it? It covers too much, from the transient grief of a motorist whose car has been dented to the howling desolation of the man who lifts a loaded gun to his temple. I call it the Beast instead—a label that casually came to mind one day and that I discarded at first because it seemed melodramatic. But on reflection, it suits this thing that is now part of my brain, something I refer to at times as "him"—though I imagine "him" less as a creature than as a force, something that has slipped outside the bounds of natural existence, a psychic freight train of roaring despair.

For most of my life, the Beast has been my implacable and unpredictable enemy, disappearing for months or years, then returning in strength. Our skirmishes have been too many to number, but when it comes to major battles, I count four: 1975, 1981, 1985, and 1989—dates that mark the onset of severe depressive episodes that lasted anywhere from six months to two years. It was during the most recent of those major battles, on a bleak February afternoon in 1990, that the Beast came closest to a final victory. I remember the moment vividly: I sat alone in the *Washington Post* pressroom at the federal courthouse, fingers poised above the keyboard of my computer. I was fearful of discovery, ready to erase my file at the sound of a footstep. But stronger than fear was the compulsion to leave some record behind, to describe the intention that had led me the previous night to pack up my journalism awards, to arrange for someone to take care of my cats, and to write a will.

"Right now I am feeling that I want to die," I typed. "I am ashamed of this. I feel it is a weakness."

The next day, under the momentary sway of a sane impulse that saved my life, I did something I had spent two decades trying to avoid: With the help of a friend, I checked myself into a psychiatric hospital. It took more than a year, many hours of therapy and half a dozen experiments with different combinations of antidepressants before I felt safe enough to say, "I am well." But eventually, I could say it. Life did not return to normal; it got better than that. In the aftermath of that terrible time, I returned to my job as a journalist and found new passion and depth in my work. More important, I stopped looking for a man who would rescue me and found a man who would love me as an equal. Today, he is my husband. Life is good.

Which is not to say that life is perfect. Because of my long history with this illness, I know it will recur; it has already, in mild form, two or three times. But now I know my enemy. I've even named him—and naming is the gift God gave to Adam; naming is power. Nowadays, what interests me is understanding the Beast, in all his manifestations. Depression is an illness that imprints itself uniquely on each personality; in a way, its mysteries point us to the answer to that ancient philosophical conundrum, the mind-body problem. Exactly how that works—how biochemical changes in the brain conspire with genetic predisposition or external events, or both, to create a disorder that can tempt the mind to its own destruction—we do not yet know.

But it begins with who we are, which begins with the place and the people we come from.

Most of my early memories are like sunlight through a tree, dappled with dread. At night, after everybody was asleep, I would kneel at the cedar chest in my bedroom, making a shrine by spreading the white sheer curtains around me. There I would bargain with God for relief from this awful sense of guilt and impending disaster. If I could be good enough, my father would not lose his job, my mother would not die of cancer, our house would not burn down. I would go to bed holding a cross made of plastic that absorbed light and glowed for a while in the dark, hoping to drift to sleep while the emblem of my Savior watched over me, a magical purplish glow. But the glow often faded before sleep came. On some nights, I drifted in and out of an anxious doze, snapped into consciousness by the crowing of my grand-mother's rooster across the cornfield from my bedroom. It might be dawn; it might be 3:00 A.M. The sound seemed an accusation aimed at me for sins I could not name.

Verily, I say unto thee, That this night, before the cock crow, thou shalt deny me thrice.

Anxiety was in the air, like a virus.

My mother was afraid. "I had a terrible dream last night," she said one day. The four of us—my parents, my sister, Nonny, and I—were in the car, at the top of a hill deep in the countryside south of Atlanta. We had been "visiting," dropping by relatives' houses on a Sunday afternoon, an old Southern custom. Now it was late. Ahead of us, the sun had burned to a dull orange and was sinking behind a knotted bramble of bare tree branches, throwing shadows across monochrome fields marked with the stubble of last summer's corn. My mother was always having ter-rible dreams, prophecies of disaster or interminable slow-motion nightmares in which she could not escape the thing that was pur-suing her. It was the legacy of her past; a childhood of poverty, the early loss of both parents, years of deprivation and abuse from relatives. From all of that she had salvaged her Southern funda-mentalist faith. Jesus was her refuge, the one Being who had never deserted her or made her feel unworthy; she loved her Savior with the fervor of an abandoned child. But even kindly Jesus warned us of doomsday, and that was what she was talking about now. My sister and I leaned over the front seat; she sat beside my father as he drove, and looked into the sunset. "The sun was blood red, like it was the end of the world," she said.

Her words gave me a chill. "What happened in the dream, Mama?" I asked. "Were we in it?"

"Yes," she said, shortly. Then she shuddered. "I don't want to talk about it." No matter how I pressed her, she would not say more. I leaned back into the car seat. How horrible it must have been, that she couldn't tell us. The dream was an omen; I believed in omens. We expected the end of the world, the Second Coming of Christ. It could happen at any moment. *For no man knows the day or the hour . . . I will come on thee as a thief, and thou shalt not know what hour I will come upon thee . . . The sun shall be darkened, and the moon shall not give her light, and the stars of heaven shall fall, and the powers that are in heaven shall be shaken.* But I knew what her dream was about: It was about me, being left behind. I was not going to Heaven.

I could not remember a time when I did not know that. The faith that steeled my mother for life, which my father accepted and which seemed to come so naturally for my older sister, did not come naturally to me.

From the beginning, my confusion centered on this thing called the Second Coming. It was supposed to be the moment of ultimate rapture for all Christians, when believers were to be caught up in the air and taken directly to Heaven. We heard the Bible verses in church. *I tell you, in that night there shall be two men in one bed; the one shall be taken and the other shall be left . . . Two men shall be in the field; the one shall be taken, and the other left.* It was a moment all Christians supposedly longed for. But every description sounded terrible, disorienting and strange to me. I just didn't get it. And the fact that this alternate view made no sense, that I awaited the Second Coming with horror and dread, was proof of my difference from others. And different, to a child, was a curse. Different meant defective.

"The angels beckon me from Heaven's open door, and I can't feel at home in this world anymore," we sang in church. But the world was my home. I was in love with the tangible; in my mind, even the letters of the alphabet possessed shape, color, texture, weight.

This was Georgia, twenty miles south of Atlanta. The time was the early '60s.

One night when I was 7, President Kennedy was on television. I said, "What is it?" The adults stared at the television and did not answer. Afterward, we had a family conference around the round oak kitchen table about what to do if a nuclear bomb fell on Atlanta. Do not get on the bus, my mother ordered; I will come get you, no matter what. At church, pale men in dark horn-rimmed glasses bent over me and asked me to suppose that godless Russians had threatened to shoot me if I did not renounce Jesus Christ. What would I do? I would renounce Jesus and go home, I thought; maybe then they would leave me alone. But I didn't say that. Telling the pale men that I was ready to knuckle under to the godless Russians was not what they wanted to hear.

The imminence of nuclear war, centered around someplace called Cuba, got tangled up in my mind with the Second Coming. I couldn't decide which scared me more: the godless Russians or Jesus in the sky, coming for the Final Judgment. Somehow I always thought both events would take place directly over the marquee of the Roosevelt Drive-In Theater, visible from our back doorstep.

My mother remembers one Fourth of July in either 1962 or 1963. She and my father had stepped out into the driveway around midnight to watch the annual fireworks show put on by the drive-in. My sister and I were asleep, they thought, in the back bedroom. At some point, between whistles and pops, my mother became aware of screaming from the back of the house. It was the two of us, awakened by the noise. We thought it was the end of the world.

I have no memory of this event. I knew only that annihilation loomed. It could happen while I was asleep, while I was pulling up my socks, while I was fighting with my sister; I could wake up from a nap and discover myself doomed to eternal Hell while the rest of my family had gone to Heaven in the Great Rapture or the giant mushroom cloud, whichever came first.

There were clear signs on at least one side of my family—my father's—that a vulnerability to mood disorders was woven into the family genes.

At some point in the 1930s, one story went, my father's mother simply went to bed and stayed there for a decade. No one knew exactly why, though there was some vague mention of "female troubles." In retrospect, it seems she simply gave up on life. My father was sent to live with his aunt in Gadsden, Alabama, while his older brother stayed at home to help care for their mother.

Years later, as an adult, I learned of another child—a girl born before my father, whose existence my grandmother rarely spoke of. Her name was Helen Faye. She had died at age three in a household accident. While my grandmother's back was turned, Helen Faye managed to climb up on a stool near the stove, where she upset a pot of boiling water. She died several days later.

My father's father was a roguishly handsome man who was one of Birmingham's first motorcycle policemen. No one in the family ever heard my grandmother call him anything but "Boy"— not in the demeaning sense also known then in the South, as addressed to black men, but as a simple word of endearment, an unusual gesture in a woman so reticent. At some point after Helen Faye's death, he left. In some versions of the story, he simply departed—went out for a pack of cigarettes, as the saying goes, and never came back; in other versions, they had fought over his decision to go look for work in Mobile. His brother found him, years later, working on the docks in San Francisco. When I was an infant, my mother says, there came news that he had remarried. My grandmother was living with my parents then—she spent most of her life, after her bedridden period, shuttling from one son's house to the other—and my mother was awakened in the night by the sound of racking sobs. By then, my grandfather had been gone for several decades. My grandmother still wore her wedding ring.

So death and abandonment took up residence in our house, trapped under a blanket of suffocating silence, and for comfort there was a kindly Jesus who might come at any moment to judge the quick and the dead. By the time I formed my first memories of my father's mother, she was a bent woman, more frail and elderly than her years, who sat on the sofa and seemed to absorb all the light and levity in the room. Her need for human contact—any kind—was insatiable, but her usual way of asking for it was to request personal favors. "Would you trim my toenails?" she would ask. "Would you wash my hair?"

Of my mother's parents I know even less.

She has a picture, taken about 1929, of two little girls standing against the side of a house. It appears to be morning. Both have bobbed hair and are carrying Easter baskets. The older one, about seven, is looking directly into the camera. The younger one, who is about three, is looking off to one side—distracted for the moment by a butterfly, perhaps, or the appearance of the family cat. Looming across the foreground are two large shadows, a man and a woman, evidently the adults who are taking the picture. The three-year-old is my mother. The shadows are her only visible reminder of her parents.

She never knew her father. He left not long after that, for reasons never explained, the way men left families in the Depression to seek work elsewhere or simply to rid themselves of the burdens of a wife and children. My mother was told that he had died. She has only vague memories of her mother—a serious, deeply religious woman with auburn hair, who worked in the Nabisco factory in downtown Atlanta, making biscuit boxes. She died of influenza when my mother was four, the winter after that Easter snapshot was made. My aunt—the seven-year-old in that picture—was told that as their mother was dying, she made her own sister promise to take care of her two little girls.

The promise was casually made and just as casually broken; poverty had made my mother's family bitter and mean-spirited. Two children, to them, simply meant a bigger grocery bill. Neither my mother nor her sister have ever spoken of their relatives with anything approaching affection. The only uncle who was financially stable, an accountant with Coca-Cola, did petition to adopt them. But the courts refused to give him custody, citing his alcoholism. For a time, my mother and her sister shuttled among the homes of various relatives, treated like the unwanted children they were. My mother remembers a family argument that ended with the two of them being pushed out of a car and left by the side of a deserted road in the country. How long they were there she does not remember; it seemed like a week, though it was probably not more than an hour. She remembers standing there with her sister in the tall grass, watching the car drive away. She was six years old; her sister was ten.

The two of them wound up as full-time residents of the Southern Christian Children's Home in downtown Atlanta. During one particularly lean period, money was so scarce that the children got a piece of bread with some pasty peanut butter for dinner at night. My mother learned to eat the bread and save the peanut butter, rolling it into a ball to eat in bed at night before she went to sleep.

My aunt left the children's home at sixteen to make an unwise marriage. My mother was luckier: She was adopted at the age of eight. Not surprisingly, she lavished her unqualified adoration on the man who came to her rescue. He was a rawboned Georgia farmer named John Derrick, whose wife, Cora, could not have children. I called him Pa-Pa. By the time I was four or five, he was retired from Southern Railway, the job he had taken to pay the bills. But at heart he was still a farmer, and up to the year before he died, he was still reflexively putting seeds in the soil. One of my earliest memories is of sitting on his lap while he fished a knife out of a front pocket of his worn overalls to peel an apple for me.

My memories of those years are primitive and sensory:

• Of a dirt road that is red clay, gluey and slick when wet. I dig it out from under my nails, find it between my toes. I walk behind Pa-Pa as he plows the upper cornfield with his white mule, Becky. It is early spring, and the crumbling clots of dirt are cold, as if the plow is opening up the winter earth to the steady spring sun. The dirt smells dark, a musky scent of manure and rain.

• Or of another spring, a few years later, as I lie on the earth outside the barn, across the dirt lane from where Pa-Pa plowed. He died on a spring day like this, a day like an old lady's idea of Heaven: a little too hot, a little too perfumed, a little too floral. I smell honeysuckle. Running under that scent, like the harsh one-note plaint of a didjeridu, is a faint animal stench from the barn. The sun is hot on my back. I lie face down in the grass, my cheek pressed to the earth, and while I sleep it seems I can feel the earth move, almost imperceptibly, toward late afternoon.

So much sadness—and yet, by the time my parents had met and married, life seemed bright, the worst hardships behind them. Pictures of my mother from that period show a beautiful woman with awkward, rounded-shouldered posture, a pose she adopted because she thought her height was unfeminine. She was slim, with red hair, green eyes and a gardenia-pale complexion. My father was skinny in those years, with black curly hair and an intense gaze that my sister would later inherit. He came home from World War II, they met while working at Delta Airlines, and they married a year later, following their version of a script that millions of returning veterans and their brides were also following. Pa-Pa carved out eight acres of his woods and cornfields next door to his own house, and my father ordered some house blueprints out of a magazine. He and Pa-Pa built most of the house from scratch, contracting out the skilled labor but mixing cement and hoisting two-by-fours themselves. My mother plastered the walls. The result was a split-level ranch house with a pine-paneled den and a two-sided living room fireplace I still recall with affection. My sister was conceived in that house in the winter of 1953. I was born two years later.

In those years, my father was getting his law degree at night while working by day in the cargo department at Delta. I was lulled to sleep at night by the sound of my mother's Royal manual typewriter in the kitchen, as she typed his school papers. The two of them were well matched. After his motherless childhood, my father soaked up my mother's unqualified love the way thirsty ground accepts water; with my father, my mother felt truly wanted at last. They honeymooned in California, stopping in Los Angeles to visit her sister, by then on her second husband. In a picture from that trip, my mother lounges against a low-slung late-1940s car, wearing slacks and looking radiant and sexy. Yet there is something—a tension in her pose, an unease in her expression—that suggests the camera had captured something from her without her permission. She was shy. But my father had a politician's gift for being with people; with him, she knew the giddy, vicarious pleasure of popularity. He played on the office softball team and won trophies, pitching left-handed; he played on the office golf team and won trophies, playing right-handed. He played in the church bowling league and brought home so many trophies that my mother stacked them in closets. He joked constantly, even in church; it was years before I realized how much he hid behind that mask of jollity. What made it effective was the fact that he was truly funny. "Did you hear what Tommy said?" people would say to each other at parties, repeating some one-liner. I was his shill, a risible child who instantly rose to his bait; nothing pleased him more than making me laugh. "After the service tonight, there will be a short elders' meeting," the minister intoned from the pulpit, and my father stage-whispered, "What about the tall elders?"—knowing that I was defenseless, that there was no way I could repress the rising hilarity.

He was impulsive. Once he came home from work, tearing into the driveway, brakes grinding, horn beeping, yelling at us to get in the car. We screamed up the road to the freeway overpass that was being built near our house, where my father pointed west toward a peculiarly brilliant red sunset. He had wanted us to see it. After he got his law degree, he moved into management at Delta, and we qualified for free airline passes. But he never planned trips; we just took them. Once he came home from work and announced, "We're going to Australia," and that weekend we did. It was the first of several similar adventures, which over the years took us to such places as Ireland, New Zealand, Hawaii—anywhere my parents had always hankered to explore and wanted us to see. My mother found this no less thrilling than my sister and I did. "Who would have thought," she would say frequently, "that an orphan from the Southern Christian Children's Home would wind up in—" In their best moments, those trips were hilarious, ad hoc enterprises. Once, trying to escape a large and oddly uninhabited airport in Auckland, we found ourselves in a rental car, stopped at the end of a road that had put us directly onto a runway. "Now what?" my mother asked, and always the eager wiseacre, I stuck my head between her and my father in the front seat. "What you do now," I said, "is locate the windsock and take off into the wind."

Sometimes rage would consume him, for inconsequential reasons—a lawn mower that wouldn't start, the mayonnaise jar left open on the kitchen counter. At those times, he frightened me; his fury could clear the room. There was something exaggerated in the way he threw a tool down or slammed a door, a fierceness that seemed to come from nowhere. In him I sensed a deep, unfathomable anger—perhaps because, even then, I sensed that I had it, too. Then it would be over. He wandered through the house, singing nonsense lyrics to popular tunes. "Toreador / Don't spit upon the floor / Use the cuspidor / That is what it's for," he bellowed; or "Lep-rosy / Night and day you *tor-ture* me / Sometimes I wonder / Why I fall asunder . . ."

For my mother, his ebullience was a tonic. She was happy. I watched her from the kitchen doorway as she stood at the sink, wearing a green striped seersucker dress, her red hair pulled off her face. Her hands moved in and out of the soapsuds; her face was calm and serious. I thought no one in the world was more beautiful. "Love lifted me," she sang in her clear, true soprano, or "He hideth my soul in the cleft of a rock. / That shadows a dry, thirsty land. / He hideth my soul in the depths of his love / And covers me there with his hand."

It was December 18, 1968, the last day of school before the Christmas holidays, a clear and chilly afternoon. My bus stopped at its usual spot, across the railroad tracks, within sight of my house. "Be sweet," my friend Necie said to me as I filed off behind my sister. The last thing I remember is a glint of sunlight on metal out of the corner of my eye.

The car had come over a slight rise, traveling so fast that I never saw it. It missed my sister by inches. I took the blow in my lower right back and went up over the hood like a rag doll. It was a week before I came to, on Christmas Eve. On the television set beside my bed, the Apollo 8 astronauts were about to make man's first journey around the dark side of the moon. I caught glimpses of it, in intervals between morphine-induced sleep, through my right eye, the only part of me that wasn't encased in gauze.

The impact had shattered the bones of my lower back and pelvis, and I had deep lacerations on the outside of my left thigh, where I apparently skidded along the road. Lesser lacerations marked me from head to toe; there was even a speck of gravel embedded in my wrist. The internal damage was also significant; intestinal hemorrhages and a bruised spleen. But the worst injury, to me, was to my face. Something metal on the car had left a ragged tear of skin that opened just below the hairline above my left eye and exposed the whole left side of my skull, miraculously missing the eye. It took six hours of surgery to put me back into human form, most of that spent by the plastic surgeon working on my face.

The accident coincided with a major growth spurt of puberty.

After three weeks, I left the hospital in a wheelchair; in three months, I was walking without a limp. But there was a slashing red scar that covered a quarter of my face, starting just above my left eye, turning the outer edge of my eye up into a distorted upward squint.

Overnight, I was no longer a child. I was that ungainly thing, an adolescent. Worse: an adolescent with a scarred face.

I never knew exactly how the accident happened. It was a time of racial tension. Martin Luther King Jr. had been assassinated the previous April, and there were dark mutterings among some people at church that the driver, a nineteen-year-old black man, had run me down on purpose, because I was white. Late in the spring, there was a criminal trial. In court, the driver said his brakes had failed. In the courthouse corridor, our families regarded each other with hostility. My family waited for some token of remorse; his family waited to see what form of injustice the court system would inflict.

After lunch, I was called to the witness stand. The questions from the prosecutor were perfunctory. Then he asked me to step down from the witness box and walk in front of the jury. He guided me down the row of jurors slowly. Some of them leaned forward to get a good look at the red scars on my face; I remember an older man who looked at me and flinched. The scars, I realized much later, had nothing to do with proving the defendant had committed a crime. But they were an eloquent, unspoken message from the prosecutor to the twelve white people in the jury box. Here was a young white girl who had been robbed of one of a woman's most valuable assets, and a black man had done it.

The defense attorney had no questions. The jury took half an hour to convict. I heard later that the judge gave him three years.

The whole thing was unbearable, so in my mind I sealed it away. Don't worry, people told me; the scars are bad right now, but plastic surgery will fix that. And so I waited. The summer

after the accident, I had the first of a series of plastic surgeries—
a day or two in the hospital, followed by several weeks spent with
a bandaged face, hiding inside the house, looking as if I had been
in a bar fight. Each time, I waited for the bandages to be
removed, to see the face I had had before; each time, I was disappointed. In fact, the only thing that could heal the scars was
the passage of time. To a fourteen-year-old, this was an alien concept. "You're a pretty girl," my mother kept trying to reassure me,
but all I had to do was look in the mirror to see that this was
untrue. And so I adopted the only tactic left to me: I tried to
ignore it.

It worked, some of the time. Once, as I was waiting at a bus
stop, a stranger inquired rudely, "What happened to your face?"
I looked straight ahead, unable to think of a reply. "Don't worry,
darlin'," said my doctor, a rakish man I had a crush on. "You're
gonna be an interestin' lookin' woman." I wasn't stupid; I knew
"interesting" was just one step up from "ugly," and ranked far
behind "beautiful" or even "pretty." Anyway, he was a living dis-
avowal of his own words. His current wife, he told everybody
proudly, was a former Playboy bunny. My plastic surgeon was a
man of medical renown who radiated an emotional chill; he
observed my face impassively, the way an artist considers his
options. In his silence, I heard an eloquent commentary on the
impossibility of my dreams.

Finally, despite her moral qualms about allowing me to wear
makeup so young, my mother took me to a Merle Norman studio. There a lady slathered my face with heavy masque foundation, dusted that with powder, dusted the powder with rouge,
then took a makeup pencil and drew a new eyebrow over my left
eye. Then she sold us a bag full of Merle Norman products. "You
look beautiful," she said, when she was done, which was untrue;
I looked embalmed. But from that moment, I never left the
house without my makeup. It maddened me, that I had to wear
makeup, that I was scarred and pasty-faced. My sister, then 15,

had grown another inch over the past year, and her face had lost its childish roundness; with her dark hair and large brown eyes, she was developing a dusky prettiness that was enhanced by the startled-doe look she turned on people when they spoke her name. It did not occur to me then that she was suffering, too, that she reacted to the attention our parents lavished on me by withdrawing further into her books and her fantasy life. As far as I can remember, there was very little discussion of the fact that she had nearly gotten killed, too. I only knew that I was jealous.

Journal entry, Saturday, May 15, 1971:

> Nonny got her hair cut today, so now I am definitely the plainer sister in the family. I always knew I was . . . She's got all it takes to be really pretty, and she's learning how to take advantage of it. As for me, I look as good as I'm ever going to look.

I had waited for adolescence like any other young girl, as if it would be a Disney dream and something magical would happen. Now, although I longed to hear my father say I was pretty, I knew it would never happen. I didn't even ask. When I came home from the hospital, he had picked me up in his arms and carried me into the house, but I felt no comfort in his touch, only embarrassment. I never knew what he thought about the accident; he never told me. We talked about it only once, years later, in a conversation that was stilted and unnatural. My mother talked about it frequently. To her, my survival was a miracle; she offered her fervent thanks that God had spared her daughter. Listening to her prayers, it seemed ungrateful of me to complain about the means by which God had accomplished this.

Once again, pale men in dark glasses bent over me at church, this time to murmur their thanks that the good Lord had allowed me to survive, and like a good daughter I echoed their piety. Inside, my rage retreated, sullen and silent. It would be years before I realized I was angry.

*   *   *

By my senior year in high school, I had fallen in with a crowd the rest of the school referred to sardonically as "creamers," as in "cream of the crop," the top of our class in an ordinary Georgia public high school. Being a "creamer" was the same thing as being called a geek or a nerd, but that was okay with me; at last, I had found a group to belong to. In geek tradition, we stuck together. We even went to the prom en masse, since none of us could work up the nerve to ask anyone else for a date. By graduation, I had garnered a number of academic honors, I played tennis, I had even acquired a boyfriend. I read constantly. My reading list was heavily male, British and 19th century, though an occasional American got thrown in: Dickens—*Great Expectations* was my favorite book—Thackeray, Hemingway, the Brontë sisters, F. Scott Fitzgerald, Thurber. My life was full of the normal teenage things—sleepover parties, clubs, working on the school yearbook staff.

But signs of chronic depression were emerging. Even before the accident, I had begun to make frequent trips to the doctor, always complaining of a variety of ailments. Some were real; others had no clear physical cause. Before and after the accident, I seemed to suffer constantly from stomachaches, headaches, a mysterious cough, strange lumps on my lymph glands—a list of ailments baffling to my doctors and worrisome to my mother, whose experiences had taught her that there is no such thing as bad news, only catastrophe. Each ailment convinced her I was suffering from a fatal disease. The family doctor referred me to an internist, who referred me to a neurologist, who gave me an EEG. It was normal. My urine was tested for diabetes; my blood was tested for leukemia. Those tests were normal, too. Finally, in bafflement, the internist gave up and wrote a prescription for Valium. I was thrilled. Not only was I getting some attention, which I craved, but the Valium meant that I was also—finally—going to get a good night's sleep.

May 1973:

It's going on 1 a.m., but I'm writing until I get sleepy. Last night I had a recurrence of all my old symptoms—insomnia, dozing off only to find myself awakened with a start ten minutes later by my own beating heart, unable to catch my breath . . . Tonight I took a dose of cough medicine with codeine, plus ten milligrams of Valium, and I hope I can sleep . . . This started about a year and a half ago, when we were going to move, and I have had problems with it off and on since then.

I was seventeen.

The anxiety was like poison ivy. It took nothing to set off that mental itch—a chance remark, remembering an event from the day before—but once it started I found it impossible to stop the cycle. My thoughts twisted and circled, my pulse hammered, I couldn't concentrate. The only thing I wanted was to make sense of this feeling—and the explanation, or apparent explanation, was obvious: I was worried about boys.

But I was a Christian, and Christian girls were supposed to have their minds on higher things. We were supposed to be happy. "Doubt," one Sunday school teacher told us solemnly, "is of the devil." I was filled with doubt, I was wormy with it. When the principal of our public high school brought a beauty queen to a football pep rally to offer her own personal Christian testimony, I sat in the bleachers with my friend Jim as, one by one, all the people around us went down to rededicate their lives to Christ. I wasn't making a statement; I just hated the emotional coercion.

I also hated my face. There were times when I silently mouthed obscenities at myself in the bathroom mirror, sick at the sight of the red keloid scar that marred my forehead. But I admitted that to no one; for years, whenever anyone brought up the subject of the accident, I would leave the room, too furious to speak. With nowhere else to direct that anger, I focused it on the most readily available target—myself. The urge to do this, to catalogue my inferiorities, was one of the earliest impulses behind the creation of my journal; enclosed in that first volume, I found scraps of paper predating the beginning of my journal in December 1969. On one such paper, dated October 23, 1969, I had written:

Basically I am a very cold and withdrawn person . . . Most [people] think I am honest, dependable and trustworthy, a fine young Christian girl. I have to state that this is, I'm afraid, mostly hypocritical . . . I have tried to be a good Christian, but because of the above-stated tendency for being hypocritical, and also an alarming tendency towards deceit and conceit, I have found it extremely hard . . . I am much worse than the drunks on the streets or the prostitutes in the barrooms, as they do not pretend to be better than they are. I cannot say the same for myself. P.S. When I read this I will probably start feeling sorry for myself.

At other times, those journal entries show that at some level I understood that my physical ailments and my mental state were linked.

April 14, 1970:

I feel fine in the middle of the day; at night I start feeling depressed, and in the morning I trace the hours on the clock til bedtime. I am really not worth all this self-pity, because I have anything that anybody could ever ask for. Well, I must not lie to myself: I have been thinking sometimes about attempting suicide because that would put me in the hospital . . . I know why I am having fainting fits, dizzy spells and general less-than-normal health; it's because of all these dark thoughts I keep thinking.

But these were episodes. For long periods, life was normal, with its normal ups and downs. Sometimes I found it hard to believe I was the same person.

June 8, 1972:

If you turn to the beginning of this epic saga, you'll read some pretty morbid thoughts on dying and suicide. "Just an adolescent phase," all you learned psychiatrists will say. Maybe so . . . But for a while I literally went through the valley of the shadow of death. I remember one summer afternoon when I was walking home from feeding the horses. I suddenly thought incredulously, "You mean, you really wanted to die? You must have been out of your mind!"

It was like flying low in an airplane, in and out of thunder-heads. The normal work of adolescence—acquiring knowledge, achieving emotional maturity, discovering sex, preparing for college and independence—took a back seat to navigating the daily storm front. I was angry, so angry. My father's black rages now seemed trivial, compared with the fury I felt but could not express. It seemed uncontrollable, and for that reason I frightened myself, sought to push it to the back of my mind. And for a long while, I succeeded. At times, when the emotional storms had abated, I felt energized, optimistic, full of myself—the adolescent version of the laughing, risible child I had been. There was a song from my senior year in high school that became linked in my mind to those times: "I think I can make it now, the pain has gone. / All of the bad feelings have disappeared . . ."

Sometimes, in black moments, my turmoil spilled out in nervous, melodramatic pronouncements; I was dying for someone to discover what I tried so hard to hide. When the Valium prescription ran out, I replaced it with over-the-counter sleeping pills, which I took by the fistful. Once, riding with a carload of friends to a football game, I announced: "Last night, I had to take ten Sominex to get to sleep." My friend Jim spoke up from the back seat. "I don't think you should take so many pills, Tracy," he said—and I treasured that remark for years, as if it had been a profession of love: He had *noticed*.

At home, the rule of silence prevailed. Once my mother found a drawer full of empty Sominex bottles in my bureau and threw them out; I did not discover until years later that she had sobbed for a day, afraid that I was becoming a drug addict. I did not tell anyone that despite the Sominex I still awoke at 4:00 a.m. with my heart pounding so loudly I could hear it in my ears. I did not tell anyone that when, in the winter of my senior year, I found out that Jim had gone out on a date with one of my best friends, I had gone home and taken half a bottle of aspirin.

I wanted to die, or get noticed, but neither of those things happened.

Over the next two decades, that formulation gradually changed. It became: *Get noticed or die.* It was only logical: An intense, narcissistic craving for praise and attention gave me the means for keeping the Beast at bay. I had few internal props, no reliable way of feeling good about who I was; I found no pleasure in being me.

Happiness, then, could only come from outside—and it was possible, it was tantalizingly close to my reach, if I could just get the right job, win the right prize, snag the attention of the right man and figure out how to keep it.

Real happiness, of course, had nothing to do with any of this.

It is barely daylight. As my mind floats up from the still pool of sleep, its first conscious act is to note the blue-gray light creeping under the bedroom curtains. Then, like a 1950s television screen coming on, objects in the bedroom gently come into view: bookshelf, television, dresser. The neighbor's dog is yipping outside, and I hear the wood flute call of a mourning dove. Drowsily, I roll over and look at my husband.

He is deeply asleep, his hand thrown outside the covers, and as I move, he stirs slightly. Soon the clock radio will come on, and the day will begin.

Last night, I dreamed of anxiety, something about being

trapped in a car in a traffic jam, in an agony of needing to be somewhere else. The car was full of people who knew about my pain but who could do nothing about it. Their helpless sympathy made me unreasonably angry. The dream was vivid; I can feel the aftermath of the anxiety now, in the muscle tension in my stomach and back. The anxiety in the dream was the diffuse, freefloating type I associate with depression. It seems odd, to dream about depression—though no different, I suppose, from having any other kind of dream-memory. Maybe a person lost in schizophrenia dreams of normal life, of taking out the garbage; I don't know. But the dreams always alarm me, because the feelings in them seem so real. I am superstitious, afraid that merely dreaming about them will release them, like an evil genie escaping from a bottle. Anyway, as far as my brain is concerned, which is more real—these dream feelings or the present, waking, moment?

Which is now, as David rolls over, half awake, and stretches out his arm to draw me close. The present comes into focus; my mind starts to fill with what I have to do today—ordinary things like my writing schedule, some gardening I plan to do afterward. These things seem lovely to me, my pleasure in them effortless. David's arm is around me; there is something nourishing in the touch of his skin on mine, the warmth of his chest against my back. We have been together for almost two years now, married for one. He is a physicist, I am a writer, our work has almost nothing in common. Not the man I'm looking for, I thought the night he first made an awkward pass at me. I told him so, and he listened, sitting there on my sofa wearing his wire-rimmed glasses—the kind, he had told me, laughing, that all science geeks wore. He heard me out. "That's okay," he had said, when I was through. "You're worth waiting for. Besides, I'm a good guy. If you stick around long enough, you'll figure that out." That story is a joke on me now, part of our shared folklore, along with the tale of our first date, when I came to the door in a fashionable silk outfit and David assumed I was in pajamas. He thought if it was silk, you wore it to bed. For smart people, we aren't too bright, I think, and grin to myself. We lie there, limbs tangled in drowsy disarray, until the radio clicks on.

This is the way my life is now.

In between this moment, and that bleak day in February 1990 when I sat in the federal courthouse pressroom and tried to compose a suicide note, lies a distance of only four years—though in psychic terms, it is a journey at least as long as everything that has gone before.

When I checked into a hospital that February, I had only the vaguest grasp of what depression is—a set of notions probably similar to those most people walk around with: *Depression is something that makes you feel sad; it's not a real illness, except when it afflicts artistic types; ordinary people like me can't possibly admit to having a mental illness.* I was wrong or only partially correct on all counts, as I learned over the next two years. It was a period of my life when most of my energy, intellectual and physical, became devoted to finding ways to understand and conquer—or at least come to a truce with—the Beast.

There were several turning points, the first one being that moment of surrender—or what felt like surrender—when I consented to become a psychiatric patient. The two weeks I spent behind locked doors in the Georgetown University Hospital psychiatric ward gave me a much-needed respite from the killing struggle to maintain appearances, a time when I could not possibly hurt myself and my body was allowed to rest. A second turning point came in August 1990, when, after months of experimenting with traditional antidepressants and their debilitating side effects, months in which my depression seemed only barely held at bay and just getting to the office every day constituted a major life achievement, my psychiatrist finally agreed to switch me to Prozac, an antidepressant drug then new on the market.

Within weeks, the mental hurricane, which had lasted for more than a year by that point, had stopped dead in its tracks. I offer no proof; all I know is what happened to me, which is that first X happened, and then Y. But it is hard not to attribute that miracle to the little green-and-white pills, difficult not to give them credit for the fact that since then I've lived something like a normal life. It's been a gift.

I'm closing in on forty—a milestone age, the point at which youth stops being a state of being I can take for granted, and becomes a relative term. It's too early for grand summary statements—but even so, I find myself weighing conclusions about how much this illness has come to define me, and how much I have imprinted my personality on it. I'm casting about for some rule, some unifying principle, by which this puzzle of my life can be seen as a whole. And it seems to me that my illness has been the product of three forces: genetics, culture and chance.

I was born with a predisposition to suffer from depression. I was also fated to grow up in a culture filled with anxiety—some the product of the times I lived in, some the product of the religious sensibilities imposed on me by my parents, who were themselves transmitting the culture they were born into. Part of it was the residual fearfulness I sensed from my mother, who could not escape her own past. And then there was a childhood accident that marred my face just as I was entering adolescence—a chance event, a unique stressor, that forever altered my trajectory.

Over time, all these things worked together—and, in doing so, they permanently altered the "wiring" in my brain, which was not perfectly "wired" to begin with. This way of thinking about depression, which scientists are exploring, is known informally as "kindling." It makes sense to me. It describes the way my brain works in other spheres: mastering an algebra problem in eighth grade, learning to serve a tennis ball—a bombardment of stimuli, a repeated reaction, the spark of comprehension, the eventual effortlessness of what had once seemed foreign and impossible.

Emotions, I believe, are also partly learned; over time, what begins as simple childhood anxiety can, in susceptible persons, become a series of stimuli that teaches the brain something new—that "teaches" it, in short, how to feel the blank apathy, the looming sense of futility and worthlessness that is the most familiar face of depression. But emotions can be relearned—with help.

Part of my recovery is the growing ability to escape the suffocating self-absorption engendered by this illness—and that, in turn, has led to the realization that the patient is only the first of depression's many victims. When I was emotionally shut down as a result of depression, the people who loved me suffered from my absence. Even the compensating behaviors I adopted to deal with the effects of chronic depression exacted a toll on other people. The exaggerated hunger for attention and praise it spawned in me often came at the expense of my older sister, who has always been as shy as I am outgoing. In my desperate desire to charm and excel, I often managed to deflect attention from her achievements, so different from mine. Depression did not create the basic differences in our personalities, but it exacerbated every point of friction—and the damage, to some extent, has been permanent. She is just one in a long list of collateral casualties; everyone else close to me has suffered, too.

In the fall of 1975, I awoke in my dorm room at Emory University in the grip of a dream. In it, I was in the basement of my old house, which had been converted into a restaurant. The light was glaring, the walls white and stark. I was eating something mushy and brown, a food designed not to give pleasure but only to sustain life. And then out of nowhere, I began to have a marvelous feeling that I had a stupendous secret: It was spring outside.

I excused myself and slipped out the door. Outside was my grandfather's old cornfield, the same field he had plowed so long ago with Becky the mule. It was covered with the stubble of last year's cornstalks; this year's planting had not yet begun. It was chilly, like the day I followed behind him in the furrows of his plow, but there was warmth in the sun. The earth was brown, the sky drab, but I could hear music from somewhere. It was faint, but growing stronger.

I took off my sweater and hat and shoes, feeling the earth slowly warming beneath my feet, letting my hair go loose. And then wolves appeared. They were my secret gods, my helpers; nobody but me knew about them, but I had actually dared to name them. They were dangerous, but I was not frightened. I felt supremely happy. I began to run across the cornfield, the wolves loping along beside me as if we were all part of the same pack, and wild, strange music filled the sky.

It is tempting to romanticize, to look back and say that dream presaged my eventual triumph over the Beast. But there is no triumph here, only wiser ways of fighting. I suspect that after all these years, the Beast and I are life partners.

But it's okay. I have an ordinary life—and though some might think this is dull, I tell you it is sweet. Ordinary life is a miraculous thing.

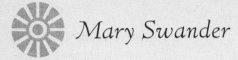
Mary Swander

AFTERWORD: SPRING CROCUSES

Several years ago Richard Solly and I sat in the kitchen of his house in St. Paul, Minnesota, the spring crocuses just beginning to push up through the flower beds lining the sidewalks outside, and talked about what it meant to be on the inside of illness.

"After my near-death experience, I had a completely different consciousness about life," Richard said. "A completely changed appreciation of things."

"You return wounded, but with a whole new sense of awe and wonder," I said.

"That's right."

Our eyes met and then we stared down into our mugs of tea. Even for veteran "survivors," a discussion of illness has its difficult and inarticulate moments.

"You think you'll never, ever lose this perspective, but as you recover, you lose it so fast. . . . You lose it so fast," Richard said.

The first dictionary definition of *recover* is "to cover over." When we find our way back from illness, we do not return to "normal," but instead carry with us a scar tissue that protects and conceals the raw vulnerability that we were forced to confront.

We scab over, and the process helps us function in the world and push on with our lives. But in this healing activity, we do lose something, and as Richard pointed out, we lose it so fast.

When we planned *The Healing Circle*, Patricia Foster and I set out to create a book that would allow a range of writers with a range of illnesses to recapture their "losses" or changed perspectives, to get them down on paper before they were forgotten. Each one of these writers has taken up the challenge with more skill and insight than we had ever imagined. Many found the creation of these essays tough going. To return to the underworld after several years, months, weeks, or even days of reprieve was not easy. The essays demanded an intense amount of honesty and self-scrutiny.

When I talked with any of the writers in this book with chronic conditions, a note of hesitancy entered our voices with the mere mention of the word *recovery*. Then we made the discovery that the concept of recovery exists more in the emotional and spiritual realms than the physical. A wound, a broken leg, or even a broken immune system can mend, but what of our souls and psyches?

Some of our authors, like Tracy Thompson, began their battles almost entirely on the psychic level. Their illnesses were of the mind, their victories invisible to most who search for the tangible markers—the burn marks, the healed stitches, or the abandoned crutches—of recovery. These writers found ways to capture the shifts in their mental worlds, the elusive province of the brain that is so little understood. These writers measured their own growth, and in the record of their accounts, the rest of us can more clearly see ourselves.

Still others, like Faye Moskowitz and Andrea Dominick, had to cut through their own denial to write their essays. Sick or well, it's difficult to confront problems, our so-called failures or weaknesses—even the relatively small, mildly irritating ones. But confront them we do, and we are generally better for it. Yet humans could not exist if they didn't have some defense mechanisms. We all walk around in denial of death most of the time, and that, in its ironic way, keeps us living. Pulling the bedsheet up over our heads does give us time to recoup. But major illness or disability won't let us stay hidden long. After a while, we are forced to gaze into our own wounds.

Which takes courage. In the last forty to fifty years, we've closeted away illness. As a culture, we have abandoned the extended family, the maiden aunts, the devoted daughters or sons who used to nurse and care for the sick. Instead, we now take our cue from the medical establishment and most often delegate these responsibilities to strangers.

In the transition, we have lost our stories and our witnesses. We no longer listen to our grandmother's recollection of her winter living in the mountains of Colorado nursing her brother through TB. What we have instead are thick medical charts filled with illegible and unmemorable notes. On a recent trip to a rheumatology clinic, I went through an hour's interview with a medical student, then the staff doctor appeared. Brushing the curtain aside, she strolled into the examining cubicle and quickly summed up and reduced my story. "So," she said. "You can't walk. You don't smoke. You don't drink. But you write."

Through the ages, there have been scores of ill writers. Keats, Chekhov, Darwin, Katherine Mansfield, and Robert Louis Stevenson come to mind. The act of writing, by its nature, is confining and solitary, and is one of the few art forms that can be accomplished propped up in bed. But until recently, writers very seldom actually wrote about their conditions. Illness should be one of the great themes of literature, Virginia Woolf pointed out in her essay "On Being Ill." She lamented the fact that for a subject that takes up so much of our lives, our novels are surprisingly devoid of the mention of illness.

In the days when my grandmother was living her hard life, illness was commonplace. Epidemics swept the country. The infant mortality rate was high. Sanitation was bad and sterile technique was virtually unknown. People got out of bed every morning understanding that by evening they could be dancing with the Angel of Death. After World War II, antibiotics, vaccines, and advances in technologies eradicated many of the deadly contagious diseases and gave us a false sense of immortality. Like Patricia, I had my own birth trauma. My mother had an appendectomy late in her pregnancy with me, and if it weren't for the "wonders of modern medicine," we would have both died.

But my mother and I survived and for the next thirty-five years our culture lived with an optimism and blind faith in the advances of science. Only when the AIDS epidemic hit and the rise of cancers and other immune system disorders began to come to light did we lose our innocence. We had to admit that we were no longer invincible. We could no longer remain buoyant. We could no longer remain silent.

In the late 1980s and early 1990s, significant works about illness began to be published. Books like Audre Lorde's *The Cancer Journals*, May Sarton's *After the Stroke: The Journal*, and Anatole Broyard's *Intoxicated by my Illness* opened the doors for a discussion of once taboo topics. Even though Confessional poets like Sylvia Plath, Anne Sexton, and Robert Lowell had long ago revealed their mental illnesses, William Styron's *Darkness Visible: A Memoir of Madness* brought the subject home to a wider audience. Illness became more profoundly political with AIDS, and an outpouring of writing now springs from that complex disease. Andrew Sullivan's essay will certainly assume a notable place in that body of literature. Finally, in a book like Susan Griffin's *A Chorus of Stones*, personal illness became inextricably linked to the most far-reaching historical, political, and ecological decisions of our century.

The Healing Circle arises out of this need to explore at last a profoundly meaningful topic. In this collection, we've attempted to tell our stories of illness in a way that will transcend our medical charts, the coldness of screws and plates, the pricks and pokes of hypodermic needles. "In a sense sickness is a place, more instructive than a long trip to Europe, and it's always a place where there's no company, where nobody can follow," Flannery O'Connor said. True enough. Illness is an experience at once illuminating and alienating. It uniquely belongs to each of us, and each of us will belong to it, for as essayist Nancy Mairs has pointed out, disability is the one minority group that we will all eventually join. If the authors of *The Healing Circle* can have no true companions on their journeys, they can at least have our thanks for mapping the way. And this book guarantees that they will never, ever lose their perspectives.

CONTRIBUTORS

Lauren Slater is the author of *Welcome to My Country* (Random House, 1996). She's at work on a book about Prozac which will be published by Random House in 1998. She lives in Cambridge, Massachusetts.

Patricia Stevens is the recipient of a James Michener Fellowship from the Iowa Writers' Workshop and a Nelson Algren Short Story Award. Her work has appeared in numerous magazines and anthologies. She lives in Iowa City.

Andrew Sullivan is the author of *Virtually Normal* (Knopf, 1996), *Untitled On Gay Marriage* (Random House, 1997) and the editor of *For Better or Worse? Same Sex Marriage, Pro and Con: A Reader* (Random House, 1997).

Richard Solly, author of *Call to Purpose: How Men Make Sense of Life-Changing Experience* (Hazelton, 1995), lives in St. Paul, Minnesota, where he is a freelance writer. He has been a past winner of a Bush Foundation Fellowship.

Pulitzer Prize winning author **Jane Smiley's** latest novel is *Moo* (Knopf, 1995). She lives with her family in California.

Mary Swander is a professor of English at Iowa State University in Ames, Iowa. Her memoir *Out of This World* was published by Viking in 1995.

Kris Vervaecke has published both essays and stories in *Prairie Schooner, Puerto del Sol, Kansas Quarterly,* and a forthcoming

Graywolf Anthology of essays about sports. She teaches writing at Coe College and lives in Iowa City.

Tom Sleigh's latest book of poetry, *The Chain*, was published by the University of Chicago Press in 1996. He teaches at Dartmouth and his many awards include grants from the NEA and the Guggenheim Foundation.

Patricia Foster is the editor of *Minding the Body: Women Writers on Body and Soul* (Anchor, 1994) and *Sister To Sister* (Anchor, 1996). She's currently working on a memoir and teaches at the University of Iowa in Iowa City.

Dennis Covington's nonfictional account of snake handling entitled *Salvation at Sand Mountain* (Addison-Wesley) was nominated for the 1995 National Book Award. He teaches at the University of Alabama at Birmingham.

Linda Hogan's most recent books include *Dwellings* (W. W. Norton, 1995) and *Solar Storms* (Charles Scribner's Sons, 1995). She teaches at the University of Colorado at Boulder.

Andrea Dominick's memoir about growing up and coping with diabetes is forthcoming from Scribner's. She lives in Des Moines, Iowa.

Faye Moskowitz is the author of *And the Bridge Is Love* (Beacon Press, 1991) and the editor of an anthology, *Her Face in the Mirror: Jewish Women on Mothers and Daughters* (Beacon Press, 1994). She teaches Creative Writing at George Washington University.

Tracy Thompson is the author of *The Beast* (G.P. Putnam's Sons, 1995) and a writer for the *Washington Post*.